Through Golden Years

Through Golden Years
1867-1943

A HISTORY OF CENTENARY PUBLISHED FOR
THE SEVENTY-FIFTH ANNIVERSARY

By LEILA ROBERTA CUSTARD

"*Through golden years Thy guiding hand
Hath led us, while these halls we trod.*"

Anniversary Hymn.
Carl Price, '98

LEWIS HISTORICAL PUBLISHING COMPANY, INC.
NEW YORK
1947

Copyright, 1947
LEWIS HISTORICAL PUBLISHING COMPANY, INC.

Preface, 2017

AS Centenary University celebrates its 150th anniversary, we look back at its long history as an institution. The Centenary Archives holds many historical school documents, but the most complete chronicle of the school's history is *Through Golden Years*, written by Centenary professor Leila Roberta Custard. *Through Golden Years* explores Centenary University's first 75 years, illustrating its growth from a coeducational high school and preparatory school to an all-girls school and later a junior college. Written between 1944 and 1947, it compiled information from archival documents and first-hand accounts from the Centenary community to create a proper school history.

Custard presented this book during the school's 75th anniversary in 1949, celebrated not 75 years after it received its charter (in 1867) but 75 years after the school opened (in 1874). Custard relied on earlier manuscripts, the autobiography of the first president, Dr. Whitney, documents from the archives of Centenary and the town of Hackettstown, and countless staff and student interviews to organize her book. She wrote copious notes as she did her research, and sent letters to staff and alumni requesting accounts of their time at Centenary. Taylor Memorial Library houses hundreds of pages of her research. She wrote on everything from the margins of correspondence to the blank pages left over from her students' examination booklets. The letters to and from students display the cordial nature of correspondence at that time; when her research time was split by a trip to Chile as an exchange professor, students wrote to her hoping that the trip would not impede her research or prevent her from finishing the book. Custard spent two semesters in Chile in 1945, and as soon as she returned, she went right back to work and had the manuscript ready before the 75th anniversary event.

Through Golden Years is truly a diamond in the rough. Within these pages lies a treasure trove of early Centenary University history in the form of facts and remembrances from its staff, faculty, and students. It is only fitting that a book published for this institution's 75th anniversary should be given a reprint on the anniversary of its 150th year.

WENDI BLEWETT

Hackettstown, New Jersey
September 1, 2017

DEDICATED
IN MEMORY OF
GEORGE J. FERRY
Trustee, 1869-1911
President of Board of Trustees,
1872-1911
IN RECOGNITION OF
HIS COUNTLESS BENEFACTIONS
TO CENTENARY
and
HIS UNCEASING DEVOTION
TO HER WELFARE

Preface

NO one person ever writes a history. An author is always under obligations to many persons for varied kinds of help. My principal indebtedness is to Professor Albert O. Hammond, whom I never saw, but who could almost be called my collaborator. Back in early 1920, the Trustees were farsighted enough to request their Professor Emeritus of Classical Languages and Literature to prepare a History of C. C. I. On October 1 of that year a neatly typed manuscript of 105 pages was transmitted to them with the title-page: "History of the Centenary Collegiate Institute Compiled from Original Documents and from the Memory of Events *Quorum pars parva fuit* by Albert O. Hammond, A.M., during forty years a Member of the Faculty of C. C. I." Several typed copies of this were placed in the Library.

When in 1944 Mr. Lewis made his generous offer to present a history of Centenary, the first suggestion was to publish the Hammond work plus a chapter which should continue the record from 1917, where it had ended. But Professor Hammond had never felt that he had had access to sufficient documents. And in the quarter-century that has elapsed so much more material has become available that it has seemed best to rewrite the history from the beginning.

Naturally this previous work has proved most useful, and its writer's "Memory of Events" is a priceless original source from which copious quotations have been made. His treatment of the problems of financing seems to be based on ample supplies of evidence, so that it has been used, with but few additions, as the basis of chapter two in the present work. It has seemed preferable to make this general statement here rather than to clutter the text with footnote references to an unpublished source.

Much reference has been made to another unpublished source which has just become available—the very existence of which was probably unknown to the school's earlier historian. This is the Autobiography of Centenary's first president, written only for his children and with strict orders that it never be published. Nothing could equal the vividness and detail of this source and of the two Scrapbooks that illustrate it, and I wish here to express my profound thanks to Dr. Whitney's two daughters, Helen Whitney Stutsman and May Vincent Whitney Thompson, for lending them.

Centenary's archives are rich with scrapbooks, programs, copies of old school publications, clippings, and pictures for which acknowledgments have long since been made to the donors. Thanks are due for several accessions sent to aid in this history, notably to Julia Carmichael Miller for copies of "The Scroll," to Mrs. Heath for programs, and to Josephine McCormick Martin for materials concerning her father. I am grateful for helpful materials loaned by Miss Laura Mack, Mr. Harold Nunn, Mr. Milton Thorp, and the Reverend Frederick C. Mooney, all of Hackettstown.

Almost my first step was to enlist the aid of the alumni without which it would have been impossible to recreate "the golden haze of student days." To those who answered my appeal either in writing or in a personal interview my sincere thanks are hereby expressed for their co-operation. I owe a real debt of gratitude to Mr. William L. Clarke who came to my assistance with a handsome collection of reminiscences and stories, and to Julia Carmichael Miller for her vivid recollections. A similar service has been rendered by the Reverend Frederick C. Mooney and by my brother, the Reverend Steward Franklin Custard, with both of whom I have conferred frequently. Interviews have been granted me by former teachers who thereby rendered valuable help: Miss Charlotte Howard, Miss Geraldine Shields, Mr. Frank V. Stutsman, Mr. Frederic A. Mets, and, by letter, Mr. William Barnard Smith.

I deeply appreciate the careful critical reading of portions of the work by Mr. William L. Clarke, Mr. George E. Denman, Mr. William H. Bacheler, the Reverend Frederick C. Mooney, Mr. Frank V. Stutsman, and my brother. Dr. H. Graham DuBois and Mr. C. Hammond Blatchford of the Centenary faculty have been most generous in giving time to the critical reading of the manuscript. And of course President Anderson has been unfailing in his stimulating interest, his suggestions, and his enthusiasm.

The drawings of the Society insignia have been done by Miss Winifred Haanes of the Class of 1947. The photograph of the Whitney Lyceum pedestal stones (showing both the original stone, one of the very few things that came through the fire, and the new one that replaced it for actual use in the Society) is a contribution made by Mr. Elmer Hart of Hackettstown. To both of these artists I am very grateful.

My sincere appreciation must be expressed also to Miss Phoebe Parry-Jones who was my efficient assistant during the summer of 1944 and to Miss Phyllis Stovel and Mrs. Olive Getchius for their painstaking, careful preparing of the manuscript.

One word more. Though this book has not been dedicated to them, it has been written with my former students—now alumnae—constantly in mind; and behind them has stood all that other much more vast body of former students of former teachers whose devotion to Centenary has been equal to mine,—students, of the far yesterdays, some of whom I now know, all of whom I can picture treading the halls of the old school. The book goes forth with whatever limitations it has—and I fear there are many—in the hope that it may help to revivify their memories and awake new appreciation of their Alma Mater.

LEILA ROBERTA CUSTARD

Hackettstown, New Jersey
February 1, 1947

Introduction

IN the spring of 1944 the president of Centenary Junior College called at the office of one of its trustees, Mr. Marion L. Lewis. The visit was purely social and was made as part of the plan of a new president to become better acquainted with his trustees. During the course of an hour's call Mr. Lewis explained the nature and scope of his own work as a publisher of historical, genealogical, and biographical studies. Many very attractive volumes were perused including several histories of colleges and universities. The new president, realizing that no history of Centenary had been published, suggested that such a history should be written, and that it would be most appropriate to begin it then in view of the approaching seventy-fifth anniversary of the opening of the institution. Mr. Lewis in his characteristically generous manner replied that he would be glad to publish such a history and give it to the College as a part of his anniversary gift. In this manner and spirit the history project was conceived.

It was important to choose an author who could do justice to the rich Centenary background. Fortunately such a person was available—the head of the history department of the College. She was a careful student and one familiar with many educational institutions and with Centenary in particular, for she had joined the faculty in 1937 and had seen the work of the Preparatory School as well as the growth of the Junior College. Her father had been a minister in the Newark

Conference of the Methodist Church, which Conference founded and nourished this institution to maturity. Her brother was a loyal and interested alumnus. She had an unusual relationship to Centenary, yet at the same time had the intellectual habit of objectivity so important to the preparation of an authentic record. Her academic background as an historian had been excellent. She was a Phi Beta Kappa graduate of Goucher College and received her Doctor of Philosophy degree from the University of Southern California. During the summer of 1944 Dr. Leila Custard began her work in a spirit of enthusiasm and devotion.

Those who have been closest to this work and have encouraged and helped in the project are enthusiastic about this phase of the Seventy-fifth Anniversary Development Program, for they realize that an educational institution assumes its character in a large measure as a result of the perpetuation of traditions and emphases which have been part and parcel of its life through the years. An educational institution is more than mortar and bricks and current budgets; it is an heritage resulting in a way of college life which becomes the central influence in shaping and moulding the lives of its students as future citizens. This inheritance at Centenary is a synthesis of the influence of faculty members, trustees, alumni, administrators, churchmen, and others who have been active in the life of Centenary Collegiate Institute, now Centenary Junior College. It was thought important as we approached our seventy-fifth birthday that we restate this tradition and make it available in a published history so that the rededication of enlarged facilities for three hundred young women planned for the anniversary commencement of 1949 would be in the spirit of this effective past.

The publication of this history is of course but one phase of the Seventy-fifth Anniversary Development Program. The marked growth in enrollment in the junior college has made it clear to trustees and administrators that the dreams of those who planned for the re-establishment of the college .work in 1929 should be brought more nearly to realization. It was felt that a general development program should be projected covering a three-year period up to 1949, the anniversary year. In the fall of 1946 a campaign was launched seeking the first $300,000 of an overall objective of $800,000. This campaign was successful. Specific projects were chosen for summer periods to be continued until the additional facilities should be completed. In 1946 the new athletic fields including tennis courts and picnic grounds were opened, the kitchen re-equipped, the dining room enlarged. In 1947 and for each summer thereafter the following projects were announced: remodelling of the library, chapel, and gymnasium; the provision for a museum of early American items characteristic of the homes in this area of New Jersey; and finally the construction of a new dormitory unit to house fifty young women. It was thought that with these additions and improvements there could be found no more ideal plant in the East for an effective program of junior college education for women.

In addition to planning for the physical needs of the College, committees of the faculty were asked to work on various phases of the academic program: curriculum, grading and evaluation procedures, field trips and excursions, programs for vocational guidance. A continuing committee on student personnel was asked to study problems and procedures in this area. It was felt that no rededication of facilities would be complete without a rededication of the faculty to an enriched program designed to meet effectively the needs of young women at the junior college level. It was planned that this intellectual and spiritual renaissance should culminate in a carefully organized academic conference to be held on the campus as a part of the seventy-fifth anniversary celebration in 1949. It was hoped that the proceedings of such a conference might be published in book form and be made a part of the literature of higher education in the junior college field.

The past becomes the foundation for the future. This history, unfolding an interesting and significant story, is an ever-present guide to the growth and development which is now taking place on the Centenary campus. Central objectives remain unchanged, the finest education for the total growth and development of human personality, for the most significant service which can be rendered to a world in transition. The publication of *Through Golden Years* should help to revive in the thinking of all who read it a respect for the uninterrupted years of Centenary's significant service and to prepare for the rededication of the institution for a broader and richer service in the years ahead.

Hurst Robins Anderson

Hackettstown, New Jersey
April 7, 1947

Contents

	Preface	ix
	Introduction	xiii
Chapter		Page
I.	"'Mid the Silent Hills Surrounded" The Vision and The Dream	1
II.	"Alma Mater Proudly Raises Halls and Tower Tall and Strong" Building a Monument to Faith and Enthusiasm	11
III.	"And Her Children Sing Her Praises" Alma Mater Gathers in Her Children: 1874-1875	21
IV.	"Sing Them Loud and Sing Them Long" The Smooth Course: 1875-1895	53
V.	"Forming Still a Noble Band" Despite Trials and Testings: 1895-1902	71
VI.	"And With Honors Still Unbounded" The Campus Expands: 1902-1908	103
VII.	Proving "Worthy of the Times" Changes: Exit Co-education. 1908-1917	127
VIII.	"Alma Mater, Live Thy Glory, Alma Mater, C. J. C.!" Further Changes on the Same Theme—Junior College—1917-1943	153

IX.	"THE GOLDEN HAZE OF STUDENT DAYS"	197
X.	"EVER SHALL HER CHILDREN LOVE HER"	245

APPENDIX

1.	The Board of Trustees of Centenary Junior College, 1947	249
2.	The Faculty of Centenary Junior College, 1947	252
	Index	261

Illustrations

	FACING PAGE
Dr. George H. Whitney	2
George J. Ferry	18
Centenary Collegiate Institute in 1874	22
The Old Building—Entrance	34
The Old Building—Dining Room	34
Whitney Lyceum Hall, 1895	38
Zeta Hall, Alpha Phi Fraternity, 1895	38
The Old Building—Parlors One, Two, and Three	40
Diokosophian Society Hall, 1895	40
Dr. Wilbert P. Ferguson	72
Centenary Collegiate Institute in 1899	78
The Fire, October 31, 1899	80
Centenary Collegiate Institute in Ruins after the Fire, October 31, 1899	86
Dr. Charles Wesley McCormick	90
The New Centenary Collegiate Institute, 1902	104
Dr. Eugene Allen Noble	110
Whitney Lyceum Pedestal Stones	110
The School Lake	120
The Canal	120
Dr. Jonathan Magie Meeker	128
Centenary Collegiate Institute's Last Football Team, 1909	132

ILLUSTRATIONS

The Last Graduating Class of the Co-educational Centenary Collegiate Institute, 1910	136
The New Building—Dining Room of Centenary Collegiate Institute for Girls	148
Dr. Robert Johns Trevorrow	170
Mrs. Editha Trevorrow	194
Hurst Robins Anderson	196
The Old Building—The Chapel	198
Professor Albert O. Hammond	202
The Chapel—New Building	222

Alma Mater

'Mid the silent hills surrounded,
Ripened by the flight of time,
And with honors still unbounded,
In her strong and lusty prime,
Alma Mater proudly raises
Halls and tower tall and strong,
And her children sing her praises,
Sing them loud and sing them long.

Ever shall her children love her,
Forming still a noble band;
While the flag that waves above her
We shall bear to every land.
Let us laud her colors glorious,
Loyal to the Black and Blue,
Let us wave her flag victorious,
Pledging each one to be true.

And when age at last steals o'er us,
Softly, like the sinking sun,
Visions will appear before us,
Of the course that we have run.
When our lives have told their story
Failing lips shall move to cry:
"Alma Mater! live thy glory!
Alma Mater, C. C. I.!"

Through Golden Years

CHAPTER I

" 'Mid the Silent Hills Surrounded"

THE VISION AND THE DREAM

LATE in the Autumn of the year 1865 two friends were spending the day together in the little village of Hackettstown, New Jersey. After dinner, the host invited his guest to walk out with him to enjoy the glorious sunshine. "We walked," says the guest, as he recalled the incident many years afterward, "from his house in Washington Street 'out into the Country' about a third of a mile, to a rising ground in a *cornfield* (after the corn was cut off). He asked me if the view was not one of extraordinary beauty—the valley twenty miles long,—the mountains on the right and on the left and just before—Schooley's Mountain, Malvern Hill—and other hills. I replied that it was one of the most beautiful views I had anywhere seen.

"Then Mr. V. said: 'I brought you here because when the Conference shall build our great new Seminary, this is the spot of all places where it ought to be built, and you are to be the President of it, you know.'

"No," said I. "I do not know any such thing."

"You certainly will be the President: *everybody* says so."

"I told him I had occasionally heard so; but I said I had no desire for it, as I had already been President of two Seminaries. 'And besides, this is 1865, and we will not *consider* it as a Conference until 1866, and then it will be long before it is built, if ever built—and really I have no desire for it.'

"Well," he said, "Mark my words, you will be our President."

"I still thought not. Two and a half years later I was elected President, and spent many years of happy life on that same spot, being President twenty-six years —1869-1895. How little any man knows his own life."[1]

The host was the Reverend Mr. Crook S. Vancleve, then Presiding Elder of the Morristown District of the Newark Conference of the Methodist Church, and his guest was the man who was to be the first President of Centenary, Dr. George H. Whitney.

As the conversation implies, events had been preparing for this prophetic afternoon in the cornfield— most of them not conspicuous, widely-proclaimed events, but the devoted, oft-repeated deeds and daily performance of God-given tasks by ministers and by circuit-riding missionaries, by bishops and by conscientious members of the Methodist Church.

A remarkable development which has been called "one of the marvels of Christianity" was approaching

---

[1] This is quoted from a unique and most valuable source, one of the most important sources for the first half of Centenary's history. George H. Whitney, after he retired, occupied some of his leisure writing his autobiography. This was intended for his children only and he stipulated strictly that it should never be published. Naturally it contains a more consecutive account and a more intimate and vivid description of Centenary life for this period than is to be found elsewhere. Permission has therefore been obtained from his daughters, Helen Whitney Stutsman and May Vincent Whitney Thompson, to make quotations from this manuscript.

Dr. George H. Whitney
President of the Centenary Collegiate Institute
1869-1895

its centennial in 1866. As American Methodism paused to observe this anniversary and to take stock of its progress, it realized that it had an unfulfilled obligation to the intellectual and social advancement of this country. The celebration of the centenary of Methodism took many forms. On the material side it was signalized by the giving of large sums of money to be invested in religious and educational enterprises. Everywhere there was emphasis on education.

Following the recommendation of the General Conference of the Methodist Church, the Newark Conference, meeting at Washington, New Jersey, in March, 1866, passed the following resolutions:

Whereas, Gratitude to God, for such a Centenary of Methodism as it has been our exalted privilege to behold should lead us to enlarged beneficence and to the setting up of some memorial which, while it should stand as a pillar with its inscription of "Hitherto hath the Lord helped us," should be an instrument for the advancement of the cause of God and the promotion of the interests of man. And

Whereas, The General Conference has recommended to each Conference the founding and endowment of at least one institution of learning within its bounds; and

Whereas, The educational wants of our people in the northern part of our State remain unmet by any seminary of high grade—one corresponding to the advance of our church in all its other departments of activity and usefulness—therefore,

Resolved, That we endorse, most heartily, the proposition of the General Conference, and recommend to our people the erection of an academic institution that shall be an honor to the church and a blessing to future generations.

The Newark Conference was at this time only nine years old, having been formed in 1857 out of the territory of northern New Jersey originally included in the bounds of the New Jersey Conference. For several years both the old and the new conferences held Pennington Seminary, a co-educational school, as a common possession and a suitable place for the education of their sons and daughters. In 1865, however, the Newark Conference deemed it best to transfer its interest in Pennington to its sister conference. Left thus without a school within its territory, it was logical that it should pass, at the same session, the following resolution—historic as the first step in the history of Centenary:

Whereas, By the action of this Conference the Pennington Seminary has been transferred to the New Jersey Conference, which leaves this Conference without any institution of the kind under its supervision; and

Whereas, The late General Conference recommends that each Annual Conference have at least one Seminary under its supervision; therefore,

Resolved, That the Committee on the Centenary of Methodism be directed to consider the subject of founding within our bounds an institution of learning worthy of the times, and that they make due inquiry as to what may be done in any of the several localities where such an institution may be desired, and report to this Conference at its next session.

At the next annual meeting of the Conference—the one hundredth anniversary of American Methodism—the Committee on the Centenary recommended the following resolutions:

Resolved, That as a thanks-offering accompanying our centennial celebration, the Newark Conference ought to raise at least the sum of $150,000 . . . . That in view of our peculiar necessity, having no Seminary under our supervision and a vast population of children and youth looking to us for the facilities of Christian education, we should be recreant to our trust if we did not avail ourselves of this great occasion to establish one, on a permanent financial basis of at least $75,000; That the locating of the Seminary be left to the Centenary committee; That the Conference Centenary committee be instructed to apply to the Legislature of the State for a charter, with powers and privileges suitable for the organization and control of an academic institution of a high order.

A very liberal charter, granted on March 6, 1867, authorized and empowered the Newark Annual Conference of the Methodist Episcopal Church

to found any institution in this State, whose object shall be for the promotion of learning: and for the purpose, ... they are hereby further empowered to elect twelve persons, one half of whom shall be members of the said Conference: and the other half shall be laymen of the Methodist Episcopal Church, as Trustees of the said Institution . . . . which said Trustees, and their successors are hereby constituted a body politic and corporate in fact name and law to all intents and purposes forever by whatsoever name the Trustees elected as aforesaid shall take and assume.[2]

No time was lost. That same month the first Board of Trustees was appointed. In April they met in Newark and chose Mr. Cornelius Walsh, Esq., Presi-

[2] This charter has since been changed to allow a larger number of Trustees.

dent, Hon. George T. Cobb, Treasurer and J. K. Burr, Secretary. The first subject they considered was the naming of the Seminary. Several names were proposed, among which was that of "The Centenary Collegiate Institute of the Newark Conference, New Jersey." This, after some discussion, was adopted. At a later date the decision was reconsidered and the last two words omitted.

Many institutions bear the name of an outstanding benefactor or a great personality, but the word "Centenary" forever uniquely carries in its connotation honor to the memory of vast numbers, many known and widely revered, many more unknown and now unnameable,—men and women who had labored for a century in the cause of righteousness. From 1766 to 1866—what a significant section of American history!—years of perplexities and decisions, of experiment, creation, and testing, of civil strife and moral contention. But the founders were thinking also of the beginning of the second century for which the new school was to educate ministers and other leaders.

Centenary—for by this name we have come more and more to call it—is a name that looks both backward to pay respect to the past and forward to greet the future with a cheer. There is a sense of round completeness alike in its resonant syllables and in its meaning —rich with overtones—which yields more and more as one ponders it.

The next question was: where should the school be located? A matter of such importance had to be referred to a special meeting of the conference,—called for this purpose a convention—which met in Newark, June 3, 1867.

The Convention directed the Trustees to procure a site "at Morristown or in its immediate vicinity." Many towns were in competition for the honor of becoming Centenary's home. First Madison sent a committee of citizens headed by Judge Potts to offer $20,000 as an inducement. Their offer was accepted, provided a site could be found. This condition apparently could not be met. Next, Morristown and its vicinity were considered. Mr. Cobb tendered a gift of five or ten acres of land or its value in money. Meanwhile Mr. Cornelius Walsh had presented a site of three hundred acres in Bernardsville. Claims were advanced also for Flanders, Washington, Irvington, Orange, Plainfield, and Newark as desirable towns.

Just before final action was to be taken, came an offer signed by ten citizens of Hackettstown, pledging themselves to donate ten acres of land and $10,000 in cash for the Seminary, if Hackettstown were chosen as the site.

It was now March, 1868—time for the Newark Conference to convene. Since July 29, 1867, the Committee had been holding meetings at various places and considering different locations but they had no decision to report. Fortunately the Conference now absolved the Trustees of their restriction as to site and suggested favorable consideration of "the liberal proposition from Hackettstown."

It was Spring when the Trustees visited the proffered site. Ah—who that has once seen it can ever forget the Musconetcong Valley in springtime? After viewing the grounds carefully they partook of a "sumptuous dinner provided by the Hackettstown committee."

The result was never in doubt—a unanimous acceptance of the generous offer presented to them and signed by:[3]

George Roe
R. Q. Bowers
Alpheus Clawson
George W. Johnson
J. H. Curtis

J. Welsh, Jr.
Caleb H. Valentine
William L. Johnson
Isaac W. Crane
David Shields.

Suitable guarantees were required that the remainder of the tract of land owned by the ten donors be so managed as not to affect unfavorably the part accepted; and a promise was exacted that the citizens "provide a good walk of stone or plank from Main Street to Jefferson Street."

More committees now went to work, among them one to procure a plan for buildings,[4] another to make inquiry for a suitable man to be Principal of the Institute. The services of Mr. S. B. Hatch, an architect of New York City, were secured, plans were presented and revised, and the contract was awarded to the Hackettstown contractors Clawson and Haszen, in accord with their bid of $78,000. Not long afterwards, Stryker and Brother also took some work under contract. It was later decided to put up an additional wing in the same style as the main building, to cost $19,350.

On August 11, 1869, at a special meeting of the Trustees, "the Reverend George H. Whitney A.M. was appointed Principal of the Centenary Collegiate Insti-

[3] Minutes of the Trustees, April 16, 1868.
[4] The Building committee consisted of: President Cornelius Walsh, George J. Ferry, J. R. Bryan, Peter Smith, J. T. Crane, and A. L. Brice.

tute, of the Newark Conference." His duty for a year was to solicit subscriptions from individuals and in church audiences after delivering a sermon or address.

George Henry Whitney was a man whose varied experience had well prepared him for this responsible position. At fourteen he had been a bookkeeper in Washington, D. C., and at seventeen he was Daily Editor of the Washington *National Whig*. "From 14 to 18½ yrs," he writes, "I studied much, made many addresses on Temperance." Late in 1848 he opened his own "select school" in Irvington, New Jersey, which he continued until, in 1851, he became a student in Wesleyan Institute, Newark. Here he remained three years studying continuously and working also as secretary and bookkeeper and later as teacher. By this time he was ready for Wesleyan University, which he attended for the usual four years, devoting some months each year, however, to teaching in select schools in East Hampton and Roxbury, Connecticut. After his graduation in 1858 he was for one year President of Macedon Academy and for two years President of Oneida Seminary.

In 1861 he entered the Newark Conference and for the thirteen years between then and the opening of C. C. I. in 1874 he was in pastorates in Somerville, Elizabeth, Newton, Plainfield, Jersey City, and Passaic. Now at the age of thirty-nine, he was entering upon work which would appeal to his varied interests and call for all his abilities.

Throughout the Summer of 1869 the Trustees met very often, wherever their members could most conveniently be gathered together, now in Hackettstown, again in Newark, and at times at the Camp-Meeting

Grounds near Denville. By September they were busy arranging for the laying of the cornerstone.

This significant event was extensively advertised. Special excursion trains were run. Seats were provided on the grounds for two thousand persons.

Centenary's President, who of course was there, made this report of the day in his autobiography:

"On September 9, 1869, occurred an event of vast importance, viz. the laying of the cornerstone of the new Institute. Ceremony—addresses, collections. Bishop Matthew Simpson, our greatest Methodist Orator made the address, and laid the cornerstone. There was a very large audience. The day was a perfect September day."

The place, he wrote, was "desolate". Not a tree—not a shrub. The town had not then grown as far as the lot. There was then no street in front of the grounds and Church Street was not opened.

But the cornfield where just four years before this the far-seeing Presiding Elder, Mr. Vancleve, had made his emphatic prophecy was now in preparation for a far richer harvest and the most important part of the vision outlined in 1865 had already been realized, the enlistment of the enthusiastic devotion of the man who was to be the guiding spirit of Centenary for more than a quarter of her first century.

CHAPTER II

"Alma Mater Proudly Raises Halls and Tower Tall and Strong"

BUILDING A MONUMENT TO FAITH AND ENTHUSIASM

THE site had been chosen, the cornerstone laid, and the Conference and its Board of Trustees were definitely committed to the heavy task which now confronted them, the building and equipping of an "Educational Institution" which should be an honor to the Newark Conference and to the Methodist Episcopal Church. The serious problem which they were now compelled to study and if possible solve, was that of the finances. The sum of money raised by the Newark Conference during the Centennial year of American Methodism and pledged for the Conference Seminary was about[1] $44,587. This sum could serve only as a beginning. As work on the building progressed, numerous changes in the original plan were found to be desirable and necessary for the beauty and symmetry of the building and for its adaptation to the work for which it was designed. Almost every one of these changes called for increased expense. The original plan was to complete but one wing of the main building, leaving the other to be completed in the future. But serious objections to this plan arose. The school was designed

---

1 The report submitted to the Conference stated that the exact figures could not be given.

to be co-educational, and it could not be opened on this basis without the completion of both wings. Besides, thousands of dollars would be wasted in tearing down what had been built up, when the missing wing should be added. It was therefore resolved not to open the school, until the main building was fully completed. This meant a large increase over the original estimated expense.

The Newark Conference showed excellent judgment in the selection from year to year of the men who formed its Board of Trustees. There were among them keen and shrewd business men, accustomed to the direction of large business affairs. These men showed in the management of the affairs of the Institute the same zeal and devotion that they gave to their own business. Some of these men remained in the Board for many years, being reelected by the Conference year after year, and during all these years they freely gave their time, their wise counsel and their money besides, to the service of the Institute. Conspicuous among them were the first three Presidents of the Board of Trustees: Cornelius Walsh, David Campbell and the Honorable George J. Ferry.

The first expedient adopted for the raising of money was the appointment of a "committee of six to be called an Educational Committee to consist of three laymen and three ministers, whose duty it shall be to travel through the Conference, holding meetings and raising monies for the benefit of the Seminary to whom shall be intrusted the whole matter of raising money." This committee was constituted as follows:—President Cornelius Walsh, the Honorable George J. Ferry, Mr. Enoch

Bolles, the Reverend J. T. Crane, the Reverend L. R. Dunn, and the Reverend A. L. Brice. The names of the Reverend J. S. Porter and Mr. H. N. Ege were added to this committee.

Four months after this the Trustees determined to appoint a Financial Agent who was to devote all his time in going to and fro throughout the bounds of the Conference, holding public meetings, soliciting individuals, and seeking in all legitimate ways contributions to the funds for building the Seminary. The first Agent employed for the year 1869-1870 was the Reverend George H. Whitney.

His autobiography brings to life again these days of long ago. Says he:

I had some 'queer' experiences; some 'funny', some illustrations of great nobility, of great meanness. My work was generally delightful and successful. But I did not thoroughly *enjoy* 'begging' from house to house, and pulpit to pulpit. The work on the Institute continued at Hackettstown, *slowly*, because the Trustees, wisely, decided not to advance beyond the treasurer's receipts— not now at least. We would soon use up the $12,000 on hand—so I must bestir myself.

Strange disappointments began at the very cornerstone laying. Mr. Whitney relates:

Mr. Cornelius Walsh, the rich layman, said to me that day: 'I cannot subscribe today; but you may rely upon it that no matter how much any man gives I will give more'.—Alas! Bro. Walsh not long afterwards failed, and really died poor. He did, however, give me $2,000 before he failed. That same day, Mr. George

T. Cobb of Morristown, who had just given $100,000 to build that Church, said to me: 'I will give you $100 today, but you may rely upon me to give as much as any man—or more'. Alas! not long after, he was killed in Virginia, by a railroad accident. 'Man proposes, God disposes.'

In contrast to this are entries such as this:

Dr. Crane came to aid me in raising money for the new Institute. It was a grand occasion and we raised $3,000!

Two other Agents were employed the following year; the Reverend J. C. Blain, and the Reverend J. W. Young. The third Agent was the Reverend C. E. Little and the fourth the Reverend J. M. Tuttle, who served two years. To facilitate the work of these financial Agents, various expedients were devised. It was resolved by the Trustees:

That meetings be held on different districts, at the most central points at which people can be reached, and that the Presiding Elders be requested to invite their preachers to meet with the District Stewards at their annual meeting to make arrangements for the meeting which it is desirable to hold at the earliest opportunity. The Secretary was directed to communicate to the Elders the action of the Board.

A committee was appointed to prepare two kinds of certificates to be presented to those who made contributions to the Seminary; those who paid one dollar or over and not more than ten dollars, to receive a certificate on letter paper ornamented with an engraving of the Seminary; and those who paid more than ten dollars to receive a certificate with a photograph of the Seminary suitable for framing. Pastors throughout the Conference were requested to cooperate in collection of subscriptions. The managers of the Camp-Meeting were asked to set apart a day to be devoted to the interests of the Seminary. During the summer a day was thus observed. The Reverend Dr. Dashiell, President of Dickinson College, was invited "to spend his vacation within the bounds of the Conference, devoting his time and talents to the interests of the Seminary, holding meetings and otherwise cooperating with the Agents."

But notwithstanding all these varied and vigorous efforts on the part of the Trustees to raise money, bills came in more rapidly than contributions. In March, 1871, the treasury of the Seminary was more than $17,000 in arrears, and this money was imperatively needed. To facilitate borrowing money, "it was moved and carried that the President be authorized to give the Trustees' note or notes to an amount not exceeding $25,000, at any one time; and that the President be appointed a committee to secure a proper mortgage to be held by a Trustee as a collateral security for the payment of said Trustee notes, said notes not to be given for a longer time than twelve months, the notes to be issued upon the written request of the building committee." George J. Ferry and David Campbell loaned $5,000 each on this security.

Meanwhile the walls of Centenary had been rising slowly. For nearly a year after the four-story walls were up, and before the roof was on, no work was done on the building because of the low state of the finances. Before the winter of 1871 and 1872 began, the roof was on and the building fully enclosed, but there was no flooring except on the first floor. Then the work ceased. Thousands of people visited the huge structure and admired it in its mute incompleteness, alike a worthy monument of the Church's devotion to the cause of Christian education and of faith in its ability to finish what it had begun.

In the Spring, the ladies of Hackettstown determined to give a dinner in the unfinished dining-room of the gaunt frame, and to take up a collection under the management of Dr. R. L. Dashiell. Writes President Whitney: "The dinner of the ladies was of course a success; but, there being no way to heat the immense (40x80) dining room, unplastered, unsightly,—the room was so cold and dismal that 'money raising' was totally abandoned."

Rescue came, however, as a result of one of President Whitney's inspirations. Let him relate the story:

Knowing the 'poverty'? or small estates of the ministry in general, but equally knowing that the ministry have ever been leaders in all educational affairs—and that *they* had projected this 'Institute'—I planned a noble gift for 'our ministers' to make to the cause. I proposed that the *ministers* from their *own* incomes (*not* from churches) should subscribe $10,000! payable yearly for 3 years. Some thought I was 'wild', 'insane', 'too far ahead of the times'.

At the session of Conference, in Morristown, March, '71, we made a special appeal from ministers, and from laymen. My proposition was well known, and much had already been subscribed to me in person. At the session very much enthusiasm was aroused by the need and glory of the great Institution now in process of erection. At the close of the 'effort' it was announced that the *ministers alone* had subscribed the noble sum of $17,252!! and the laymen $15,248, thus making a grand total of $32,500.

"This magnificent gift," states the Trustees report to the Conference of 1872, "rescued the Institution from its position of danger and gave to its affairs such a prestige that the entire year now closing has felt its influence."

When it is recalled that many ministers of those days received only six hundred dollars a year, or less, one's imagination is not hard pressed to picture the many sacrifices and privations that made possible the raising of C. C. I.'s "halls and tower tall and strong."

In November, 1872, George J. Ferry proposed "a plan for proceeding confidently to the speedy completion of the building; viz. to raise either in cash or by valid and unquestionable notes $30,000, payable during the next five years in annual and equal installments; upon this to place a mortgage upon the Seminary property to the amount of $30,000." He offered to contribute $5,000, on the above conditions and also to cancel the $5,000 note which he held as security for money previously loaned. David Campbell also offered $5,000 on the same conditions, to which was added $4,000 previously subscribed. The plan of Mr. Ferry was unanimously adopted. In two week's time, subscriptions under this plan had amounted to $18,500. On April 2, 1874, David Campbell, who had served the Board of Trustees as President honorably and faithfully for four years, resigned his office. The Honorable George J. Ferry was elected President in his stead. The long and arduous struggle with the problem of the finances had been continued for four years and the building was now approaching completion.

It must not be forgotten, too, that this work had been proceeding during "hard times." The terrible Black Friday of September 19, 1873 had blasted fortunes in a day and inaugurated a depression that laid a heavy hand on American life for several years to follow.

It must have been with a feeling of heart-felt relief that on May 14, 1874, the Trustees voted that September 9, 1874, "be fixed upon as the day for opening the Seminary." A prospectus prepared by Dr. Whitney was adopted and 10,000 copies were ordered to be printed. The fee for board and tuition for the Academic year of 36 weeks was fixed at $275 exclusive of extras. A deduction of twenty-five per cent from regular rates was given for children of ministers, thirty-three per cent for students preparing for the ministry.

The main building had been completed and dedicated. The first President had been chosen and the school opened. And yet the harassing financial problem which had for four years taxed the sagacity of the Trustees had not been fully solved. With the opening of the school new and heavy expenses had necessarily been incurred. The furniture for the building had cost nearly $17,000. A barn and other out-buildings had been erected. The grounds had been adorned under the superintendency of the Reverend C. E. Little with 200 trees and 800 shrubs. These and other necessary expenses had so greatly increased the debt that early in 1875 the Trustees were obliged to borrow $32,000 secured by a mortgage on the Institute property. A policy

GEORGE J. FERRY
Trustee, 1869-1911; President of Board of Trustees,
1872-1911

of retrenchment was now adopted. Expenditures were scrutinized and minimized. The meager salaries of the Teachers and other employees of the school were cut down and vigorous efforts were made to raise money to relieve the financial situation. In November, 1881, a gleam of hope appeared on the dark horizon. Mr. George I. Seney of New York promised Dr. Whitney a gift of $15,000, on the condition that the Trustees would raise the remaining $17,000 required to pay off the mortgage, before the annual meeting of the Newark Conference. This was only four months distant. The time was short. Was it possible to meet this heavy condition? The Trustees resolved to begin again a vigorous campaign for financial contributions; and in addition to all the sacrifices which they had previously made, they pledged their names for new and generous subscriptions. George J. Ferry subscribed $4,000, H. M. Gillette $4,000, J. C. Allen $1,000, and other Trustees lesser sums, amounting in all to $11,700.

An appeal was made to the Presiding Elders of the Conference to aid them in securing contributions. But the people throughout the bounds of the Newark Conference, having been so often called upon for money during the past sixteen years, were getting "weary in well-doing," and contributions came in slowly and in small sums; so that when only about two months remained of the time within which they must raise the $17,000, or else forfeit Mr. Seney's conditional gift, one of the Trustees, yielding to discouragement, offered the following resolution:

Whereas, the Board of Trustees find a lamentable lack of interest in the Hackettstown Institute on the part of the laymen of Newark Conference as to paying off the funded debt, be it therefore Resolved, That it is with feelings of deep regret that we are obliged to decline the generous offer of G. I. Seney and that this Board deem it unadvisable to make any further effort at this time to liquidate the funded debt of Hackettstown Institute.

However, there were other men on that Board, that were not easily discouraged. Mr. Ferry increased his former contribution by $1,000. Mr. J. C. Ludlow added to his subscription $200, and the resolution quoted above was laid on the table. It would seem that the crisis now reached had inspired an increased public interest in the matter, for at the next meeting of the Trustees, held only three weeks later, additional subscriptions were received amounting to $2,775, more than enough to complete the sum of $17,000, and thus, with the aid of Mr. Seney's gift now available, to cancel the mortgage.

On March 30, 1882, the school stood for the first time free from debt. Remembering the years of struggle, the Newark Conference tempered its rejoicing with a resolution urging that the property be hereafter kept free from any encumbrance. Would that it had been possible ever after to follow this counsel.!

CHAPTER III

"And Her Children Sing Her Praises"

ALMA MATER GATHERS IN HER
CHILDREN: 1874-1875

WHEN in August of 1869 George H. Whitney accepted the presidency of Centenary Collegiate Institute, he probably had no idea that fully five years were to pass before he should stand before the school as its head. Several times during those years he had had the opportunity to step into the leadership of a flourishing organization. Cazenovia invited him more than once. Pennington sought him. Then, too, the Board of Bishops elected him to found the mission that the church had decided to establish in Japan. "All of these and other similar offers," says Whitney, "I declined, desiring to finish and organize the Institute which I flattered myself should be the finest and most successful Seminary the Methodist Church had yet produced."

Now September of 1874 was rapidly bringing a Day which was to stand forever as the dividing line between the time when Centenary Collegiate Institute had never been and all the years of her history—Opening Day.

What multiform preparations had been going forward all over the campus! What interest they had aroused! It is said that on pleasant Sundays during the whole five years "very many, even multitudes came many miles from all the surrounding country to gaze upon the big building." Among the plain country folk it was a common remark: "What great fools these Methodists are to build so mighty a house as this—they'll never in the world have it half full."

In the last feverish days of completion, President and Mrs. Whitney were greatly aided by the Reverend A. L. Brice. Says the President:

> To get the furniture into the house and properly placed in so great a house was an extraordinary work of labor—chiefly because the furniture did not reach the town in time, and we found it difficult to get enough men to help in the work.

At last the building was in readiness, "a noble structure . . . . within and without. The interior was fresh, clean, spotless, handsomely, tho' not elegantly furnished."

The Day, September 9, was bright, clear, beautiful indeed. Its dawning light shone upon President Whitney busily writing his Inaugural Address. "So overwhelming had been the demands upon my time for many weeks," he explains in his *Life,* "that I had not yet finished writing my "inaugural address" the night before. Thus on the morning of "opening day" I rose at 4 o'clock, went to a 4th story room, No. 46 on Ladies' side over our own rooms, and there for three hours wrote until I finished—what had been *planned* and thought out for months over and over again."

The event had been heralded far and wide. The President of the Morris and Essex Railroad furnished a great number of passes from the cities. Special excur-

Centenary Collegiate Institute in 1874

sion tickets and coaches were provided. Fully five thousand persons came[1]

The Trustees had secured a great circus tent for the front campus in which thousands could be seated. Here at ten o'clock the service for the dedication of the building was led by the Rev. Charles N. Sims, D.D., substituting for Bishop Janes, who was too ill to be there. The star speaker invited for the occasion was the Governor of New Jersey, the Honorable Joel Parker, a staunch Presbyterian who told that Methodist crowd much about their own history. Many notable personages were present. The Hackettstown *Herald* commented: "This is altogether probably the most distinguished body of people ever met in Warren County."

At twelve o'clock a big dinner was served in the dining hall by the ladies of Hackettstown. Nine hundred were seated. At either end of the President's table was a huge, handsome cake, gift of the two rival bakers of the town, each cake supposed to be presented with a neat speech. "But," writes the President, "as we never sat at the table that day, we did not see the cakes or taste them, or hear any speech. So busy were we that dinner came not to us or we to dinner."

In the afternoon, the chapel, packed with an audience of seven hundred, was the scene of the Inaugural Exercises. The Honorable George J. Ferry presented the keys of the Institute to the President, who then delivered his Inaugural Address.

But Opening Day meant more than dedication and inauguration formalities. After all, a school exists for its students. Picture then, boys and girls—accompanied

[1] This is President Whitney's estimate.

by fond fathers and mothers—going through the process of registration. The first student to inscribe her name in the original record book[2] was Flora Green, of Orange, New Jersey, a "transfer" from Orange High School.[3]

Actually, however, the first students to be enrolled were Colin S. Carter, and George Carter, who had been entered two months earlier by their father, a newspaper editor in Middletown, Connecticut, where he had known George H. Whitney as a student in Wesleyan University.

One hundred and eight boarding students registered and a number of day students. All were asked to state, with other information, their "Aim in life." Of the "Female Boarding Students", nine wished to become teachers, one a missionary, one a journalist. Two sought to "Be good and do Good"; two merely to "do good". The others had no expressed objective. Their ages ranged from thirteen to twenty-two, the average being seventeen. All but six were Methodists.

Of the "Male Students," twenty were preparing for the ministry, seven wished to enter business, six had chosen to become lawyers, five merchants, three farmers, two physicians, two teachers, one a missionary, one a banker, and one an undertaker. Fifty of the total number of boys in attendance that year had not chosen a vocation. The youngest of them was ten, the oldest, thirty-two! There were several entries of ages ranging from twenty to twenty-seven.

2 Still in existence and still legible, though charred and stained before its rescue from the fire of 1899.

3 Now Mrs. W. P. Richards. She visited her Alma Mater to participate in a historical pageant, as recently as 1940.

Enrolment details complete, the student had next to be guided to his or her room. This too was largely the President's work. Reconstruct in imagination these lively scenes:

To assign all those 108 their rooms during that eventful day was a work of really prodigious labor and difficulty. Of course the Faculty aided me nobly in every possible way. But not one of them had ever met one of those 108 or one of their 108+108 fathers and mothers—while *I* had corresponded with *all* and had seen most of them—*none* of them would accept any service from *anyone* but myself. So, *often* and often when I would accompany a father, mother, daughter—to a room on 2nd, 3rd, or 4th hall—50 or 100 would follow me to see me, to ask questions, etc. etc.—crowd into the room densely packing it, crowding me into the remotest corner—so that I had to plead with them to go out of the room—so that *I* could get out to give all a chance to converse with me at earliest moment. My dear wife was similarly besieged—and so were some of the faculty.

At last the visitors departed. Evening came. Students and teachers sat down to eat together for the first time.

"After supper", concludes the President's story of this day, "we held our first chapel service. . . . I made a brief address of welcome, explaining some few duties and requirements and wishing all a good night's rest."

The President's Inaugural Address was described by Professor L. H. Batchelder, of Centenary's first faculty, as showing "far-reaching plans—a key-note speech." It did in fact give clear answers to the question which he felt all were with perfect justice asking, namely: what are the plans and aims of the school and how shall they be carried out?

Condemning showy, superficial training, President Whitney asserted that Centenary Collegiate Institute was designed to be a school of *sound learning,* "thorough in discipline, thorough in training, thorough in culture,— an institution that will lay broad and deep foundations on which may be built the most accomplished and brilliant scholarship . . . ." I will not sacrifice thoroughness for numbers" .. . .

Thoroughness he considered the essential principle of true success. It must have pleased his hearers to learn that this rule of life was to apply to all of school life, when he added:

We are determined not that this shall be a *boarding house with a school attached* to make it seem literary; but that it shall be *strictly a literary institution* with a home attached—with that attachment so necessary in this mortal state—a good *cuisine.*

But with President Whitney the process of education was by no means confined to books. "The students," he insisted, "must be taught to comprehend the difference between mere book-knowledge and culture . . . . There is such a thing as grace in education, ability to speak when speech is needed, as well as ability to be silent when silence is golden."

Another principle strong in Dr. Whitney's creed was the inculcation of the love of the beautiful. He goes on, expanding this idea:

There is indeed, and we hail it with profound pleasure, a growing tendency towards the aesthetic in education. The boy shall learn music as well as the girl. The young man shall study drawing and painting as well as the young lady... All this adorns the home, and what is life without home, and what is home without the love of the beautiful? That is a better home whose walls though not rising to lofty ceilings are adorned with the daughter's pencil and brush; that is a more attractive and hence a better home where are heard the strains of music from the skilful fingers and cultivated voice of the beloved children of the household... Now what should be our aim? Undoubtedly we must combine the excellence of the solid training school with the finer and more aesthetic element of a first-class education.

Of kindred importance in Dr. Whitney's mind is the social training of the young. They must learn the finest art of all, that of creating successful home life. Said he:

Men are not always in the market place or in the stock exchange. There is something better than money and beef and stock. Money and paintings and statuary do not constitute in themselves a happy home. Men want *homes*. Arithmetic and Astronomy, and Greek and Physiology do not make homes. The social element is the sunbeam that gilds all the pictures on the wall with beauty and with grace.

A good school, in Dr. Whitney's opinion, should teach the amenities and graces of life. "Students ought not to be mere animals at the table or boors in the parlors. *Refinement* in company is part of a first-class education."

Speaking of the advantages and disadvantages of a "foreign education", he stated his belief that:

Somewhat kindred to the influence of travel is the study of history.—History shows the successes and the failures of the past both among individuals and nations; and the thoughtful student of history becomes a philosopher finding out the causes of success and failure. History must be considered one of the most important studies in our curriculum.

The religious element of education, he thought, must never be overlooked. With utmost sincerity he announced:

We wish to acknowledge with much emphasis that this is a religious school, and more than that, it is a Christian school. . . . We teach no sectarian dogmas, we demand no adherence to creeds, but we reverence God's word, and make its teachings our sole guide in morals. We wish parents to feel that the safeguards of a Christian home are thrown about their sons and their daughters in this place. We wish with all our souls to help their children to possess a true manhood, a true womanhood—that is, a manhood of truth, a womanhood of truth.

Concluding his speech, the President asserted:

It is not too much to ask that from these walls may go forth the spirit of sound learning, with an influence that shall be felt not only in every hamlet in our State, but in all parts of this great country. Our youth are the flower of the State. Why may they not become an honor to the nation at large? Hundreds of young men and women shall here doubtless receive a new inspiration of truth and go forth with broader views of life, to be successful in all the avenues of trade and commerce; to shine in the professions, to adorn the homes over which Providence shall call them to preside, and to bless their fellow men with thousand-fold power.

In harmony with these ideals was the motto which he proposed for the school, "All done, and all well done."

High standards these, concrete and definite. No less clear was the need in those days, as always, for an institution that stood ready to advance them. In 1874 there were in all the United States only seventy schools of this grade. There were only four recognized high schools in the State of New Jersey.

President Whitney's ideals were shared, as he said in his Address, by "the cultivated gentlemen and ladies who compose the faculty. To select these," he confides in his autobiography, "was a labor indeed. I felt the heavy responsibility. For five years I had been ever receiving applications. . . . After untold difficulties I announced the Faculty only a few days before opening." It was as follows:

Dr. Whitney[4],
    Professor of Mental and Moral Philosophy.
Reverend Henry C. Whiting, A. M.,
    Professor of Ancient Languages.
Loring H. Batchelder, A. B.,
    Professor of Natural Science and Mathematics.
Edward A. Whitney,
    Professor of Commercial Department[5]

---

4 In 1873 the degree of Doctor of Divinity had been conferred upon President Whitney by Wesleyan University. During the first two years, he took upon himself the teaching of five classes daily—"when," says he of himself, "he should have had not more than two."

5 "He was", writes the President, "my brother, much beloved . . . He was of great service to the school and to myself he was simply invaluable. He was with me for twenty-one years—dying a few months before my own departure from the Institute in 1895." He was also the cashier and bookkeeper of the Institute.

Joseph S. Smith, Professor of Phonography.
Professor Charles Grobé, Musical Director.
Miss Martha A. Wragge,
   Preceptress, Belles-Lettres and French[6]
Miss Fanny Gulick, M. L. A.,
   English Literature and German.
Miss Anna Nicholl, M. L. A.,
   History, Painting, and Drawing.
Miss Stella Waldo, Piano and Organ.
Miss Laura J. Hanlon, M. E. L.,
   Piano, Organ, and Vocal Music.
Edward A. Whitney, Librarian.

C. C. I.'s Annual Catalogue announced:

The design of the institution is to afford to young people of both sexes the amplest facilities for securing a superior education at the lowest rates compatible with real excellence.[7] By thorough Classical, Scientific, Commercial, Literary, and Aesthetical Courses of Study, young men are prepared either for the higher classes in College, or for the Theological Seminary, or for business and social life.

This preparation for the higher classes in College called for work of high grade covered in three years. The classes were called the Junior, the Middle and the Senior.

   6 A lady was always a "teacher." Only the men were called "Professors."
   7 The cost of board and tuition for all grades for the academic year was $275. There were extra charges for courses in Modern Languages, Music, Phonography, Drawing and Painting in Water Colors, Oil Painting, Wax Flowers, and Fruit. Two dollars was charged for the use of carpet! Three dollars per term covered the cost for use of piano or organ for practice.

Below this in grade was an Academic Course for both "Ladies" and "Gentlemen," comprising in the first year the study of Arithmetic, Geography, Grammar, Reading, Spelling, Penmanship, Composition, and Declamation; in the second year, Bookkeeping, United States History, Physiology, Latin, Mental Arithmetic, Algebra; plus Reading, Spelling, Penmanship, Composition, Letter Writing, Declamation and Calisthenics. With this preparation many students advanced into one or another of the higher courses.

Centenary thus became a model high school. But this was by no means all. It was by design and not by mere chance, or for reasons of euphony, that the school had been named Centenary *"Collegiate"* Institute.

Having been authorized by the State to found "any institution whose object shall be for the promotion of learning", and having resolved to establish an institution "worthy of the times," the Conference had determined on a forward-looking, even a pioneering policy. These were the years when women were just being considered "college material," in the hope that they might perchance possess intelligence enough to study the same courses as their brothers. Few were the colleges devoted to their higher education, fewer still the co-educational opportunities.

Thus C. C. I. was in the very front of educational progress in announcing in its Catalogue:

The Department for Young Ladies is a regularly chartered College, and is empowered to confer degrees upon those ladies who complete the prescribed courses of study..... Ladies who pass a satisfactory examination in the four years' College Course of Study receive a

Diploma, conferring the title and degree of MISTRESS OF LIBERAL ARTS—M. L. A. Those ladies who satisfactorily complete the Belles-Lettres Course receive a diploma, with the title and degree of MISTRESS OF ENGLISH LITERATURE—M. E. L.

The "Ladies' College" continued for twenty-two years, until Dr. Ferguson's administration. By this time the present large women's colleges were well under way and the Methodist Church had a first-rank one of its own, the Woman's College of Baltimore, now Goucher College.

There were in the school ten Departments of Instruction: English; Ancient Languages; Mathematics; Natural Sciences; Intellectual and Moral Science and Belles-Lettres; Modern Languages; Music; Drawing and Painting; Commercial; Normal.

The year was divided into three terms: two of thirteen weeks and one of fourteen weeks. Pupils were received at any time during the year, but it was emphasized, "It is of the first importance to be present on the opening day of the term."

All students were required to bring "certificates of moral character. Any known to be immoral," stated the Catalogue, "will be rejected." Examinations were given to determine assignment to classes. "Candidates for the Ladies' College and Belles-Lettres Courses will pass an examination on the studies of the Academic Course or an equivalent."

The four years of the Ladies' College Course were devoted to the study[8] of Greek, Latin, French, Algebra,

8 The list follows the order of subjects, term by term, throughout the four years.

Geometry, Rhetoric, Outlines of History, German, Natural Philosophy, Mythology, Mental Philosophy, Trigonometry, Civil Government, Greek and Roman History, Chemistry, Astronomy, Moral Philosophy, Logic, Political Economy, English Literature, Botany, Geology, with an elective course in Elements of Criticism and Evidences of Christianity. Essays, Elocution and Calisthenics were featured throughout the whole course. Latin Composition was required during the Sophomore Year.

Remembering Dr. Whitney's devotion to "thoroughness," we can feel sure that the "Young Ladies" earned their degrees M. L. A. and M. E. L.

The total registration for the three terms of the first year was 251; of these 180 were resident students and 71 day students. Since there was good train service, many day students came from all the neighboring towns.

The largest Department in the school was that of Music. During the first year, eighty-seven were studying instrumental music—piano, organ, violin, flute, guitar—and seventy-two vocal music. The work of the department included also Ensemble singing, Theory, Harmony, Composition, and History and Aesthetics of Music. The management of the school stated:

> It is our design to render these departments worthy of the patronage of those who consider a musical education to be more than a mere showy appendage to a fashionable and superficial education.
> An unusually comprehensive course has been adopted, embracing all departments of musical culture.
> Every effort will be employed not only to secure the most thorough and rapid advancement of the pupil, but

to render the study enjoyable and profitable in every respect, and to inspire a love and admiration for the art.

There was a "Normal Class" for those intending to teach.

The students were apparently very much impressed with the work of the music department (obviously it was the one which could make the most immediate and conspicuous display of its attainments) for they devoted to it a very large proportion of space in the first publication called "The Scroll"—with subtitle—"Devoted to the True, the Beautiful, and the Good[9]. They spoke almost lyrically of "the bright musical future in store for our beloved Institute."

In point of fact, throughout the years the department steadily grew in numbers and the excellence of C. C. I. as a school of music was widely recognized. In 1894, *The Journal* of Elmira, New York wrote of C. C. I.:

The Fine Arts and Music are special features. There are few schools in the United States that have the facilities for musical instruction possessed by this institution."

True to his emphasis upon the cultural and aesthetic, Dr. Whitney introduced into Centenary a feature which, he says, was never before known in any preparatory

---

[9] This was the first paper ever published by C. C. I. students. Volume I, No. 1 was dated December 15, 1874. Its Editor was Thomas James Bass and the assistant Editors were J. W. Slaght and S. A. Johnson. No copies of any later numbers are to be found. The fact that Thomas J. Bass, who hailed from Dundalk, Ireland, was expelled during the first year may indicate that this was the first and only number.

The Old Building—Main Entrance

The Old Building—Dining Room

school. This was a course of "Lectures by able speakers from abroad." There were fourteen lectures the first year, with topics—choosing different types—ranging from "Chisel and Brush" and "Glimpses of California" to "Strange Phases of Human Nature" and "Curiosities of Love." They were open to the townspeople for a nominal charge, and according to all accounts were looked forward to with pleasure by all. Dr. Whitney speaks of the labor it required to secure the right speakers with the small means at his command, but he adds:

> I found these distinguished men ready to come at my entreaty and I am happy to say that so greatly delighted were they, all and every one, that to a man they were glad to come again—even tho' they knew they would receive far less pay than generally elsewhere. But they always delighted in the intelligence of our audience, and the splendid welcome all received among us.

Another point that had to be stressed was what Dr. Whitney called "expression in education." Said he: "Education ought to do more for a man than to make him a mere encyclopedia."

This principle he carried out in the Friday afternoon exercises which were thus described in *The Scroll* of December 15, 1874, at the close of C. C. I.'s first term:

> These exercises are conducted on the above day at 2:45 P.M. Their object is to give amateur speakers self-possession in public speaking, to store their minds with standard pieces of oratory enabling them to form a correct style and to promote fluency of speech and suavity of manner.
>
> Many of our friends from the town have seen proper to patronize us with their presence on these occasions.

For this we thank them, and in so doing cordially invite them to come as often as they can, for they may rest assured that they are always welcome.

This exercise has been of great practical use, as many who could not speak publicly at the beginning of the term are now rather far advanced in the art; many whose voices became tremulous and whose cheeks tingled with blushes, now sing with ease and composure, while others have just discovered a new talent which they have resolved to improve.

During the past term there have been nineteen pieces of vocal and instrumental music performed. The Singing Class has sung on four different occasions.

Twenty-three young declaimants have been heard from the platform, twenty-two compositions have been read, sometimes by others than those who wrote them, but more frequently by the writers themselves. Thirteen recitations have been given, making in all a very fine exhibit of which we are by no mean ashamed.

A more complete account is this one of Professor Albert O. Hammond, who joined the faculty in 1878.

The students were divided into groups alphabetically, and each group assigned to a Teacher for training and criticism. Then the entire school assembled in the Chapel where Dr. Whitney presided. The names of a dozen or more students, who had prepared the best essays or delivered the best declamations, were given by the Teachers to Dr. Whitney who now called these students forward to repeat their essays and declamations before the school. As this was considered a high honor it had a very stimulating effect, encouraging them to do their best. Dr. Whitney was a strong believer in the art of extemporaneous speech. He endeavored to train the students "to think upon their feet," so as to fit them for public debate in the future. Hence he called for volunteers among the young men, who would agree to come forward to the platform on any Friday afternoon when their names were called, and discuss for three minutes any topic which he might give them,—the topic to be announced after they reached the platform and faced the audience. If they could not think of anything to say, they were expected to stand for three minutes mute before the audience. There was no lack of volunteers, who agreed to undergo this ordeal, and it was a valuable experience to the volunteers and furnished much amusement to the school.

Many students of these days have spoken with appreciation of these exercises, admitting their trepidation at the beginning but expressing gratitude for the valuable training. What better preparation could there have been for the many students who were looking forward to becoming preachers and lawyers?

In this year of beginnings, the students too had ideas on education and they lost no time in putting them to use. On September 11,—their very first Saturday in C. C. I.—five young men, W. M. Trumbower, J. H. Stitzer, C. S. Benedict, H. H. Rusby and A. C. Van Syckle, held an informal meeting and decided they needed a society organization for mutual improvement and practical utilization of the forces acquired in the daily class drill.

They proceeded to organize a literary society which they wished to call the Whitney Lyceum and sought authorization for taking such a step. "Their request for permission to name it thus of course I could not wish to refuse," wrote President Whitney. "Thus it was begun, and under the most happy auspices. The students who were thus banded together were picked young men." From *The Scroll* the further fact is gleaned that it was "composed principally of those young gentlemen who propose entering the ministry." The membership soon was enlarged so as to include students whose interests centered in other vocations, but consistently it attracted the earnest, purposeful young men.

The second oldest organization in C. C. I. was a Society among the gentlemen, called the Philomathean, founded, according to *The Scroll,* also in the same September of 1874, by O. A. Stevens. This was known as the Hackettstown Chapter of the Philomathean Fraternity. In the Fall of 1885 an opportunity was offered for wider influence by uniting with the Alpha Phi Fraternity, and of this the Society became the Zeta Chapter. Increased prosperity came with the new relationship. Zeta aimed to be the best chapter in the Fraternity. In 1889 the *Alpha Phi Annual* carried these paragraphs about Zeta Chapter:

> The work done in Zeta Hall is not inferior to that done in any preparatory school in the country. The young men are trained in debate, discussion, impromptu speaking, essay writing and journal work. Our system is so arranged that we can get out of our members a large amount of work. Discussions on parliamentary questions often come up, and pains are taken to settle them correctly. The members who have gone out to take an active part in other organizations rise up to bless the time they learned points of parliamentary law in Alpha Phi Hall.
> The moral side is not neglected and it might be said that the journal is one of the best instruments used to brighten the moral nature of the student. It criticises and puts facts with telling force, sparing none, but deal-

Zeta Hall, Alpha Phi Fraternity, 1895

Whitney Lyceum Hall, 1895

"AND HER CHILDREN SING HER PRAISES" 39

ing out its blows to those who allow themselves to come under its lash. "Long live the journal" says every active member and alumnus.

The work of Whitney Lyceum was of the same nature as this, according to "Whits" who have been interviewed. No written description has been found.

Only during the first year did the young gentlemen hold the monopoly of societies and secret ritual. The "ladies" were busy with the opening of school in the Autumn of 1875, and on September 19, their Society, numbering twelve members, was organized under the leadership of Miss H. Emma Stitzer. They chose to call themselves the Diokosophians, which means, "those who live according to the custom of wisdom." Their headquarters for the first year had to be one of the music rooms.

Then history repeated itself. The girls needed another society. Here is Dr. Whitney's story:

After a few months other young ladies desired to form a society. Permission being granted, the "Evergreen" Society started under very happy auspices—with a golden Crescent and bangles for a "pin" or badge. Later the ladies were disgusted with both name and "pin" and came to me for counsel. We changed the name to "Peithosophian", and the "pin" to a very attractive and appropriate device.

The President could scarcely be expected to remember the exact dates of these student events. Actually, several years elapsed before the girls who were "a little less sedate" determined to organize. Records show that the second select circle—to which it was at first intended to admit no other members—first met on Saturday, October 4, 1879 and was composed of the Misses Chaplain, Morrow, Stevens, Richardson, Ellis, and Porter. Finding that they derived much benefit from their meetings, they decided to open their membership to others and signalized this by calling themselves Peithosophians, or "persuaders to wisdom."

These names lie open to the interpretation of all who know Greek. Not so were the mottoes adopted by each society. These guides to good living were closely guarded secrets. Their initials only were public property, appearing on the society pins as part of their beautiful cabalistic meaning, and on all other insignia and on printed matter such as programs of public meetings. Members of rival Societies sometimes fitted facetious interpretations to the letters, such as the translation of the Philomathean's M. V. S. Q. H. into "Maude Valentine studies quite hard."

Whitney Lyceum's secret letters were V. N. A. F.; Diokosophian's are still S. E. V.; and Peithosophian's, D. V. V. Some old-time members have suggested that the full texts of these secret mottoes be now included as part of this history. More have quailed at the idea —so thoroughly have they learned obedience to tradition. Current members and officers of the present day Societies have reacted variously: one imparted the information with a scared quick glance all round to see if any one might be listening; another thought best to refuse; a third simply evaded the question! Tradition shall be respected. One statement only: such mottoes as have been divulged express the highest and most beautiful ideals. What a theme for an essay!

The Old Building—Parlors One, Two, and Three.

Diokosophian Society Hall, 1895

All the Societies met regularly every Saturday night, engaging in literary exercises, parliamentary practice, debates, mock trials, orations, and the reading of the society paper.

Election to the office of "Critic" was a high honor. The Critic criticized everything, sternly but fairly: manners, dress, deportment, and especially *English*. One Fred Hannon, later a professor at Drew, was said to know all the rules—and exceptions—of Brown's *Grammar, verbatim!* Often he would say, "That violates Rule XVI, exception 7 of Brown's *Grammar*." There would be a roar of laughter—instantly stopped by the gavel—but if challenged, Fred would bring out the book, and challenges soon ended!

By February 26, 1875, the Whitney Lyceum was ready for its Inauguration Programme, held in the chapel and largely attended by townspeople. This was the first public performance ever given by the students in the C. C. I. chapel—six months after the Institute was dedicated. It was a fine program.

Thus was set a precedent, followed on June 18, by the Inauguration Exercises of the Philomatheans.

In every succeeding year of their existence each Society presented an elaborate Anniversary Program on the Friday evening as close as possible to the date of its founding. At its conclusion, the students would go gaily from the chapel to the parlors for a "social." The Societies were thus agencies contributing to the social training envisaged by President Whitney as an important element in education.[10]

10 More will be said on this subject in a later chapter.

It proved fortunate that C. C. I. was a large building. Says the President:

The fifth story in the tower had two very large rooms—about thirty-six feet long, sixteen feet wide, ceiling twenty feet high.
The front one of these I gave to the "Whitney Lyceum." They fixed it up very nicely—with some help from me—and year by year made it better, until in a very few years the room was truly elegant, not suffering by comparison with any literary society *anywhere*—in colleges or elsewhere.
I gave the *back* room to the second Society (when formed) for *young men*.
To the Ladies I assigned the only place the time afforded—a back room on fourth floor of ladies' halls.
... In a short time I gave them a better location. I had removed a partition between two *large corner* rooms front on fourth Hall—one of the "towers." It made a fine place. For many years the Diokosophian Society Hall has been indeed "a thing of beauty and a joy for ever." . . .
To the Peithosophians I gave a room in the rear of the Diokosophian—across the hall—same size, style—identical. They have made their hall equally beautiful.

The society rooms became the pride and joy of their members. Their furnishing and beautifying were of course the responsibility of the Societies—business projects affording valuable practical training.
From the beginning, then, the Societies were warp and woof of the fabric of C. C. I. life. They were,—to paraphrase the statement of a student historian, George R. Graff, writing in "The Hackettstonian" of June, 1892,—not under the direct supervision of the

"AND HER CHILDREN SING HER PRAISES"   43

President; they did not recite to the Faculty or receive material support from the Trustees; and yet they were equal to at least any one great branch taught, in their practical preparation for success in life. If the students considered them valuable, no less so did the President. As he looked back over his years at C. C. I., he paid them this beautiful tribute:

These Societies grew in power and interest. They met every Saturday night. The unity between them and myself was delightful, and even remarkable. Indeed they became a genuine help to my authority and discipline during my twenty-one years of Presidency. I *ever* found these young men and ladies ready to listen to my slightest wish. I treated them frankly and so they treated me—from '74 to '95—on all occasions.

The student point of view coincides with that of the President. Writes a member of the class of 1884:

In school discipline the Societies were a powerful adjunct. Woe betide the student guilty of chronic misbehavior. He or she would be brought to trial, admonished or expelled.

The following illustration is contributed by one of the alumni:

At one of our big inter-school base-ball games, the whole school in attendance, a "Deik" was caught flirting with a member of the visiting team. She was called before the faculty and censured. Then before the "Deiks" in meeting assembled, and after a formal charge and abject confession, she was again censured.

These were by no means the only organizations. *The Scroll* of December, 1874, after describing the

Societies, went on immediately with the topic of "Physical Advancement"; the word "athletics" appears nowhere in their account. But let the students speak for themselves:

> Physical advancement has not been neglected either among the ladies or gentlemen. The former have several croquet sets which are often used on the fine sunny days on the greensward where science is put into practice very often to the amazement of those unacquainted with it.
> The Trustees are about furnishing a ladies' Gymnasium where calisthenics will be taught by an experienced instructor.
> The latter body have a large Cricket Club consisting of twenty-five members, Thomas J. Bass being President, J. W. Slaght, Vice-President, W. J. Galloway, Secretary and W. Willcocks, Treasurer. This club has regular meetings every Saturday during the season and often have they been cheered and fired with ambition by the presence of numerous spectators who had come to witness the several matches and to applaud while the laurel of victory was placed on the brow of the winning eleven.[11]
> There is also a Base Ball Club called the "Eutaws" consisting of nine members, R. Dalrymple being Captain, W. Galloway, Secretary and C. Hemmingway, Treasurer. This Club has never been beaten *by any* rival, although three hard fought games were contested for.
> The Trustees are now erecting a Gymnasium for the young gentlemen at a cost of about $3,000. When this is completed we can give a more definite account of improvement in avoirdupois and muscle. If some of the students advance in their literary duties as far as they

---

[11] Cricket had a very short popularity in C. C. I. Students of the Eighties say they never heard of it.

have in their physical, they may indeed each be termed Modern Mental Hercules.

Rating greater prominence than athletics and considerably more space, was the subject of religion. Again let the students' own words re-create the past:

The Religious Exercises of the Seminary are conducted on three days of the week. On Sunday morning at nine o'clock there is a class meeting held by the students in the Chapel, which has resulted in much good, not only benefiting those Christians who give their experience but also many of those who do not make profession of religion.

At 2:30 P.M., the same day the regular Berean Lesson is discussed, illustrations being used on the blackboard to convey more fully the character of the lesson to the minds of the class at large. Numerous hymns are sung and the meeting is brought to a close about 3:30 P.M.

Again, in the evening at 7 o'clock there is a general prayer meeting conducted by one of the Faculty, held in the same place as the above meeting at which all students are required to remain. Many precious seasons of grace have been enjoyed at this service.

The plough-share of God's Spirit has upturned many sterile furrows in the hearts of unbelievers. Seeds of righteousness have been sown, which have been gently moistened by the dews of His grace, turning the waste ground into good soil whose seed has "sprung up," bringing forth, some an hundred-fold, some sixty-fold and some thirty-fold, all now growing as sturdy trees in the garden of the Great Husbandman.

At the religious meeting on Tuesday night some seventy-five Christians stand up for Jesus and often have the voices of new born babes in Christ been heard lisping the first faint notes of the song of Moses and the Lamb.

On Friday at 7 P.M., in the Chapel there is another prayer-meeting composed of and conducted by the students; the attendance on which is not compulsory, but to which nearly all the young people remain. To show the beneficial effects resulting from this means of grace we will simply state that within the past term seven souls have been enabled to lean upon Jesus and trust him as their Saviour.

This picture is not quite complete. It overlooks the daily—including Saturday—chapel services, night and morning. The omission is eloquent, however. Chapel apparently was so much a part of life that the students would no sooner have thought of mentioning it than they would have printed the fact that they had three meals a day.

Not so with the President, however, who gives it much space in his Autobiography.

Immediately after the "opening day" I determined that our "Chapel Exercises" should be as attractive and profitable as possible. Though from the very first they were "Compulsory" as to attendance, I never in all my years' stay heard that the students considered them a "bore". Indeed I frequently heard that the students were always glad "to go to Chapel." Young people do not like "long" exercises about most things, especially about religious matters.

The general program was night as well as morning: Scripture (responsive); Hymn—three verses sung; Prayer—always brief. Sometimes after prayer I made brief announcements and occasionally brief remarks—explanatory or humorous or didactic. The singing even from the first was superior. Nearly or over 200 to 250 voices—young ladies and young men in the prime vigor of young life—cheery—hopeful—happy! oh! how they

"AND HER CHILDREN SING HER PRAISES" 47

sang. Often and very often—indeed almost always—it was grand, inspiring and the fame thereof filled the town and brought many listeners.

Probably because it was not a student-led service, the Wednesday night prayer meeting was not referred to in the student account of religious life. But Dr. Whitney writes of this:

At once I instituted a Wednesday night prayer and praise service—of which I had charge in person throughout all my years. These occasions were full of interest, delight and profit and have been talked about and written about in all the years.
I organized also a Friday night prayer meeting—to be ever in charge of some young man of the Y.M.C.A. of the school—or occasionally a lady. The same glorious results followed these meetings. In both always there were "testimonies" from many concerning Christ's love and power to save. Many, very many, conversions occurred in all the years—from the beginning.
A goodly number of the young men of the school each year were students for the ministry. Many private prayer meetings—not in the Chapel—were held in all the years—with notable results.
Alumni of these years, too, have stressed the importance of these meetings and their results.

The student account of the "religious exercises" of Sunday also must be supplemented. Another eloquent omission,—attendance at Church.

But the guiding spirit of the school gives graphic details of Sunday at C. C. I.

On Sundays the school went in a body to the Methodist Church in Hackettstown in the *morning*—the ladies going two by two in line, with some teachers in front and some in the rear. The men did not go in procession. In the church the ladies had seats assigned them in a body, and the gentlemen elsewhere, in a body. The school, of course, made a large and most interesting addition to the pastor's audience.

On Sunday evenings, from the very first Sunday, in all my 21 years (of course with occasional exceptions) I had the students all in the Chapel. It was my pleasure and great delight to see these young bright immortals before me, and I resolved to preach (briefly) to them my very best efforts to help them build up a grand, blessed manhood and womanhood. Doubtless many would have preferred more frequently to go to the Church on Sunday nights. I, of course, frequently let all go to hear the pastor on some special theme—or a stranger. Once a term the custom was to send all to the Presbyterian Church—to the delight, usually, of all.

But the rule was—every Sunday night to be in a body in our own Chapel. The organ and music of so many voices was grand. I spoke briefly—but with all the experience, study, and fervour I could command for Christ's sake—for their soul's sake.

As pastor of churches, I had felt my responsibility; and now I felt that I was doubly a pastor, having a greater responsibility than ever—for all these young souls were away from not only their own churches, but away from their homes.

Happy indeed I am here to record in 1899 that hundreds of times I have heard of the blessedness of those Sunday night addresses with the blessed singing of those young people and often their testimonies and prayers. God was indeed with us in all our Chapel services. I determined that with God's help this should be a "religious school"—not a school simply with a little religion thrown in for the sake of name only. God was with the school in all its years.

"AND HER CHILDREN SING HER PRAISES" 49

So the days passed and the first year of C. C. I. was coming rapidly to its closing week. In the class rooms preparatory reviews were given for the Annual Examinations to be held for two days in the Chapel, before the Examining Committee.

Then the exercises of Commencement Week: the Baccalaureate sermon, the first annual Vincent Prize Contest in Oratory, the first President's Reception—"with guests from many and various parts—" and the first Commencement followed by the first Commencement Dinner—an event which like all the others became traditional in the annals of C. C. I. until well into the nineteen hundreds.[12]

Perhaps, since the hospitality of C. C. I. became so much a part of her tradition, a word of description of the old-fashioned abundance will not be out of place.

For Students, Trustees, all Ministers and their Wives, all strangers from a distance—specially all parents of students from a distance, and their friends, the "Commencement Dinner" was always a great affair—beautiful to see—delightful to eat. Everybody was *satisfied*, everybody was *happy*—the Seniors and their friends—all students and their friends—all felt the charm of the occasion. Ice cream of several kinds, and in *very great* abundance was always at the close—the dishes were large, very large—and a second one if desired.[13]

This was a Commencement but there was no graduating class. Many students had applied for admission

---

[12] The writer remembers distinctly eating the delicious commencement dinner along with family and relatives on the occasion of her brother's graduation with the last class of boys in 1910.

[13] Dr. Whitney's autobiography.

into a final year of work which would lead to graduation—as it would have led in the schools where they had been studying—but Dr. Whitney, resolved to set the highest standard possible from the very start, had refused.

During the year the President had never left the school, though he had received invitations to speak in a number of different places. As he looked back over the months, he made two summarizing comments which paint in a background that suggests the multitudinous details that add depth and reality, light and shade, to the picture of C. C. I. life that has been drawn.

The weeks and months and terms passed swiftly on during our first year. Very many happy events there were. My wife and I had innumerable joys, and innumerable cares and anxieties.

Everything was *new* and everybody. Patience inexhaustible was needed and the wisdom of Solomon.

Cases of joy, of fun, of frolic, of dignity, of pain, of sorrow. Incidents ludicrous, farcical; incidents full of nobility and of meanness—*multum in parvo*—the world itself in miniature—all was there.

The gas pipes leaked, the gas smoked, the gas machine was defective. The steam pipes leaked, the pipes burst, the boilers were defective, the tubes occasionally broke down. Sometimes—many many times I wanted Job to come to me to teach me patience and courage under mountains and worlds of difficulty! . . . .

It had been a year of marvelous work and of very great success and of great joy to us all. No one had died; no special sickness, no marked wrongs occurred. Of course some mischief there was among the 251 students enrolled for that first year.

Beside the names of two students of that year stands

an asterisk, explained in the footnote by one word—
"Expelled." This one little symbol speaks volumes,
though there are no data extant regarding the incidents.
One further quotation from the President—"I learned
much that year! ! ! !"

And Centenary Collegiate Institute was off to a
most auspicious start.

CHAPTER IV

"Sing Them Loud and Sing Them Long"

THE SMOOTH COURSE: 1875-1895

CENTENARY was now entering a long course of consistent progress, prosperity, success, and good will.

Came with the roses of June, 1876, the first graduation exercises, for twelve who received degrees from the Ladies' College and for sixteen young men who had completed the College Preparatory Course. Presently began the testing of their preparation in colleges and universities. Followed then reports like this from the New York *Daily Graphic* in 1878: "In the Wesleyan University recently the Freshman prize for the best preparation was carried off by a student of Hackettstown." This record was repeated the next year. C. C. I. students took a generous share of prizes everywhere.

Continued the *Graphic,* commenting on Centenary's work:

The science course is wider than in any similar institution, the students having special facilities for thorough work in the chemical laboratory. In the College Preparatory Department the courses are unusually thorough.

Changes in the curriculum are interesting. More

electives were permitted in the College courses. The College Preparatory work was lengthened to four years. A special curriculum preparatory to the Theological Seminary was developed which drew students from thirteen different Conferences.

Just as a careful business enterprise has its accounts expertly audited, so this school yearly welcomed a Committee of Examiners, generally from ten to fifteen in number, scholarly men from four different Methodist Conferences and from chosen Presbyterian churches. The examinations were oral and were conducted by the teachers in the presence of the committee, who were invited to ask freely whatsoever questions they pleased. They occupied two days and were a severe test of the faithfulness of students. In addition, every other aspect of school life was scrutinized.

Here is a typical evaluation of the academic work of 1878-1879:

> The Institute is also most highly favored in the possession of a very superior corps of teachers. ... It is very plain to be seen from the attainments, thoroughness and enthusiasm of the board of instruction here, that the teachers are not mere accidents or experiments; they are individuals who, unlike many, are making the work of a teacher a life-work and not a mere financial convenience or stepping-stone to other departments of literary excellence. ... The actual results of teaching are what we want in order to determine the character of a school. These results we have honestly sought to ascertain. The examinations, which we believe to have been both full and fair, revealed not only a high grade of excellence, but a degree of advancement, in many cases, which pleased as much as it surprised. The

"SING THEM LOUD AND SING THEM LONG" 55

amount of the work done and the thoroughness with which it was done, were points which shortly [sic] attracted our attention. The elementary training is remarkably thorough and exact.

Definition, rule, paradigm and principle, are matters of constant drill. The devotion and excellence of particular teachers have, in not a few cases, awakened a kindred spirit of enthusiasm in the pupils. We have seen nothing which looked like mere superficiality, empty show or terminal sham.

And at the end of these decades, examiners were still saying:

The corps of instructors is both ample and able. Among them are professors, who, in technical scholarship and competency, are the peers of those filling the same departments in our best universities.

Students were still capturing their full share of honor prizes.

The following commendation of the work of the Music Department in 1894, proves that it had realized the high expectations held out for it in 1874:

While we would not say in the sense of comparison or displacement of other studies that superior attention is given to music, yet Hackettstown Seminary has always had a high standing for its proficiency in this department, and this high grade is now fully maintained. The exhibitions of the students both in vocal and instrumental music left nothing more to be desired. The special three years course in music, including harmony and composition, is so thorough that it is equal to any school of the best grade, and its graduates are eminently fitted for the position of instructors.

Here is the 1880 Committee's comment on another phase:

We have found the moral and religious tone of the school marked and elevating. There seems a settled purpose to unite things secular with things spiritual. We may say of the whole course, as was once said of Dr. Arnold's at Rugby, "It is not based so much upon religion, as it is itself religious."

Compare with this Dr. Whitney's own notation made on his visit to Rugby in 1885:

It is consummate conceit of course, but from 1869, from my election then as President, I had ever had Rugby and Arnold in view.

Of course the Committees studied the government of the school. Very modern sound these descriptions, though written in 1885 and 1893.

The discipline of the Institute is peculiar and striking. It is a system of directed and guarded self-government. There is no machinery about it. . . . The government as we witnessed it is both fraternal and paternal. It is sympathetic, brotherly, and kind. The government which believes in and cultivates manliness, honor, friendship, and love must be beneficial to the governed. We are not surprised at the success it has won here. As a result of this system we notice the manly and womanly bearing of the pupils, and the development of self-control in their characters. . . . Somehow Dr. Whitney seems to love every student and every student to love him.

Beside these observations place these words of the President which reveal his methods and the sources of his strength:

Cases of "discipline" would fill a volume. I claimed to be *"just"* at all hazards. I endeavored in every case to act as I would wish a teacher or President to act in case *my son* or daughter were away at school and to be disciplined. The result is that after 21 years (I write in '99) of disciplinary administration I do not recall a single instance in which my conscience condemns me for being too severe. I think I was sometimes too lenient. I was obliged occasionally to *expel*—but *never* without the most *exhaustive* investigation and *never* in anger or in temper. My patience, my "piety," my conscience, my manhood—were all "tried" a thousand—yea ten thousand times. But I always endeavored to remember that every case involved the *destiny* of an *immortal*—and I tried to act in the fear of God. . . . To govern so large a school of 250 students and fourteen to sixteen *teachers* was a herculean task and I so felt it and only God's grace and strength gave me power to succeed.

The report of 1883 praised the social phase of school life:

The atmosphere of the institution is that of home. The courteous bearing of the students toward the teacher and each other has been a subject of observation and approved by the Committee. Much of this spirit is doubtless due to the refining influence of the building, in its architecture, appointments and rich adornments of art.

Another group of observers said:

Many things improve with age. This is true of this school. The passing years have beautified the lawn and given growth to the trees, so that it seems like a very pleasure garden.

In June, 1891, the Hackettstown *Gazette* neatly

summarized C. C. I.'s upward course and in these beautiful words placed the credit where it always justly belongs:

The school has been a success from its opening; it is more successful today in all that goes to make a school of this character a success than ever before in its history. The faculty is stronger, its standard is higher, its accommodations greater, its facilities better than they have ever been, and its graduates are taking rank in the higher educational institutions that reflects only credit upon their *alma mater*. It has won for itself a prominent place among the educational institutions of the land, and holds that place by deserving it. Dr. Whitney, to whose wise direction and executive ability much of this is due, has made Centenary Collegiate Institute his monument. His name is inseparably and ineffaceably associated with it.

Meanwhile, friends of Centenary had been expressing their joy in her success through gifts that made equipment more adequate and adornments more beautiful. By the opening of school in September, 1876, a fine pipe organ had been installed in the Chapel. A gift of geological casts from Dr. John H. Vincent[1] and cabinets of minerals and botanical specimens became the nucleus of a museum. In 1883, Mrs. Mary F. Graves added to this a set of physiological casts presented as a memorial of her daughter Carrie, a C. C. I. student who died shortly before the Commencement at which she would have been the valedictorian.

1 Dr. Vincent, Editor of the Methodist Sunday School lessons, later was elected Bishop. He was an intimate friend of Dr. Whitney and frequently visited the school and addressed the student body. He offered the Vincent prizes, also.

A large room over the Chapel was furnished, making a most attractive library and reading room. Books were added each year. Several rooms were equipped as an infirmary. Fire escapes were placed upon the building.

During the summer of 1885 the new gymnasium for Ladies was built. During the next year a laboratory building was erected, greatly strengthening the Science Department. The year 1888 brought a new laundry with new equipment. In 1889 was built an ice-house. Two summer-houses had been built upon the lawns. In 1890-91, the new gymnasium for young men was completed. All buildings were at this time furnished with electric lights—a great improvement on the former method of lighting by gas manufactured by a machine on the grounds.

President Whitney took great interest in the parlors and was constantly on the lookout to beautify them. There is a pardonable ring of pride in his words:

Our Institute parlors were three in number,—counting the front Hall, four. They all (4) opened together by sliding and folding doors—making a length of about 100 feet, a width of about fifteen, with high ceiling of fourteen feet. With a splendid velvet carpet, with pianos in three of the rooms, with handsome chairs and sofas, many tall windows making fine light by day, with chandeliers and gas and later, electric light by night—there was a splendid sight. By degrees I placed the most elegant pictures, paintings, engravings, photographs plain and colored—in the front hall and the three parlors. In the square front hall, with its handsome carpet of linoleum—its many splendid *large* and small pictures, its fine white busts and elegant Parisian Crystal

Chandelier—the visitor on entering at once found himself, as *many* constantly expressed it, in an atmosphere of culture and refinement. When this fine Hall and the similarly decorated and adorned parlors were all thrown together and brilliantly lighted, . . . it made a scene of beauty and blessing never to be forgotten!

In this beautiful place he delighted to have receptions and "socials."

The first improvements had been made during years of financial depression in the seventies. In 1878 the rates for board and tuition were reduced to $225 per year.

By 1886, C. C. I. was so financially stable that the Trustees were able to appropriate and pay the sum of two thousand dollars as the school's contribution toward the building of the new Methodist Church in Hackettstown—in view of the large number of students who made this their church home.

A few years after this the Trustees were requested to contribute to the Preachers' Aid Society ten per cent of the net receipts of the school. For seventeen years so great was the prosperity of C. C. I. that it was possible to make these gifts.

In this connection must be mentioned other "invisible" gift items revealed in this paragraph from the Trustees report of 1889:

The Trustees do not receive as much money as they could profitably use for enlargement and improvement. This is to a great extent owing to the fact that, while the school is full, there is a large number of scholars from whom no financial profit accrues to the Institution. We do not mention this by way of complaint, but rather by way of explanation. During the present year the discount of 25 per cent, which is made on the bills of the children of preachers, and on those of young men preparing for the ministry, amounts to about $5,500. This is the gift of this Institution to the ministry of the Church, and we rejoice that the Church has enabled us to make it. It can be readily seen, however, that, because of this, some needed improvements must be slow in coming.

Centenary's halls were crowded to capacity year after year and students had to be turned away. In her tenth year as many as sixty students were refused for lack of room. Writes Dr. Whitney, "In all those 'refusing' years, two students were in every room and three in about ten rooms on ladies' side."

All this proves the effectiveness of Dr. Whitney's "hobby" mode of securing students: "make the school supremely (! ? !) *attractive* and *worthy* of success—and success will come! Twenty-one years justified the hobby," he declared.

Dr. Whitney's yearly vacations at Ocean Grove were partly given over to the interests of the school. Here he had the inspiration for the first Alumni meeting—the seed idea of the flourishing Alumni Organization of today. Let him tell about it:

I determined to have a C. C. I. "Reunion by the Sea." I worked very zealously to bring it about. Thus I succeeded in having the *very first* Sea-side Reunion ever held in America by *any* Educational Institution.

In July 1878—four years from Dedication we assembled at Ocean Grove at the Sheldon House during several hours of the day. There were very many students—alumni of the four years and other students and friends. At night in Educational Hall, Asbury Park, we had an audience of 2000—crowding the Hall.

The *so great* a multitude surprised us, and gave me great joy to know what an impression our young folks had the opportunity of making for C. C. I. It was a magnificent success. Our "lovely girls" and brilliant young men acquitted themselves grandly, in oratory, recitations and music. And I then decided to have such a Sea-side Reunion of C. C. I. every 5 years.

These reunions became immensely popular, and were repeated in 1883 and 1888. The fourth, postponed to 1894 because of the Chicago Fair in 1893, brought together "a gloriously happy company" of two hundred and fifty at a brilliant banquet—long remembered as the "Great Reunion of '94."

These occasions reflected much honor on C. C. I. Verily her children were singing her praises, singing them loud and long.

One reason for this loyalty and success remains to be mentioned. Both Trustees and Examining Committees had recognized its vital importance. One group had urged: "The ability to pay generous salaries to the teachers and thus secure the best possible instructors and *retain them permanently* would give to the Institute an influence and a power which could not be measured."

Fortunately not all the financial resources had gone into buildings and equipment. Some had been devoted to making salaries attractive enough to offer some splendid teachers opportunities for worth-while careers. These living links between the past and the present and the future give a school continuity and stability so necessary to its dignity and development. This, combined with Dr. Whitney's care in selecting teachers, resulted in a well-knit, devoted Faculty, many of whose members remained from year to year.

Obviously only some outstanding examples can be named. Five of the original Faculty remained long at C. C. I. Edward A. Whitney has been cited as the President's brother and right-hand man. Miss Stella Waldo was on the Faculty until 1892, Miss Anna Nicholl until 1886, Professor Batchelder until 1881 and Miss Gulick until she left to marry Professor Batchelder in 1882. Into his place in 1884 came Professor E. F. Cuykendall, who held his position through the rest of Dr. Whitney's period and was in charge of the Institute while Dr. Whitney was in Europe in 1885. Professor C. F. Thomsen and E. L. Stivers of the Music Department were on the Faculty for a number of years. Mrs. Susan George Jones, too, must be mentioned, referred to by her superior officer as "a very valuable Preceptress and a fine earnest teacher, remaining with me seven years."

In 1878 Dr. Whitney selected to head this Department of Classical Languages a man who was to serve Centenary longer than any one else ever has to date. Albert Overton Hammond, scholar and gentleman, stood by C. C. I. through prosperity and adversity, gaining the sincere respect and even reverence of generation after generation of C. C. I. college preparatory students. For forty-six years, from 1878 to 1924, he held the thread of continuity, serving under all the Presidents except the present one. Mrs. Hammond, too, joined the Faculty in 1881, teaching art until 1893. Together they served C. C. I. a total of fifty-eight years! People look twice at a school that can call forth such devotion from such admirable personalities as these.

Looking back to his first years here, he seemed to be deeply impressed by the religious activities of the years 1879-80. The following narrative from his pen reveals much about Mr. Hammond himself, too.

During the winter of 1879-1880 a great religious revival swept through the school bringing almost every student under its influence. After the regular evening chapel service, the President or one of the Professors would make a short address ending in an appeal to begin a Christian life. All who would do so were invited to come forward and kneel at the front seats. The Christian young men and women then gathered about their comrades and earnest and fervent prayers were offered in their behalf. It was not long before prayer was turned to praise, as we listened to the joyful testimonies of those who had found the peace which comes from the knowledge of sins forgiven,—the "peace which passeth understanding." These meetings were of such intense interest, that it was very hard to dismiss them, and often they were protracted to a late hour. On one occasion, the meeting was dismissed two or three times, since on each dismissal, it would begin again spontaneously. The students were not content with the meetings held each evening in the chapel, but both young men and young women conducted religious meetings daily in their rooms. Denominationalism was at a discount. No one was asked whether "he followeth with us." There was in the school a Roman Catholic young woman, whom every one respected for her truly Christian character. No young woman was more active than she in seeking to influence her fellow students to begin the Christian life. There were also two young Jews in the school, whose minds became deeply impressed with what they saw and heard. When their parents learned of this, they promptly took them out of the school. One of the converts during this revival was Geo. P. Eckman, who afterwards became Editor of the New York Christian Advocate. Pre-eminent in Christian effort among his fellow-students was Abram S. Kavanagh, who was afterwards known as Rev. A. S. Kavanagh, D.D., Superintendent of the Methodist Hospital in Brooklyn and District Superintendent in the New York East Conference. The influence of this religious revival did not quickly pass from the school. For years after this, the school was noted for its strong religious character. A year or two later a member of the New York East Conference brought to the school his son, who was inclined to be somewhat wild, and said to the writer, "I have brought my son to this school with the earnest hope that he may here be induced to begin the Christian life, more than for any other reason." Before the year was ended, it was my privilege to write to that father that his hope had been fulfilled.

As years went on, visitors and examiners found one fault with C. C. I.—it was not large enough. Every year it was urged that the building be enlarged. This Dr. Whitney always declined to consider, as did also the Honorable George J. Ferry, President of the Board of Trustees. "No," said they, "hard times come, small pox may come, fevers, unpopularity, no endowment,—all say: 'do not enlarge'."

Events were to prove the wisdom of this decision. True, great years were ahead, notably those of 1889 to 1892—but in 1893 broke a financial panic, followed by one of the worst depressions in American history. Registration declined, but still there was what could be called a comfortably full school and all was "merry, cheerful, happy, full of work and order and hope."

Everything and everyone indeed, except the guiding spirit of it all. As early as 1888 his Journals reveal that Dr. Whitney's health "was being surely undermined." At length, in February 1889 came a crisis. For ninety days he ran the school from a reclining chair, as he wrote, "in agony simply unspeakable and inconceivable," writing letters, consulting constantly with Faculty, governing the school, knowing all its details, and with the aid of his brother Edward, who was cashier and bookkeeper, managing all finances. Finally at the end of April came a very serious operation.

Years of improved health followed,—broken, however, by further spells of illness. "I kept my Trustees frankly posted," he wrote, "on all my case. I frequently suggested that I would resign. But no resignation would be listened to. Thus I accepted my agonies and my duties, and worked on—as if nothing were the matter—as well as grit and grace would allow." In 1892 he was reelected for another period of five years.

Obviously he could not travel about or be very active but, though he continued to grow worse instead of better, he kept at his post, was usually in Chapel, attended all the "sociables," anniversaries and receptions of the four Societies, and chatted and smiled and "told stories" just as he ever had done. The addresses at Vespers, Chapel services, and other religious meetings were never interfered with by illness and, as he never looked sick, a stranger would never dream but that he was in perfect health—such was the testimony of those who knew the truth. Of these occasions he related, "One *very* strange and *blessed* fact was that *never* did I suffer while I was preaching or giving these addresses —or *any* addresses."

Professor Hammond, working with him through these years, said,

> His sufferings were intense, but he bore them with the patience of a martyr. Never did we hear from his lips a murmur or complaint. However, he was unable to attend to his duties, and for many months the students seldom saw his face, and he was obliged to delegate his authority to others. But delegated authority ceases to function at its source, discipline falters and the morale of government declines. This, notwithstanding the faithful efforts of the Teachers, took place in the school. And as this state of things continued for two or three years, the prestige of the school was lowered, the number of students declined.

Still as the school opened in 1894 he was able to say:

> I may say, and I say it certainly with a proper sense of pride and humility—that not one of the past twenty years failed to pay current expenses, and some profits—some years very large profits—but profits every year. *Such* a statement can be made of *no* other school in Methodism, for the past hundred years. And in all these twenty years, even the least good of them, there was *no day* that I could not pay every debt I (we) owed in five minutes delay!

The statement held equally true at the end of his twenty-first year.

Early in March, 1895, President Whitney sent his

resignation to the Trustees, who this time were obliged to accept it, with appropriate resolutions.

During the Commencement season Dr. Whitney was honored at a meeting held on the campus by the Trustees, and at other banquets and receptions by students, townspeople and friends; and he and Mrs. Whitney received many substantial tokens of affection.

Included always were words of appreciation for Mrs. Whitney. Indeed this history would be incomplete without recognition of the important part she played in C. C. I. during these twenty-one years. Her husband in his autobiography refers to her again and again as his "help-meet," his helper always and everywhere. This tribute from the Trustees is a beautiful expression of gratitude:

We cannot close this report without reference to the help which Mrs. Whitney has been to her husband during these years of earnest toil. Quiet, refined, strong of character, she has been to him a tower of strength, and to the prosperity of the school a great element of success.

She had excellent taste and judgment. Managing the housekeeping affairs and the servants admirably, she was a wonderful executive. She was the hostess of the school, beginning the home-like atmosphere for which C. C. I. has ever been noted. Says her husband: "The blessedness of Mrs. Whitney's work and success every way for twenty-one years will never be written."

Many times during these years Dr. Whitney had been offered the presidency of various seminaries and also of institutions of higher learning: South Dakota

University, Dickinson College, Hamline University, and Wesleyan. Nothing could swerve him from his determination "that this school should surpass *any* in attractiveness, in neatness, cleanliness, taste, beauty, religious ideals: a great ideal indeed! But, under God, I *had* that great ideal and bent every energy of body and soul to reach it."

Always, he said, he felt that he was "on trial." Any account of success or outstanding achievement closes with the words, "To God be all the glory and all the praise."

CHAPTER V

"Forming Still a Noble Band"

DESPITE TRIALS AND TESTINGS: 1895-1902

1. *The Administration of President Ferguson*

THE Trustees chose as Dr. Whitney's successor the Reverend Wilbert P. Ferguson, then pastor in Patchogue, Long Island. A Canadian by birth, he had graduated from Victoria University, Toronto, and from Drew Theological Seminary. Then thirty-two years of age, he had already led a life of varied experiences,— as assistant pastor on a large circuit in Canada, as pastor of churches in Illinois, and as Professor of Latin in Iowa Wesleyan University. Returning to the ministry, he had transferred to the New York East Conference, where he had made such a reputation as a "hustler" that he seemed eminently fitted to maintain and to advance C. C. I.'s high standards. He was inaugurated on October 23, 1895.

His inaugural address, on the subject "Educational Progress," was a confident summary of the history of education, concluding with the statement that the questions of what education is and whither it should tend and upon what broad principles it should be carried forward are no longer in doubt. It was merely a matter now of determining what subjects are of most value, and what methods most effective for the training of character, the real education to true manhood and true womanhood. He summed up the constituents of a sound and thorough education as these:

(1) character; (2) culture, which is the power to apprehend and relish the beautiful in conduct, in art, in literature, and in nature; (3) critical power, and mainly in the two great elements of accuracy and sympathy; and (4) power to work hard and endure pressure, to turn off large relays of intellectual or other work in a short time. Especially noticeable is it that mere knowledge is left out of this list; that the heresy has been discovered, that education is mental only. A higher, richer, broader notion now prevails. The *whole man* is to be educated. The gymnasium under a scientific director, and out-door sports under safe restrictions, must be used as a method of discipline, of inspiration, and a cultivation of the best qualities. The class-room must find in it a fallible teacher and a fallible pupil— both of them students together of all the problems of life and science, the teacher being a guide with torch in hand to lead the way and a friend at the side in holy communion and with constant encouragement. In worship, private and at chapel, in Bible-study, in the activities of Christian associations, in aggressive evangelism, and indeed in all the phases, activities, and associations of student-life, reverence for truth, devotion to God, and love of our fellow must be cultivated, emphasized, glorified.

He entered upon his duties, young, vigorous, alert, ambitious. Professor Hammond tells us that he had a fine voice, a pleasing presence, and that he was an excellent preacher.

Dr. Wilbert P. Ferguson
President of the Centenary Collegiate Institute,
1895-1900

"FORMING STILL A NOBLE BAND" 73

Immediately he set to work to enlarge the student body. In this he was eminently successful, raising total enrollment to a high-water mark of 283 in 1897-98. In order to accommodate more young ladies, it was necessary to move the president and his family into a house rented by the school, and even to provide temporary quarters in the kitchen extension for seven additional students.

The new President was especially eager to bring in more day students. Large numbers came in by train from surrounding towns. Many residents of Hackettstown attended C. C. I.

Change and experiment were the order of things educational, as the century neared its close, and President Ferguson was fully in accord with this mood. Copying the University Extension idea, he began in 1896 an evening commercial school in Washington, New Jersey, a branch of C. C. I.'s Commercial Department. For a year this flourished. Then it ceased to justify its existence, mainly, it was said, because so many young people were obliged to work during the evenings in the organ factory.

Dr. Ferguson's first Catalogue, that for 1896-97, indicated a distinct break with the past. No mention is made of the Ladies' College. Actually, degrees continued to be granted until 1898, however, at which time it was announced that no further degrees of any kind would be conferred.

Recent graduates had been enrolled in Vassar College and in the Woman's College of Baltimore. Girls were now receiving diplomas in a "Ladies Classical Course" preparing them for college work. In 1896, the

Woman's College of Baltimore (now Goucher) made available a four-year competitive scholarship.

The work of the school was now arranged in six courses: Classical, Latin-Scientific, Greek-Scientific, Scientific, Belles-Lettres, and Academic. Dr. Ferguson originated the Department of English Literature and appointed as its head the Reverend Charles Wesley McCormick, Ph. D., D. D., who was at that time pastor of the Hackettstown Methodist Church. He also enlarged the scope of the Commercial Department, so that students were instructed in the theory and trained in the practice of modern business methods "comprising coal business, lumber business, shipping and commission business, jobbing, manufacturing, joint-stock companies, banking, etc." It was moved to new separate quarters and provided with a regular banking counter.

"The English Bible was a required study throughout the Junior and Senior years," writes Professor Hammond. "The Bible itself was the principal textbook. Instruction was given in Biblical Geography. Lectures in the classroom and on Sundays in the chapel before the school, were a feature of the course."

The terminal examination plan was done away with for all students whose class standing averaged above 75 and who had not taken more than seven cuts from class.

Following the trend of these years, Dr. Ferguson made athletics a notable feature of C. C. I. life. The word "Athletics" now replaces "Gymnastics" in the Catalogue and in student writings. About this time, too, "young ladies" become "young women," and young gentlemen" are now "young men."

A "Director of the Young Men's Gymnasium" was added to the Faculty in June, 1896, who in a year or two was a full-time athletic teacher and coach. The spacious grounds of the rear campus were graded, a running-track was laid out, baseball diamond and football grounds were provided, and a grandstand was erected for spectators. Regular coaching of teams began and the fame of C. C. I. in all kinds of athletics spread far and wide.

Other parts of the campus were used for laying out eleven tennis courts and for croquet and quoit grounds. Tournaments among the classes aroused such enthusiasm that it was "not unusual to find students practicing at 6 o'clock A.M."

An Athletic Association was organized to which was appropriated one-half the receipts from the fees for athletics.

In February, 1896, appeared the first issue of *The Hackettstonian*, Centenary's first monthly student magazine. Stated the editor, T. J. Elliott, "We have long felt the need of a school paper, but for some unknown reasons the matter has never before been brought to an issue. The four literary societies of school endeavored to supply this want."[1] The contents were highly literary in character: excellent original stories, essays, and poems by students and faculty members. There were good editorials, news items, jokes, and always Alumni Notes. Indeed, it was intended to be a medium of communication between students and alumni.

Another new feature was noted by Professor Ham-

1 There had been an annual called *The Chronicle* in 1886 and 1887 and one called *The Hackettstonian* in 1892.

mond. He says, "During four months of each year, President Ferguson delivered in the chapel every Friday morning an address upon current topics, literary, political, and sociological. . . . These gave the students an outlook upon national and world-wide conditions, which they had neither time nor opportunity to secure for themselves. The young women were organized into a Current Topic Club, meeting twice a week under the Presidency of a Teacher," usually Miss Laura G. Thompson, teacher of History. Miss Charlotte Hoag, the Preceptress, also gave "Parlor talks to the young ladies."

In the lively election year of 1896 the young men took an active part in politics by organizing a Sound Money Club. While they admitted that their endeavors had not exactly decided the election, their celebration of the triumph of the gold standard left nothing to be desired, complete as it was with noisy parade, fireworks, and a huge bonfire on the campus. "But," concludes the account in *The Hackettstonian,* "let us maintain the gold standard in our scholarship, and be careful to utilize every minute of each hour; let the ratio be 60-1."

The C. C. I. Glee and Mandolin Clubs were active during these years.

Socially, too, life was freer. There was more liberty to go about in the village. "Sociables," held almost weekly, were largely attended. In April, the evening chapel services were omitted because of warm weather, but, concludes the news item, "it is to be hoped that the omission will not lessen the spiritual fervor of the students."

Along with these enlarged liberties went a relaxation of rules, treating students individually, placing all students upon honor, cultivating self-government. A senior hall was established for the men, with special privileges granted in order to prepare them for the larger liberties of college life. Acting under counsel of the Faculty, they appointed a Board of Censors to control and maintain discipline. No smoking was allowed, even off campus.

The enthusiasm of the Alumni continued unabated. At the regular quinquennial seaside reunion, held in 1899 at Ocean Grove, demands were made for annual gatherings of the sons and daughters of the beloved Alma Mater.

During these years more and more worthy young men and women were being enabled to attend Centenary, too, because of increased opportunities for student self-help through employment and also through scholarships. The President personally raised the money for five scholarships annually. Besides these, there were two that had been in existence since Dr. Whitney's last year through the gift to him by Mrs. Hurley of Washington, D.C. of $1,500 as a memorial to her deceased son, who had been guided into the Christian life while a student at C. C. I. The children of ministers, and young men studying for the ministry, were allowed a discount of thirty-three and one-third per cent from the regular rates.

The surplus funds of the Institute, supplemented by gifts from Trustees,[2] friends, and loyal citizens of Hackettstown, were expended on improvements. A

[2] The Board of Trustees had been enlarged by granting representation to the New York, New York East, and Philadelphia Conferences.

brick addition to the rear of the north wing of the main building, five stories in height, provided superior bathroom facilities for the young men. A fine Otis elevator was installed in the ladies' dormitory. Students' rooms were refurnished. The parlors were recarpeted and refurnished. Ten new pianos were purchased. There was new flooring in the classrooms and new chemical and physical laboratory equipment. All the exterior and interior wood work had been painted.

The outlook for the future seemed brighter than ever. True, there was great need of additional accommodations for the work of the school, but in 1899 there were also lively hopes of supplying them. For 1899 was bringing C. C. I.'s twenty-fifth anniversary and great plans were being made for a fitting celebration. The Trustees had approved a suggestion of President Ferguson to raise $25,000 for a new building as a memorial of the first quarter-century, to be a chapel and to house the music department. An endowment fund was another objective.

During the Commencement season of June, 1899, the formal commemoration exercises were held. Among other honored guests sat the surviving ex-members of the Board of Trustees; the survivors of the original contractors of the building; and the survivors of the original donors of the land. Dr. Whitney was unable to be present because of the state of his health but he sent a letter expressing his undying interest in the school.

Dr. Freeman, Secretary of the Board of Trustees, read a history of Centenary which he had carefully prepared.[3] The most appropriate event of the celebration

---

[3] This history seems to be lost

Centenary Collegiate Institute in 1899

was the unveiling of two portraits: that of Dr. Whitney, the gift of the Alumni, and that of the Honorable George J. Ferry, who was then completing a quarter-century as the president of the Board of Trustees, given by the Board. It was a beautiful tribute to Mr. Ferry, a man who deserves the highest consideration of every friend of this school.

Not for long did these valuable portraits adorn the chapel, however—not even until the end of 1899. For the anniversary year was also to be Centenary's most critical year. Midnight of October 31 transformed all this glowing promise into a mass of smoking ruins.[4]

The fire which started in the basement, in painters' supplies which had just a few hours earlier been brought down from the Diokosophian and Peithosophian Society rooms, was probably the result of spontaneous combustion, though, as in most calamities of this sort, the true cause will probably never be known. No time was lost by the night watchman, who discovered the fire, and the four men teachers whom he summoned. They quickly agreed upon a plan for arousing the 215 sleeping students, teachers, and employees. One summoned the local fire department, who quickly had three sets of hose in operation. A bucket brigade was formed but the water could not be thrown with sufficient force.

4 The story of the fire is based upon the following sources:
Report of a Committee of Investigation appointed by the Trustees.
The Hackettstown Gazette.
The Washington Star.
The Warren Republican.
The Christian Advocate.
Professor Hammond's History.
Personal recollections of those who were students at the time, and of citizens of Hackettstown.

Though the woodwork was extremely dry and the painters' supplies added to the fury of the flames, and the strong west wind drove the flames toward the main building, yet all these circumstances combined were not so baffling as the uncertainty of how and where best to combat the flames. The presence of a high-pressure boiler in the basement kept the firemen from entering and the heavy, pitchy smoke precluded their working effectively or safely in the dining-room. And yet within a half hour so well did the firemen apparently succeed, that all believed the fire had been fully extinguished.

But scarcely five minutes later, a large flame was seen in the chapel and the organ was all ablaze. The fire had steadily crept up a wooden flue that covered the chain reaching from the organ motor in the basement up to the organ, and had just as stealthily but more surely worked its way up the back stairway and entered the organ from the rear on the third floor and had entered the library also on the fifth floor. Students used the Institute hose on the library room and the firemen turned their streams on the chapel, but all in vain. The rooms were as inflammable as the basement and dining-room, and allowed a free circulation of air. In an incredibly short time these rooms were all ablaze and the wind drove the consuming flames into the halls of the dormitories. Now no human effort could save the property, and crackling flame and fiery fury were everywhere present. The wind veered and burning embers were carried nearly one-half mile to the home of Professor Hammond, which a student rescue party heroically saved. But this change of wind defended the neighboring village homes and lessened the extent of the catastrophe.[5]

[5] Extract from the report of the fire prepared by the Executive Committee at the request of the Board of Trustees and presented to them on January 18, 1900.

The Fire, October 31, 1899

Meanwhile, one member of the Faculty had taken charge of each floor and with the greatest order possible marshalled the students out. Some boys were able to pack their trunks and save much of their clothing. Mr. Terrill, the bookkeeper, was able to rescue many of the records from the safe and to assist in saving some furniture and pictures. He lost practically all of his own possessions, however. The smoke in the girls' dormitory was much more dense, probably because the shaft of the new elevator served to carry the flames aloft more quickly.

Robert O. Mathews, a divinity student, dashed through fire and smoke warning the occupants of the girls' dormitory to get out. The girls were obliged to leave their rooms attired in bathrobes and night clothes and without opportunity of saving anything. Nothing but the nerve and superb presence of mind of the preceptress, Miss Charlotte J. Hoag, saved them from panic and sudden death. After waking her charges, Miss Hoag assembled them in an upper hall east of the tower and then from memory and without mistake called each room by number and the names of the girls rooming in it. All were present—about sixty-five—except one girl, who appeared before many moments. Then marshalling her little battalion, she marched them in perfect order and under complete control to the boys' gymnasium. The roar and blaze of the fiery furnace behind them, with sparks and flames that rose two hundred feet into the air made a background of glare and sound that contrasted strangely with the pale faces, scanty clothing, and bare feet of this never-to-be-forgotten procession. A mighty shout rose from the crowds, involuntary tribute to the calm self-control of this heroic woman.

Dr. McCormick and other professors had meanwhile been no less active and vigilant in getting out and checking the roll of the young men.

At two o'clock the old tower clock struck as if tolling the requiem of the historic structure it had so proudly graced; then as the last stroke died on the air, it plunged to the ground, along with the tower, with thundering noise. To those who heard it, it seemed the stroke of doom, the knell of C. C. I. Nearly every one of the onlookers was in tears. Soon after, all the floors fell, and the inside walls with them. At four o'clock naught remained but the gaunt outer walls, portions of which kept falling throughout the whole of the next day. The wreck was then complete, except for the two gymnasiums, the chemical laboratory, the barn, and the ice house. Only well-directed effort saved these buildings—work done in the face of imminent danger of an explosion from a large quantity of gasoline only a short distance away. In fact, the gas house, which communicated with this veritable mine of explosives, was twice on fire.

All the students, professors, and help lost some of their personal belongings; a great many lost everything, and not a few escaped with their night clothes only. The students, partly clad and wrapped in blankets and comforters, were a weird sight as they flitted hither and thither in the fierce glare of the flames.

Great as was the destruction of property, nothing could exceed the joy of all that not a life had been lost. Nor had anybody suffered a serious injury.

During the progress of the fire various homes nearby were thrown open for the refugee students and teachers, and all possible hospitality and help were extended by the citizens of Hackettstown.

Even the darkest tragedy has its comic relief. This came early the next morning when old William, the cook, was on his way from his home at some distance from the Institute to start the duties of his day. The uproar and tumult of the night had not reached him, nor had he heard a word about the disaster. He always looked up Church Street at the clock, and when he did not see it, he thought that he must be losing his sight. He asked a passerby whether he could see the clock and was told that the school had burned down. "Ach, mein Gott!" exclaimed William, "And I left my best shoes there last night!"

President Ferguson had been absent in Canada during all this tragedy, and, while seated with his sister at the breakfast table that day, he received the news of what had happened to his school.

Next morning, Professor McCormick, who customarily acted as president during Dr. Ferguson's frequent absences from his post, assembled students and teachers in the Methodist Church. After this they were allowed to go home, many of the girls in comical combinations of borrowed clothing.

The first thought that had occurred to the President, he relates in a letter of appreciation to the people of Hackettstown, was St. Paul's verse, "Cast down but not destroyed," and indeed this thought seemed to animate everyone. As early as November 7, announcements were on the way to students and parents that C. C. I. would continue its Fall term.

Monday, November 20, was set as the day for reopening of classes. Several hotels in Easton and in nearby resorts immediately offered their facilities for housing the school, and considerable study was given to the possibilities of The Dorincourt on Schooley's Mountain. It was deemed wisest, however, to accept the active cooperation offered by the citizens of Hackettstown, who had risen magnificently to the crisis.

Houses were opened to take in students as lodgers. A number of homes, including the Methodist parsonage and Dr. Holden's residence, were vacated in favor of the students. Those soon acquired the dignity of "Halls," each bearing the name of the Faculty member who was in charge. The basement of the then-unfinished new Methodist chapel became the Centenary kitchen and dining-room. The Presbyterian chapel was used for recitation rooms until the completion of the Methodist Chapel, which, with its galleries divided by folding doors, was admirably adapted to the use of the school.

The students returned in unexpectedly large numbers and were joyfully greeted by President and Faculty at a reception in the Presbyterian Chapel. Comments *The Hackettstonian* (which carried on awhile despite obstacles), "A more happy company of young people it would have been difficult to find, for they were joyous over their return to the duties and pleasures of C. C. I."

The sixty students who had suffered the most burdensome losses—of whom forty had been wholly or partly self-supporting—continued at school with the aid of a relief fund contributed by churches and Epworth Leagues. Five hundred dollars had been raised by a benefit concert given by citizens of Hackettstown.

There was more than usual of social life—social evenings in the chapel and occasions when the young ladies of one "Hall" would entertain those from the various other homes. In June, the usual closing events took place and a class of forty-three graduated.

The work of the year was commended as "remarkably successful," but the expense of running the school under these conditions was far greater than had been anticipated, and instead of the usual surplus, the end of the year brought a heavy, embarrassing deficit. It brought to an end also the term for which Dr. Ferguson had been engaged.

Long before this, however, everyone knew that there was to be a change in C. C. I.'s leadership. "Before the fire," writes President Ferguson in his letter to the Trustees, "I had fully determined not to seek re-election, that I might be free to carry out plans which have been maturing through a long series of years." The great disaster had seemed to him a summons to reconsider, but apparently the Trustees had not seen eye to eye with him in plans for immediate rebuilding. "Believing that unanimity is essential to the surest success," he resigned as early as January 24, 1900. The resignation was accepted without comment and a committee of five was appointed to select a new President.

On March 12, 1900, the committee "was authorized to engage Dr. McCormick to superintend the interests of the school the ensuing school year. The designation of title to be left with Committee." Two weeks later, with title of President assured, Dr. McCormick was excused from school duties as far as possible in order to attend to the work of the Building Committee.[6] In April, Dr. Ferguson, having been appointed pastor of St. Luke's Church, Newark, had to arrange to divide his time between Hackettstown and Newark.

2. C. C. I.'s Fate in the Balance

Does history repeat itself? At this point Mr. George J. Ferry must surely have thought so! Here in 1899 and 1900 were the same frequent, anxious Trustees' meetings, the same Mr. Ferry requesting, as before, seasons of prayer for Divine Guidance on the same problems as in those years of the Seventies and Eighties. He was presiding over an entirely different body of members, but there were some of the same possible benefactors to be approached.

Though themselves determined to rebuild, the Trustees had to secure the sanction of the Conference. First action came in the form of advice from a Convention of Ministers and Laymen of the Newark Annual Conference held on November 23, which passed the following Resolution:

Resolved, That we approve the rebuilding of the Centenary Collegiate Institute on the proposed group plan and we are of the opinion that the resolution of the Newark Conference which prohibits the trustees from incurring debt should be repealed, if necessary, at its next session.

Active at this Convention along with Mr. Ferry was the same George H. Whitney, sharing his vision

[6] Milton E. Blanchard, Chairman; William H. Murphy, A. H. Tuttle, Dr. Whitney, President McCormick.

Centenary Collegiate Institute in Ruins after the Fire, October 31, 1899

of a bigger and better C. C. I. rising like the fabled Phoenix gloriously from its ashes. Watching from his retirement, he saw that the school's fate hung in the balance as he wrote in his autobiography: "Throughout the bounds of the Conference 'talk' went on. *Many* said 'Never build it up—we need no such schools anymore.' The bad history of discipline for four years had discouraged many. *Many* said 'we *must* and will rebuild'." At the Convention he "felt that there was considerable apathy."

As six architects began to prepare plans and bids, several consulted the Whitneys. Mr. O. S. Teale, who eventually was awarded the contract, spent "very many hours" in the Whitney home in Plainfield working on plans for a new group of buildings.

On March 12, Dr. Whitney, "feeling now well enough," accepted the place on the Board of Trustees left vacant by the death of the Reverend Dr. J. M. Freeman, for many years its Secretary, and compiler of the first history of Centenary. And in April, the Newark Conference enthusiastically elected Dr. Whitney President Emeritus of C. C. I.

The entire amount of the insurance had been collected—$116,500, but at least $140,000 additional would be required for rebuilding. The original team, twin Titans of enthusiasm, Ferry and Whitney, were exerting every effort to secure funds enough to encourage the Annual Conference to stand behind the rebuilding plan. Pledges of $10,000 from Mr. Ferry, Mr. William H. Murphy, and Mr. Hudson Hoagland of Dover headed the list, with other thousands promised on certain conditions; lesser thousands followed, from Colonel E. L.

Dobbins, J. W. Jackson, Robert A. Cole, Mr. Halls and others; many subscribed sums in the hundreds. The citizens of Hackettstown gave $5,200. The Alumni were helping, also.

Yet some had other ideas. Dr. Whitney wrote:

> During these months before April there was *much* talk, pro and con, about the "necessity," the "certainty," the "uncertainty" of building up again C. C. I. Meanwhile the $116,000 of insurance funds began to tremble in the balance. Some said: "Don't use a dollar of it for a deficit." Some said "Use it." Some said "Do not rebuild—give the $116,000 to Drew Seminary for young Ministers." Some said "Do not rebuild—give the $116,000 to the Fund for old preachers—this will be splendid." (This latter "took"). So like a shuttle-cock the question flew to and fro.

The Conference unanimously empowered the Trustees to rebuild; yet, with the impassioned speech of Mr. Ferry ringing in their ears, they gave only $7,000 of the $30,000 he had asked. "Mr. Ferry never got over *that,*" wrote his co-worker.

Still the Board wanted more financial security before acting, and it was not until September 28, 1900, that they finally executed the contract.

For several months the Board could not decide whether or not to continue the school during the rebuilding. Nevertheless, they had engaged a number of teachers. In June they finally voted that school should not reopen. This necessitated making equitable arrangements with these teachers—all but *one*. With Professor Hammond they drew up a contract.

Every loyal Centenarian owes a debt of gratitude to

Professor A. O. Hammond for his determination that the banner of old C. C. I. should not cease to wave, no matter what her tribulations might be. Let us hear from his unassuming pen the story of:

3. *The C. C. I. Day School.*

The Trustees had resolved to rebuild. The new building could not be ready for occupancy under a year. What could be done during this year to retain the breath of life in C. C. I. and to prevent the scattering of the students to other schools? The heavy debt incurred in holding the majority of the students together after the fire to the end of the school year forbade a continuance of this plan under the same conditions. Moreover, the Trustees, in view of the heavy expenses soon to be incurred in erecting the new building, did not feel justified in assuming any financial obligations for the coming year. Nevertheless, it was very desirable that there should be no break in the history of the school. Hence, Dr. McCormick, the President of the Institution, and the Board of Trustees requested Professor Albert O. Hammond to open and conduct the school during the year 1900-1901, and to gather in as many of the students as possible, with the understanding that he should be financially responsible for the undertaking. The proposal was not very attractive, but after careful consideration, Professor Hammond accepted it and undertook the work.

He determined in the first place, on the ground of economy, to discontinue all departments of work save one, the College Preparatory Department. A Circular was printed and sent out to the students inviting them to return and continue their studies in this department.

Thirty-four students responded to this appeal and were on hand at the opening of the school in September. The school assumed the name of the C. C. I. Day School. A hall was rented in the town where the students met for recitations. The students boarded in private families. Miss Hannah M. Voorhees, a recent graduate of Goucher College, who by her superior merit had won the five hundred dollar scholarship of that College, and Professor Hammond were the only teachers. Between them, they conducted sixteen classes a day—eight classes each—throughout the year. The students were chiefly members of the Junior and Senior classes in the College Preparatory Course. The grade of scholarship maintained during the year was unusually high, probably for two reasons: first, because a large proportion of the students were pursuing advanced work; and second, because of fewer side issues to draw off their attention from their studies.

The Society Anniversaries were held as usual. The Commencement exercises were held in the Chapel of the M. E. Church at the end of the school year. President McCormick presided. Reverend Charles L. Mead, who had been elected Bishop of the M. E. Church at the General Conference, delivered the Commencement address. Professor Hammond made the address to the graduating class and distributed the diplomas, the regular Centenary Collegiate Institute diplomas, signed by the teachers, by Dr. McCormick and by George J. Ferry, President of the Board of Trustees. There were eight graduates in the class of 1901—one young woman

Dr. Charles Wesley McCormick
President of the Centenary Collegiate Institute,
1900-1902

and seven young men. With one exception they all went to college. The receipts were sufficient to pay all the bills at the close of the year. The report of the Trustees for this year said: "It is worthy of grateful mention that, notwithstanding the enforced partial suspension of the school for a year, there will be no break in the continuity of its history—no year in which it will not have a graduating class."

4. *The Administration of President McCormick*

No man ever assumed his duties as president of C. C. I. with better educational preparation than Charles Wesley McCormick. A graduate of Wyoming Seminary, a Bachelor of Arts and a Master of Arts from Wesleyan University, he had received his Doctor of Divinity degree from Syracuse University in 1897 and his Doctor of Philosophy degree from New York University in 1898, the same year that he became the pastor of the Hackettstown M. E. Church.

In May 1899, he had been elected to teach English and History in C. C. I. and to take over administrative duties equivalent to those of a Vice-President. His election was hailed by the students, according to *The Hackettstonian* of June, 1899, "with universal favor and high expectancy of good to the school. . . . As pastor he has been so successful in local affairs, ... so attractive personally and as a preacher to the student body, that he enters upon his work with an unusual town prestige and student favor."

Assuming the title of President on June 1, 1900, he devoted his efforts during that year to securing additional subscriptions and to working with the Building Committee. Also busy raising funds were the Reverend J. A. Cole, financial agent, and Dr. Whitney, working particularly among the Alumni.

On December 1, 1900, in the presence of a large crowd who braved inclement weather conditions, the cornerstone of the new building was laid; directly behind it had been placed the old cornerstone, carefully preserved after the fire. This impressive service, usually one of the functions of a bishop, was very appropriately performed by C. C. I.'s President Emeritus, who also made the address at the service which followed in the Methodist Church.

So rapidly did the work proceed that within three months the Architect and the Building Committee assured the President that it would be safe to arrange for opening the school that Fall. At last beginning to concentrate on matters of administration, President McCormick chose a strong Faculty and prepared an admirable "Prospectus"—clear, concise, scholarly. Under date of April 5, 1901, he sent forth a letter to "Friends of C. C. I." asking co-operation in completing and furnishing the school, in replacing the lost library and in securing students. He expressed warmest thanks to all who had helped, and especially to "those men who, having given largely for the erection of the old building, are now among the most zealous and energetic in the erection of the new." In closing he pledged:

The old motto, "A *thorough* School, and a thoroughly *Christian school*," is still ours, and in such a school we believe we shall, in some measure, attain to our ideal, "A Christian Education for Christian Service."

One of Centenary's cardinal dates is September 23, 1901, the Opening Day of the New C. C. I. Dedicatory services had to await the completion of chapel and recitation rooms; consequently this day was not one of crowds and wild enthusiasm. One visitor, the only representative of the Board of Trustees, was the President Emeritus, coming also for the purpose of enrolling a foreign student from Japan whose guardian he was. How busy his thoughts were, contrasting those two Opening Days, twenty-seven years apart, he confided to his Journal.

Appropriately enough, he slept at the school that first night, and at Chapel—which had to be held in the dining room—he made the very first speech in the new Institute, just as he had done in 1874.

The student body consisted of 102 boarders and 52 day students—a good beginning, considering the fact that a large number of former students had scattered and found homes in other schools. It was not to be expected that many of these would again break school ties. Wrote Dr. Whitney: "The new President and his wife were both very happy and made a fine impression upon everybody. . . . I left the second day, September 24, feeling that the skies were bright."

During many weeks the teachers conducted classes amid the din of saws and the pounding of hammers, until finally the classrooms were finished.

One improvement—long overdue—made by President McCormick was the inauguration of a Sub-Preparatory Department. Regular final examinations and frequent tests were again features of the academic life, even to the extent of requiring a special examination to qualify for the final one, if a student had been absent too much from classes. Places on athletic teams were only for those who maintained the required grade. The scholarship was high. C. C. I. had been placed on the basis of the certificate plan of entrance into Colleges and Universities.

Dr. McCormick was greatly interested in the cultural subjects. He improved the Art Department.

"The social life," writes the President's daughter, who was an impressionable little girl at this time, "was mostly centered around the four literary Societies. They had weekly socials (no dancing of course), picnics, hay rides, and in winter skating on the canal. There were literary programs and debates. There was a good football team, fair baseball and track teams. Tennis courts were used by both girls and boys." Thus C. C. I. was off again to an auspicious start.

In a few months the building stood complete in every detail of construction and furnishing. The latter had been the problem of a special committee composed of: the President, Mr. Blanchard, Mr. Teale, Mr. Ferry, and the President Emeritus. Writes Dr. Whitney:

> As Trustee of C. C. I., as member of the Building Committee, as member of the Furnishing Committee, I was very busy constantly—attending Committees, begging money, looking up furniture, etc. etc., doing as much work for months as if I were President, but being *only* President Emeritus—and *LOVER* in general of the great Cause.

At Conference time a number of churches had agreed to furnish a room apiece. When asked to speak,

Dr. Whitney bound himself to furnish the *largest room* in the building *completely*—the Chapel.

The tangible proofs of his efforts were all about him in the Chapel on December 5, 1901, as he made the Dedicatory Address—for he had again been signally honored by being chosen to dedicate the new buildings, as a year before he had laid the cornerstone. Now he could make public acknowledgement and pay tribute to those who had responded to his calls for help and he did so in these words which ought to re-awaken gratitude in the hearts of all who have ever called Centenary their Alma Mater. It is a familiar still-lovely scene which he is describing thus:

Assembled in this Chapel, as we admire its beauty and perfection, allow me to say that in its equipment we are indebted to our former students—or their relatives; for it has been a pleasing thought that the students of other days would gladly respond to an appeal to equip and furnish the new Chapel in memory of the glory of the old chapel. The splendid organ which has so greatly delighted us today is the gift of a lady of the class of '83, now married, residing in Toronto.[7] The noble great central memorial window—of the star and the angels—yonder, with the two adjacent beautiful windows and the three below, are the gift of a lady of your town whose daughter was here a student, and the equal gift of her sister, of Newark, whose grandson was here also;[8] but the windows are a memorial of the giver's father.[9] Those two splendid figure windows of Saint John and Saint Paul are the gift of two

---

7 Mrs. C. D. Massey (Anna Vincent Massey).
8 Mrs. Nancy Dill and Mrs. Richard Vanhorne.
9 Mr. Daniel Axford.

students of '94, of Greenwich, Connecticut, who concluded to join themselves never to part, and to give a window apiece in memory of that blessed optimistic event.[10] That handsome window with the emblem of the crown is the gift of a lady of far-away Minnesota, whose niece was a student of '91, but the window is a memorial of the giver's father, one of our former citizens.[11] The handsome window with the emblem of peace—the dove —is the gift of a lady of Brewster, New York, whose son was here, of the class of '95[12] As you sit in your comfortable opera chairs, you may remember that over a third of them are the gift of two former students, a sister of '79 and a brother of '82, of Plainfield, New Jersey: another goodly number of chairs are the gift of a young man and lady of '83 who later joined their hearts, and who live in Westfield, New Jersey. Another fine block of seats is the gift of a young man of '91, and a lady of '93 who concluded later to join their hearts and pocket-books and abide in Madison, N. J. Another, just received, is the gift of a little more than a third of these seven hundred seats from a young man and a lady, both of '83, who a few years later also resolved never to be put asunder and to spend the rest of their lives in the splendid capital of the Nation.[13] .... The nucleus of our Library is already the gift of a few friends. A suitable library is indeed a very great want; and the need will be surely met.

You must perceive that the beautiful and valuable gifts for this splendid chapel amount to thousands of

10 Mr. and Mrs. W. F. Lockwood.

11 Samuel Albertson, given by Mrs. C. C. Cokefair.

12 Mrs. Julia A. Storm, in memory of her son, Frank A. Storm, 1895.

13 Mr. and Mrs. Odell Smith. Other donors mentioned in Dr. Whitney's *Journal* are: Miss Annie Burgess, now Mrs. Yerkes; George Burgess; J. W. Pearsall; Mrs. Hurley, in memory of her son Frank. Of course this is not a complete list. It has not been possible to identify all of the givers mentioned above.

dollars. Many other students have most notably contributed—some with much sacrifice—other thousands of dollars for these great buildings.

All honor we give today to our splendid body of students—four thousand of them—scattered over all the land and truly over all the earth, many of them occupying the highest positions in the professions and in business life. They are a magnificent tribute to the glorious history of the old temple; and an earnest of the glory of the new. It is also the monument of your farseeing and wise trustees; it is equally a monument of the many generous and cheerful givers—a few of very large sums; many of small amounts—all worthy of praise; and surely it is also a monument of faith and works in a thrice-blessed cause.

On this day President McCormick delivered his Inaugural Address. Of him Dr. Whitney said:

President Dr. McCormick is a fine-looking, impressive man, of about forty-five. He made a most admirable impression on the audience in general. And thus again a good start!

Thus with joy and hope began the new regime, but alas! it was not destined to end in like manner. There was in waiting another calamity.

On December 20, when the Christmas vacation began, the school was paying expenses, and there was hope of closing the year with a small surplus. During the holidays, a few persons in Hackettstown had become ill with smallpox. More cases were probable. President McCormick notified all students to remain away a week longer. In a few days the order was changed to "until further notice."

The pleasant village of Hackettstown, with 120

of its citizens smitten with the dread scourge, was quarantined, cut off from the world. The pest-houses were filled. Everyone was afraid of his neighbor; friends crossed the street rather than meet. Stores were closed; schools, churches were closed. Wide circles were made around houses where fluttered the yellow flag.

The few who were in C. C. I. dared not leave the buildings for any reason. All employees who could be spared were temporarily discharged. All were vaccinated. Writes Josephine McCormick of these days:

There were only a few students and teachers at the school. We were all quarantined and the mail had to be fumigated each day before we were permitted to have it. To help pass the time some of the teachers edited a daily magazine or news sheet and I wish that I could find some of the copies. I recall that they were illustrated and they must have been very funny, for grown-ups laughed and laughed.

At last, after six weeks, the school was allowed to re-open. By dint of much correspondence, the President had kept the loss of students down to twenty-nine, but of course there were no new students entering, as usually happens at mid-year.

Add to this sad financial loss the fact that the buildings had been dedicated with a great debt of $65,000, with interest at five per cent.

"The fact is," wrote Professor Hammond, "that no President of C. C. I. ever had in one year so many serious difficulties to contend with as fell to the lot of Dr. McCormick." He was exceedingly discouraged. He saw no prospect of ever being able to work in the field where his talents really lay—teaching and governing. Raising money, he felt, was not his forte. Therefore he informed the Trustees that he was not a candidate for re-election; furthermore, he requested that he be released on April 1 from his contract, which ran till July 10, 1902, in order that he might take an appointment at the next Annual Conference. The Trustees consented, passing at the same time the following resolution:

Resolved: That the Trustees of Centenary Collegiate Institute in accepting the resignation of President Charles W. McCormick do assure him of their continued love and esteem as a Christian gentleman and educator; and would express their sincere appreciation of the conscientious, faithful and laborious service he has rendered the Institute in a most critical period of its history. They would also express to him their desire for the largest usefulness and happiness in the pastorate to which he returns.

5. *Dr. Whitney Returns*

It was now March 11, 1902, and after April 1, C. C. I. would be without a President. The Trustees at once set to work to find the man who would pull the school out of its slough of despond and place it once more on the high road to prosperity. This man was not far to seek, being one of their own number, an accession in 1898, at the time that the charter had been revised so as to increase the number of Trustees from twelve to twenty. He was the Reverend Eugene Allen Noble, a graduate of C. C. I. in the class of 1885. At this time he was the Superintendent of Seney Methodist Episcopal Hospital in Brooklyn, an institution which he had managed so successfully as to attract public attention. He was deeply interested in his Alma Mater and eager to serve her, but he could not be free to enter upon his new duties until July 10.

The Trustees were in a dilemma. There was no Professor there at that time who could step into the breach. The solution came as a happy inspiration—let the President Emeritus become Acting President for this interval. "Thus," writes Dr. Whitney, "thirty-three years after the first time I was elected President of C. C. I. I was elected the second time! A strange event most certainly."

Things went back into their old grooves. All irregularities of discipline and management arising from the broken sequences of school life were smoothed out. The Lecture Course, which had been discontinued for two years, was resumed. The "Anniversaries" occurred as before and the four Societies as in years past, wrote President Whitney, "were a glory, a right arm of power, a help—great help to the school; a great discipline for the members. . . . They were a blessing to myself, and to all who belonged to them, or who were in any way influenced by them."

Thus the first year in the history of the new C. C. I. ended happily for the students and for all. Perhaps the happiest person of all was George H. Whitney, as he wrote:

And *NOW* that the *new* great splendid building was at the end of its *first year* of history, behold I was the President, and graduating the *first* class in this *NEW* building! It was a great honor! A great coincidence, strange indeed!

A strange coincidence, yes, but a fortunate one for those who love Centenary, for it binds together the old and the new. It enables us to picture George H. Whitney treading these very halls; to feel still brooding over Centenary the spirit of her Guardian Angel.

CHAPTER VI

"And With Honors Still Unbounded"

THE CAMPUS EXPANDS, 1902-1908

DR. Eugene Allen Noble brought to the presidency much enthusiasm and a unique preparation. A student during Dr. Whitney's best years of leadership, he had followed C. C. I. tradition in choosing Wesleyan as his University and in marrying a Centenary schoolmate, Miss Lillian W. Osborne of the class of 1887. After completing his theological studies at Garrett Biblical Institute, he had served as pastor of churches in Bridgeport, Connecticut, and Brooklyn, New York. Then came administrative experience as Superintendent of the Methodist Hospital in Brooklyn which would stand him in good stead. Similar value inhered in his term as Trustee of C. C. I. from 1898 to 1902, during her years of gravest misfortune, from which she was now struggling to recover. Imbued with the spirit and tradition of Centenary, and identified with her past, he certainly took up his work on July 2, 1902 with no illusions as to the realities of the present and the necessities of the future.

His formal Inauguration was deferred until the Commencement of June, 1903, in order that it might be combined with another long-planned-for event—the bicentenary of the birth of John Wesley, founder of

Methodism. C. C. I. had been chosen by the Newark Conference as the most appropriate place for its celebration.

Again the Lackawanna ran a special train to Hackettstown, bringing many distinguished guests. The Governor of New Jersey, the Honorable Franklin Murphy, D.D., whose father, Mr. William H. Murphy, was an honored member of the Board of Trustees, presided, and introduced the orator of the occasion, Bishop Andrews. The aged Bishop Bowman was also an honored guest.

For the fourth time in his career of devotion to C. C. I., George J. Ferry presented to a president the insignia of his office, the keys of the institution. He congratulated Dr. Noble on the success of the school during the year of his incumbency. The President's Inaugural Address stressed the importance of Christian education.

The students' estimate of their President was summed up in three words: "strong, fearless, progressive;" and this phrase strikes the keynote of his years in office. There were no spectacular departures. Development continued along the lines of traditional patterns—an unfolding, a rich flowering, an expanding along many radial lines.

Emphasized still were College Preparatory Courses: the Classical, the Latin-Scientific, the Scientific. A new Modern Language Course had no college entrance objective. Study of the Bible, taught by Dr. Noble himself, was required during each year of a regular course. The Conservatory of Music remained unchanged. The Department of Commerce now classified its Courses as:

The New Centenary Collegiate Institute, 1902

Commerce, Banking and Finance, Accounting, and Stenography. German or Spanish or French was required.

Continued were the Friday Rhetorical exercises required of all students and the Friday evening formal exercises in the Chapel, where the best writers, speakers, and musicians gained experience in public performing. As before, the three-minute extemporaneous speech was featured, for, wrote the President, "The conditions of modern life require ready and accurate expression in public speech and in composition."[1]

The high scholastic standing of C. C. I. is attested by the installation on her campus of the Zeta chapter of Alpha Delta Tau, the honor society for secondary schools which corresponds to Phi Beta Kappa in institutions of higher learning. Only senior honor boys were eligible to it. Other chapters were in Jacob Tome Institute, Phillips Andover Academy, Phillips Exeter Academy, Evanston Academy, William Penn Charter School, Brooklyn Polytechnic Preparatory.

There were faculty members who rejoiced in this recognition and who should be given credit for it. Dr. Noble was able to retain throughout his period some of the stronger teachers of the years past, and to attract and inspire other admirable teachers to devote their best years of service to this school, thus giving it an influence and a power which could not be measured. Much excellent work was done, of course, also by teachers who remained for shorter periods. Unfortunately, space permits mention here of only the outstanding personalities who maintained the tone of the school through

[1] Catalogue, 1903.

all her vicissitudes of fortune. Foremost were Professor Hammond and Miss Charlotte Hoag, who was Preceptress, teacher and friend of all from 1898 until shortly before her death in 1909. Carrying the thread of continuity from the previous administration through this one were: Miss Anna May Mirteenes, of the Academic Department, Miss Mary Gray, teacher of Painting and Drawing, and Mr. Albert E. May, Accountant. Excellent appointees of Dr. Noble's were these, whose devotion to Centenary extended many years beyond that of the President who chose them: Professor George Edward Denman, who will be remembered by many boys as Athletic Coach and House Master from 1903 as long as there were boys here; Professor Frank V. Stutsman, who taught Science, and carried various other responsibilities from 1904 to 1925; Miss Charlotte Howard, another C. C. I. product returning to serve her Alma Mater, who worked in the Conservatory of Music from 1905 till 1934—except for a short interval; Mr. Frederic A. Mets, who joined the Faculty in 1906 and, except for a short period of service in the first World War, gave his characteristically untiring energy as teacher of Piano and Organ, and for many years as head of the Music Department, until June, 1946.

Student life, always vigorous, for the most part intensely earnest, and creative, took on an added vividness as it deepened old channels of interest or uncovered new ones. Much Centenary history was made during this first decade of the new century.[2] Most spectacular

2 What is said here of student activities—athletics, Societies, Clubs, religious organizations, etc.—is true generally of the whole period between the re-opening of C. C. I. in 1901 and the end of the co-educational regime in 1910.

"AND WITH HONORS STILL UNBOUNDED"   107

was the development of athletics. Here is the story of what lay behind this success:

> The first time Professor Denman appeared on the field at C. C. I., he made a short statement of his intentions concerning the team, which was that if all candidates would do exactly as he directed, he would do whatever was in his power to put out a winning team. This principle he has adhered to thoroughly ever since, and he has shown that there is a great deal "in his power." Defeat falls from him "as water from a duck's back," as he works again for a future victory.
>
> Although football is his specialty, yet he coached a green baseball team into such form that it was able to defeat Blair Hall's well-trained nine. In track, even though he never ran a race in his life, he is able to inspire the men with some of his own indomitable courage and grit. He is so typically energetic himself, that he can never tolerate on one of his teams a man of an indolent or irresponsible temperament. A few more years of such efficient supervision in athletics and our school will have reached the position among the surrounding schools which it held before the fire.[3]

These were the days when the Alma Mater Song, then "The Blue and Black," reflected the prowess of the Teams.

>   Let Blair Hall's royal Blue and White
>   Be ever fair to see,
>   And may we cheer old Pennington
>   With songs so glad and free.
>   Our hearts are with the Blue and Black,
>   And may we never sever
>   The tie that binds our hearts to thee,
>   And C. C. I. forever.

3 *The Hack*, 1905.

And may the boys of Easton High
   Throw out a mighty cheer,
And may Wyoming's verdant hills
   Grow fairer year by year.
Our hearts are with the Blue and Black,
   And may our great endeavor
Raise high the glorious Blue and Black
   And C. C. I. forever.

Baseball and Football Teams traveled far and wide, playing full schedules each season with the stronger high schools, such as: Erasmus Hall, Easton, East Orange, Newark, and Brooklyn; with other "Prep" schools, among them: Peddie, Pennington, Blair, Dwight, St. Paul's, the "Preps" of Bethlehem, Allentown, and Princeton; and with Freshman and Sophomore teams of Manhattan, Columbia, Fordham, Lafayette, and Wesleyan. And of course the verdant hills re-echoed the cheering from year to year as games were played on C. C. I.'s own Athletic Field.

The net results of a season were generally very satisfactory, too. Take the football record, for instance: the team of 1903, under Captain Garrison, scored five victories out of eight games; 1904; under Captain G. A. Palmer, three out of seven; 1905, under Captain Harman, seven out of eleven; 1906, under Captain H. W. Faraday, two of eight; 1907, under Captain Fuller, three and two ties—one with Blair Hall—out of eight games. The team of 1908, under Captain Crane, was probably the best of all these years, winning seven out of nine games, with a victory of 12 to 6 over C. C. I.'s ancient rival, Blair Hall.

By 1904, victory began to perch on baseball banners, too. In that year, under Captain Day, the team won more than half the games played; in 1905, under Captain Gorham, eleven of seventeen. The team of 1906, under Captain Palmer, was claimed to be "the greatest collection of ball players that has ever worn the colors of the "Blue and Black." Out of nineteen games, C. C. I. gained sixteen victories. W. DeMott and D. H. Valden were notable players. In 1907, under Captain B. H. DeMott, eleven out of seventeen games were won, and in 1908, under the same captain, nine out of twelve. "Hisen" DeMott, Pitcher, and D. H. ("Piger") Valden, Catcher, were the outstanding combination among the "Prep" schools of their time.

At the same time, the Trustees declared that "all athletic sports should be designed for health rather than for 'the selfish hope of a season's fame' .... The cultivation of sound health is with us, and should be in all schools, the first object of all forms of athletics; and it is our intention to eliminate all games that do not stand this test."

A track team was formed in the Spring of 1904. Succeeding Track Teams won laurels and gave C. C. I. a high ranking in track athletics. C. C. I. men were always creditable participants in such events as: the University of Pennsylvania Relay Meet, the Brooklyn Polytechnic Institute Meet, the New York Athletic Club Meet, and the Interscholastic Meets of Columbia, Princeton, University of Pennsylvania, Wesleyan, Lehigh, and Yale. Once they stood second among forty-three schools. In 1906, at the New York University Meet, in securing first place in the one mile relay, the team broke the Greater New York Interscholastic record and established a new one of 3′.34″. The school, with only five men entered, held second place in the Meet as a whole. Later that year, the team won the Wesleyan University Interscholastic Meet, piling up 35 points as compared with the 22 points of their nearest competitor. The relay team on this occasion, composed of: R. W. Bacon, '06, G. W. Sutton, '06, H. W. Faraday, '07, W. H. Bacheler, '08 broke all previous American records for the mile relay for preparatory and high schools, making the time 3 minutes, 30 and one-fifth seconds. In 1907, two new Interscholastic records were made in the Wesleyan Meet (as well as two new school records) by Faraday and Camp, the former covering the 440 yard Dash in 51 seconds and the latter the 880 yard Run in 2 minutes, 5 and four-fifths seconds. An additional school record was made there in the 220 yard low hurdles by Kilpatrick, time 27 and four-fifths seconds. Other outstanding track records by C. C. I. boys were those made by H. L. Bryant, '05, who did the 120 yard high hurdles in 16 and four-fifths seconds and by W. H. Bacheler, '08, who did the 220 yard hurdles in 26 and one-fifth seconds. In 1908, the C. C. I. team won the New York University Meet from more than thirty of the foremost schools.

Camp's record for the half-mile and the one mile relay record remained unbroken for several years and, indeed, even after C. C. I. had become a girls' school, she for a while still had the distinction of holding all records for United States preparatory schools and high schools. The story goes that the President was once astonished to find in his morning mail a reproach-

DR. EUGENE ALLEN NOBLE
President of the Centenary Collegiate Institute, 1902-1908

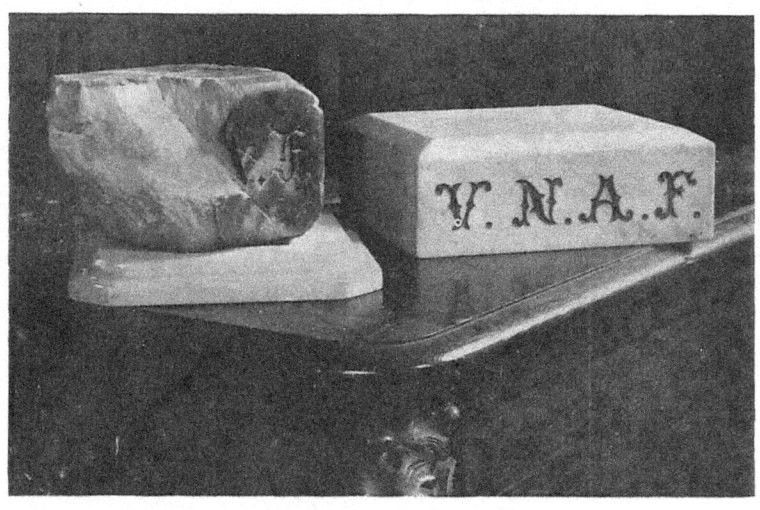

(Photographed by Mr. Elmer Hart, Hackettstown, New Jersey.)

WHITNEY LYCEUM PEDESTAL STONES
The one at the left is the original stone which came through the fire.

fully challenging invitation to enter a C. C. I. track team in a forthcoming athletic meet!

Other interesting careers could be mentioned but space allows reference only to the remarkable work of H. W. Faraday, winner of many firsts, breaker of records in 100 yard Dash—10 and one-fifth seconds— and 440 yard Dash—51 seconds. Prominent in athletics from 1905 through 1908, he was President of C. C. I. A. A. in 1906, and Captain of both Football and Track Teams in 1907, and of Track Team in 1908.

Professor Denman inaugurated Indoor "Gym" Meets, cross country runs, and "Hare and Hounds" runs which became popular.

The Athletic Association was perhaps the strongest organization on the campus and its monograms, awarded on certain terms to outstanding players of football, baseball, and to successful track contestants, were eagerly contended for and proudly worn. A medal was given for the best work on the Annual Field Day. Over and above all this was the All-Round Athletic Championship. In determining the winner of this distinction, the scope and quality of ability in all sports were considered. The winners from 1904 on were:

1904—John Crane Day
1905—Gerald Andrus Palmer
1906—Arthur Boynton
1907—D. Harvey Valden.
1908—Fred E. Linder
1909—Arthur B. Irving

Suggestions that the girls enter this competitive athletic life were presently in the air, eventuating in 1906 in three girls' basketball teams, each with its coach:

Professor Hall for the Senior team; Professor Tressler for the Juniors; Miss Maclay for the Underclassmen team.

The students' gratitude to Professor Denman was very sincere. A few expressions of this, indicating the tremendous influence for good which he wielded, are well worth quoting:

The athletic season, which has just been finished, has been a very creditable one to C. C. I. To the one person who has done most to bring this about all praise is due. He, not only with his instruction on the diamond and track, but by his spirit, his manliness, his Christian honor and self-respect, has done for sport at C. C. I. what countless victories alone could not have done. In spite of discouragements and defeats, he has loyally kept on and has helped both the sports and the life at C. C. I.[4]

Beloved by every man with whom he comes in contact, throwing off discouragements and turning them into inspirations, always the advocate of true sport, Professor Denman has won the respect, love, and confidence of every fellow in the school.

In years to come, when we sit down and count the blessings of our school life, we will have no greater one than the acquaintance and friendship of this man.[5]

So much "history" was being made by the Athletic Association that a distinct need began to be felt for some medium to record and preserve for posterity the prowess of C. C. I. True, there was *The Hackettstonian* whose continuity had been not too seriously broken by the years of calamities, its Editor and other Staff mem-

---

4 *The Hackettstonian*, June, 1904.
5 *The Hackettstonian*, December, 1905.

bers being elected by the different Societies. But an annual to summarize the events of the year was wanted. There had been one in 1892, called *The Hackettstonian*, but it had not perpetuated itself. At the suggestion of Mr. Harry H. Runyon and with the backing of Professor Denman, the idea of an annual began to be seriously considered. At that time neither of the two upper classes formed early enough in the year to complete the task successfully. The only other organization powerful enough was the Athletic Association. So, in the Fall of 1903, a board was selected and work was begun. The result was the first *Hack* "Running between the Centenary Collegiate Institute and the General Public, controlled by the Athletic Association and containing Interesting Personalities and some baggage, driven by E. Raymond Riegel, chief." All the staff were boys. The first *Hack* was dedicated to Dr. Whitney. It was a very clever publication and set a high standard for succeeding "Hack Boards" to emulate. Any profits from the *Hack* were applied to the support of the Track Team. A deficit was made good by the whole Athletic Association.

If scholarship and athletics were aligning C. C. I. beside the best schools of the United States, no less so was its religious activity. The Young Men's Christian Association, active on the campus since 1879, was sending its delegates to State Conventions and student Missionary Conferences. As a result of participation in the Students' Missionary Convention held at Princeton in 1907, the boys organized a Mission Study Class for the purpose of studying foreign missions. It had twenty members in 1907. Equally strong was the Young Women's Christian Association, organized in 1888, which sent its group of delegates each Summer to the Conference at Silver Bay on Lake George. In 1908, C. C. I. entertained the meeting of the New York and New Jersey Territorial Committee of the National Board of the Y. W. C. A. from March 7 to 9. Y. M. C. A. and Y. W. C. A. secretaries and other officers of the national organizations visited the campus each year, as did also the organizers of The King's Daughters, a religious organization which had two circles very active on the campus, called "The Willing Workers" and the "Sunshine Circle." These latter groups held fairs yearly to raise money for their enterprises, local and foreign. There was also a strong Young Women's Missionary Society. Both the "Y's" had large memberships and reported most interesting meetings, attended by sixty or seventy, each week. And not interesting only. Students were working for favorable effects on conduct and life, too. Commented the Editor of the "In and Around School" section of the student magazine:

This organization [the Y.M.C.A.] has always been one of the main factors in school, to influence fellows for a better life.
The Christian spirit of a school influences all other life, and while we continue to bask in the blessing of such meetings we need have no fear for discipline.

The School regularly observed the Day of Prayer for Schools and Colleges.
In another way, too, C. C. I. was connected with a national organization—she had on her campus the Zeta Chapter of the Alpha Phi Fraternity. Delegates

from Hackettstown were sent to the annual conventions, and the 27th annual convention of the Alpha Phi Fraternity was held at C. C. I. on December 4 and 5, 1903, in Zeta Hall.

Social life still centered around the Literary Societies whose public Anniversary Programs were becoming more and more elaborate, time-consuming, and expensive. To bring these activities within more reasonable bounds, different experiments were tried. The anniversaries of the brother and sister Societies were celebrated in a joint program, the Whitney Lyceum and the Diokosophian together, and the Alpha Phi with the Peithosophian. Then in 1907 the festivities were combined into a union anniversary of all four Societies. To chronicle this *The Hackettstonian* put out an "Anniversary Number" with pictures and reprints of speeches. But the problem apparently was not solved, according to an editorial which observed:

The combined festivities did not diminish in elaborateness; but, in fact, were more resplendent than former celebrations; they did not appreciably lessen the consumption of the students' time; it cannot be said that they represented the students' regular work and ability to any greater extent than did former ceremonies; and, from general indications, the slight curtailment of expenses will not be of any great consequence.

Beside and outside of these there were growing up other societies and many special clubs, providing so many diversions under which the students "suffered" that on one occasion they felt constrained to ask the instructors to make the examinations as light as possible!

The long-established Current Topic Club among

the girls, meeting Tuesday evenings, was paralleled by the Fact and Fiction Club among the boys, meeting for a half-hour before Chapel on Thursday evenings. For both of these Miss Charlotte Hoag was the "Speaker," as she was also for the Travel Club. "Fact and Fiction" was disbanded in 1908, the boys ceasing to support it.

Clubs appear, disappear and re-appear under new names. The Cercle Français of 1904, fades out to be replaced in 1907, under the direction of Professor Hyde, by the French Club. There was also for a time a German Club. There was a movement to start a debating team and join an interscholastic league but this seems not to have matured at this time. A Camera Club was active for awhile, and for several years a medal was offered for the best collection of pictures of the lovely scenery of the "sweet little Warren County balliwack" cuddled in the beautiful valley of the Musconetcong.

Musical Clubs also flourished, dropped, died, and were revived under the successive names: The Mandolin-Banjo Club; The String Glee Club; the C. C. I. Concert Band; finally The C. C. I. Orchestra, which was vigorous for some years.

The humorous fun-makers' Clubs, too, entered their pages in the *Hack;* for example, the Cabbage-Head Dramatic and Musical Club. In what connection should be recorded the existence of the Fusser's Club?

More lasting were the mysterious secret "Dormitory Societies." Of these the discreet historian dares to no more than quote the students' own account written in December, 1906.

"AND WITH HONORS STILL UNBOUNDED" 117

There seems to be a doubt in the minds of some as to the value of dormitory societies. As to whether there is any foundation for such an attitude remains yet to be seen. Probably like most other things, there can be an abuse as well as a use of such organizations. The chief objection to them in the minds of some is, that they are cliques. Yet nothing is more natural than that certain people of similar tastes and dispositions should associate, either in the formal folds of a society or simply by the ties of common sympathies of pursuits. This has always been, is, and always will be. It is based upon human nature, and like all human things is liable to abuse, beside being capable of considerable good.

In the year nineteen hundred, a few kindred spirits, for the sake of obtaining a closer fellowship, organized themselves into the Delta Lambda Pi. The initiation of John Day and his contemporaries has been crowned with success. The torch of fellowship they lit has burned from year to year, warming many a heart brought within the scope of its cheery influence. The keynote of the society is brotherhood; not athletics, which belongs to the school in general, nor literary merit, cherished by the literary societies, but good fellowship. A bunch of congenial fellows drawn together by common likes and aims. A "hail, well met" hearty crowd, not shirking the storms of life but enjoying the sunlight. Good times we have enjoyed together and better are in store.

The fall term of the school year 1904, witnessed the birth of a second society among the boys. Several fellows drawn together by the desire of more intimate social life and the knowledge that there was room for such an organization, formed the "Spook and Spectre" Dormitory Society. "Bob" Bancker, "Dud" Palmer, "Walt" Clark, "Abe" Fretz, were among those who were willing to take up the task of its formation, and it is due to their strength and purpose that Spook and

Spectre has progressed so nicely, and maintains its present firm footing. Vigorous resolutions to advocate all that stands for the best in school life, to become closer knit in the bond of fellowship and mutual progress, are commendable features.

Each Society had its "Frater" or "Soror" "in Facultate." Delta Lambda Pi had a mascot—Togo, Professor Denman's dog.

The dormitory societies on the girls' side are flourishing. The new members of the Alpha Epsilon are Misses Griffen, Hagerty, Geoffroy, Backus, Coonrod, Harris and Derry. Those who have lately been taken into the Phi Delta Delta, are Misses Hay, King, Ashley, Sanford and Olmstead.
The "Knife, Fork and Spoon" are still doing good service. Miss Morton has taken Miss Davis' place as the "Fork;" Miss Geoffroy takes Miss De Ponthier's place as the "Knife," while Miss Noe still holds the position of the "Spoon."
Two new societies have been formed; the Phi Delta Pi, composed of Misses Carnrick, Wendler, Byrnes, Sanford and Olmstead, and the Pedestrian Club, whose members are as follows: Misses Dunlap, Ryan, Mittag, E. Hutchison, H. Hutchison, Hanna, Fletcher, Baker, Olmstead, Wendler, Byrnes, and Sanford, with Miss Maclay to chaperon the walks.

"Eating Clubs" too were in good standing and out-in-the-open. These were called "Cauldron and Pestle" and "The Animal Cracker Club." An "After Chapel Club" may have been of this number but suspicions point to a "bull-session" purpose, rather.
Indeed, C. C. I. Alumni had their clubs, too. There

were for many years a Wesleyan C. C. I. Club, a Woman's College of Baltimore C. C. I. Club, and for a time also a Syracuse C. C. I. Club.

The real vigor of a school is seen in its traditions. Many Centenary traditions date from this period of beginning afresh after the rude intrusions of calamity. A most dignified, meaningful, distinctive, and beautiful tradition was the Salamander Ceremony[6] commemorating the fire. The class of 1901 deserves great credit for originating this, and it is unfortunate in the extreme that this uniquely Centenary tradition was allowed by later less imaginative classes to die out. Nor has any substitute ever been suggested.

A less expressive custom—found on most campuses—begun at this time, was the observance of May Day. The Seniors of 1907 began it, using May 31 for a stately procession led by a May Queen and a May King with their court. The program included an address by Professor Denman, a May-Pole dance with ribbons of the class colors, humorous races and stunts, and refreshments dispensed from decorated booths.

Begun as a "Junior Spread," a Junior Banquet developed, with an elaborate program of toasts. The Seniors revived for themselves a custom popular in Dr. Whitney's day which had included the whole school—the day-long Excursion by train to Delaware Water Gap. The Senior "Pleasure Trips" were varied: sleigh rides, straw-rides to Budd Lake or Cranberry Lake, excursions to Delaware Water Gap, picnics.

It became traditional for all students to attend the Methodist Church in a body on the first Sunday of

---

[6] This ceremony will be described in the chapter on student life.

the school year, and the Presbyterian Church on the last Sunday in October. At commencement time the class tree was dedicated. At this time the Alumni came back in large numbers, and it became customary also for a number of Alumni to return to observe the starting of each new school year.

A frequent visitor at C. C. I. in these years was George J. Ferry, still President of the Board of Trustees. On most of his visits he addressed the student body and *The Hackettstonian* recorded these occasions with warm enthusiasm. The second volume of the *Hack,* for the year 1905, was dedicated to this man who—"By his constant munificence towards, chivalrous confidence in, and magnanimous loyalty to our Alma Mater, has contributed inestimably to her success."

Spontaneous and exuberant as was this student life, there was still a noticeably conscious effort to achieve better school spirit. Always there seemed to be some boys who violated the cleanliness and order of the boys' parlor, always those less desirable personalities —then as now—who are the most voluble and conspicuous. Periodically the editorials contained pleas that the better students exert continuous influence to keep the tone of the school high.

These were the days of football rallies, C. C. I. yells, marching songs, class songs, school songs. Most of the songs that Centenary has date back to these years. Examples are: "Returning to C. C. I." Written by Lydia E. Byrnes (Thompson) '07 with music by Grant Colfax Tullar, C. C. I. 1891.

"The Fire Songs." Written by Professor Clifford W. Hall with music by Professor Frederick Schlieder.

The School Lake

The Canal

"The Salamander Song." Words and music by Carl F. Price, 1898.

"The Praise of C. C. I." Words and music by S. Quackenbush (1905).

"The Song of Tribute." From *The Hack* of 1904, anonymous.

"Hail to C. C. I." Words and music by Lydia E. Byrnes (Thompson) '07.

"June-Tide." From *The Hack*, 1906, anonymous.

"Parting Song." Words by Beulah M. Sanford (Osborne) '07.

A few songs were produced in response to a general appeal put out by *The Hackettstonian,* which in December, 1903 published a song by Mr. Harry H. Runyon (1905) entitled "Alma Mater—C. C. I." Apparently its outstanding merit was not recognized at once, but the song appears again in the school magazine for December, 1907, with this request:

> In looking over some old issues of the "Hackettstonian," the song printed on the first page of this issue was found. It was written by Mr. Harry Runyon in 1903. It would be a good plan, if the students would learn this song and add it to their collection of school songs.

Finally when the first and only book of C. C. I. songs, *A Year of Song,* was published in 1910—a collection edited by the well-known writer of songs and hymns, Carl F. Price, C. C. I., 1898—this song entitled simply "Alma Mater" stands in the place of honor. Thus began Centenary's "Alma Mater" song.

Back of, and a part of all the events of these

years, moved the President, "strong, fearless, progressive," meeting his own problems, making his own decisions. Enrolment was brought up to the point where all rooms were occupied, and maintained there, despite the necessity of raising rates to $375 a year. In 1906 there were 241 boarding students. Dr. Noble was successful as a financier. He inaugurated a regime of extreme economy. Each year showed a net gain of receipts over expenditures in the current expenses of the school, the surplus of 1908 being six times the size of that of 1903.

All the money that could possibly be spared was applied toward the cancellation of the debt which stood in 1902 at $67,000. The Trustees had pledged and secured through their own soliciting $50,000 of this. The presiding Elders, Ministers, and Churches had co-operated in this effort. Also a portion of the Twentieth Century Thank Offering had been allotted to Centenary. These combined efforts were so successful that when Dr. Noble resigned, the property was free from debt, and in 1909 the cancelled mortgage was presented to the Annual Conference with the statement: "And now the most stately buildings and the best-equipped secondary school in Methodism, . . . valued at $200,000, is entirely free from debt."

Many improvements had been made. In 1903 the grounds, much injured by the fire and the process of rebuilding, were put in order and landscaped, the expense being met by the Honorable William H. Murphy, one of the Trustees. The rear walls of the new buildings presented a rather bleak appearance. Dr. Noble wisely planted ivy about these walls which are now covered with a luxuriant growth which has added greatly to the beauty of the buildings.

In 1903 the gift of a tower clock was announced but all that the public knew was that the giver was a citizen of Hackettstown. It was not until after the donor's death that his name was found to be Peter A. Welch, the father of Bishop Herbert Welch.

An improvement of immense value to the school and one for which the students ought ever to remain grateful was the construction of a swimming-pool adjoining the boys' gymnasium. It was completed in the Fall of 1908.

Just about the time that the debt was beginning to shrink appreciably and the yearly surplus was demonstrating a healthy upward trend, occurred an event in the annals of Hackettstown real estate that was big with importance to C. C. I. Here is the story in the jubilant words of the Trustees, reporting to the Newark Conference in the Spring of 1906:

> The small plot of ground which we have owned at Hackettstown has long been recognized as too restricted for our needs. There is not enough campus room for athletic purposes; and there is not enough room for the possible extension of our work in ways that may be desirable and necessary. By a stroke of singular good fortune a property came to our attention which we have often wished to own. A prohibitive price had been put upon it, and we balanced regret against hope. What we wanted we could not get. During the past year a proposition was made that permitted us to hope again; and the substance of things hoped for we can now report. A valuable tract of one hundred and eighteen acres, within the town limits, and only a short distance from

our campus, has been purchased by us, and will soon come into our full possession. It would seem strange that we could purchase this property when we had so little money; but again the love which is loyalty and responsibility and liberality has been shown, and we take pleasure in presenting to the Newark Annual Conference, as their possession, without encumbrance of any sort, one hundred and eighteen acres of choice land located less than five hundred yards from our present location. As soon as the lease of the present tenant expires, we shall begin to improve this holding, and we are sure that the ideals and plans for the school will be easier to realize because of this possession. We desire to emphasize the fact that this property is not encumbered, but is given free and clear to the Newark Conference by its Board of Trustees.

At the same time another plot of two acres adjoining the school property was purchased, and a lot across from the front campus which had been intended as a site for a President's home was sold.

The Trustees regretted that they could not immediately develop the land as they wished, and in 1906 the School Farm was leased for a year, with the lessor reserving right to construct a dam and possibly a golf links. Plans called for a new athletic field, a golf course and a skating pond. *The Hackettstonian* for October, 1907 reported progress: "During the summer extensive alterations have been made. The farm buildings have been remodeled. New stock has been secured. The products of the farm have gone far toward improving the school menu. Part of the farm has been reserved for golf links and an athletic field. The work on the improvements has been retarded not so much because of a

"AND WITH HONORS STILL UNBOUNDED"   125

lack of funds, but because of a dearth of the right kind of labor."

In May, 1908, an appropriation of $3000 was granted for improvements on the farm property and on November 8, 1908, the committee appointed on the construction of a dam reported that the work had been accomplished at a cost which was $635 less than the amount authorized. President Ferry of the Board of Trustees made a report setting forth the advantages gained from this work. The school lake was now a reality.

Before this, however, the man who had watched the campus expand under his presidency had sent to the Board of Trustees the following letter:

May 28th, 1908.

To the Trustees of Centenary
    Collegiate Institute,
        Newark, N. J.
Dear Brethren:—

    I beg to present herewith my resignation as President of Centenary Collegiate Institute.

    This step has been taken after great deliberation. I have been elected to the presidency of the Woman's College of Baltimore; and after going over the matter with care and prayer I feel that the election ought to be accepted by me.

    My work at Hackettstown has been rendered cheerfully and loyally. If any measure of success has come to the school through me, praise should be given, primarily, to the members of the board of trustees for their support and cooperation. To one member of the board, your honored president, I owe a debt of gratitude which can never be paid. He has been more than friend, and almost a father. With kindnesses unnumbered and a loyalty unhesitating he has stood with me in my work; and I love him and honor him. What he has done for me has brought this election about; and I shall hope to serve the church in the new field and in every way as he has served the church at Hackettstown.

I shall consider it an honor to continue at Hackettstown until such a time as you may appoint. Knowing the work of the school so well I shall gladly aid my successor; and if you think me worthy of election to your board of trustees I shall be pleased to serve the school that way. Praying God's blessing upon the institution which has been a part of my life and shall always be, I am,

Sincerely yours,
(signed) Eugene A. Noble.

The Board accepted this resignation with resolutions of regret. All too short had been these halcyon days of expansion and elaboration of traditional designs. New educational ideals were forming. Change was in the air and the Trustees were fully aware of it, as is clearly evidenced by their discussion of it in their Report to the Annual Conference made in April, 1908.

Feeling that the vacancy created by Dr. Noble's resignation should be filled as soon as possible, lest detriment come to the school, they did not defer action. Dr. Whitney nominated the Reverend J. M. Meeker, D.D., Mr. Blanchard seconded the nomination, Mr. Ferry endorsed it, and the others concurred, making unanimous the election of Dr. Meeker as the next President of C. C. I.

CHAPTER VII

Proving "Worthy of the Times"

CHANGES: EXIT CO-EDUCATION. 1908-1917.

"NO president of C. C. I. entered on his work under such cheering conditions," writes Professor Hammond in his History, "and with such bright prospects of a successful administration as Dr. Meeker. He was well and favorably known in Hackettstown, for he had been pastor of the M. E. Church there a few years before. The citizens of Hackettstown heard of his election with joy and when he came, received him with an ovation. A large company of citizens accompanied by a band of music assembled on the grounds in front of the Institute to do him honor. J. C. Allen of Hackettstown, a former Trustee, delivered an address of welcome and Dr. Meeker made a gracious reply."

This is but surface cheer, however. Place beside it the facts in this sentence from Professor Hammond's preceding chapter: "When Dr. Noble left, no debt existed, all bills were paid, and there was a neat balance in the treasury." Still the product of these factors is not necessarily "bright prospects." We can see this now, with the easy wisdom of "hind-sight," but let us for a moment go back to the last six months of 1908, assemble all the pieces of the then-known picture, and see whether their edges fit together to create a vista of unclouded prospects.

First take the financial situation, a basic factor in any enterprise. The school still had no endowment; there had been practically no accretions to the small nucleus of the Hurley memorial fund of $1500 given under Dr. Whitney's regime back in 1895. Buildings and equipment were new but the heyday of their newness was closing; soon maintenance, repairs, replacements would be a considerable item in the budget. Even before President Meeker took office, expenses had been running too high and the school was being managed on a very narrow margin, too close to admit of always seeing the way out. There are indications that the financial structure in 1908 was none too firm. Mr. Ferry's letters to the new president contained cautious warnings and insistence that "we must be able to pay our debts when they come due."

The Farm was a liability even though it afforded basis for this attractive paragraph on "The Seminary Farm" in the Catalogue of 1908-1909:

The purchase of a near-by farm property has given the School an opportunity to expand and improve its facilities. It makes possible a Golf-links, comprising nine well-located holes, with good hazards, and of good length. Students are privileged to join the Golf Club, and to share in all the contests. A pond for skating is being constructed, and will make a beautiful body of water, fed by hundreds of bubbling springs, which now flow into a well-stocked trout brook. A large and quite unusual Athletic field will be put in shape as soon as it is possible to utilize a field of about eight acres,

Dr. Jonathan Magie Meeker
President of the Centenary Collegiate Institute
1908-1917

lying nearest the School. The rest of the farm property is under cultivation, and all produce is intended for the consumption of the School.

The potato blight struck in 1908; and the 4000 celery plants had not done well. The project threatened to be a perpetual problem and Mr. Ferry admitted as much in his letter of August 19, 1908:
"The farm owed us a good deal of money, as it always will. It was not bought for profit, but to increase our acreage, and to give the students a place to go for recreation instead of in the village." Moreover, signs pointed to an augmenting rather than a diminishing of this kind of liability, for it was already evident that the school authorities ought to connect the farm with the campus by the purchase of the approximately fifty intervening acres.

Another grim, sad, inescapable fact to be reckoned with was the imminent loss of Centenary's great tower of strength, Mr. Ferry. Then seventy-nine years old, he had for several years past been pleading to be relieved of the responsibilities of the presidency of the Board of Trustees. Plainly he could not be counted for much longer. Would it ever be possible to replace a man of such generosity and devotion? The wise counsels and enthusiasm of Dr. Whitney would soon be things of the past, too.

If the school situation was not reassuring, neither was that of the nation or of the world as a whole. The panic of 1907 was not a matter of memory only. In the world there was mounting international tension.

So much for financial aspects. Turn next to the

educational scene. The founding fathers of C. C. I. had resolved to establish an institution "worthy of the times." What times? In the realm of education as in the physical world, only the organism that can adapt itself to its environment survives. The Trustees must do much more than see that bills are paid. "To be charged with the responsibility of managing a school where youth is trained is a serious obligation," they reported to the Newark Conference in April, 1907. "There are many factors in the problem of secondary education which are not even imagined by many people; in fact, it is the hardest problem in the whole question of education. While we do not claim to have found the ultimate solution, yet we have worked diligently during the past years to understand our work."

In studying their data for 1908, they found much significance in a noticeable increase in the number of applications from girls and a decrease in the number from boys. Further, they were keenly aware of conditions which made them ask "whether the sort of work which we are doing at Hackettstown should continue." They described the trend away from education for culture toward the ideal of utility and technical training, and summarized the debate then going on in the United States over the place and work of secondary schools in a revised scheme of education. They placed before the Conference the consideration of the question of separate training for boys and girls, as well as diverse courses of study, and even suggested that they request the University Senate or the Board of Education of the Methodist Church to co-operate in determining what changes would best meet the needs of the times. In this inquiry the whole educational landscape of the Methodist Church had to be considered.

One more factor must be taken into account before we can measure the brilliancy of the prospects for C. C. I. and for President Meeker in 1908: the personality of the President himself. How historians love to debate the determining influence of personalities upon history!

Jonathan Magie Meeker had prepared for college in The Hudson River Institute, Claverack, New York, and entered Wesleyan University, from which he received the degrees of M. A. and D. D. After graduating from Drew Theological Seminary, he earned his Ph. D. degree in New York University. He served many prominent charges in the Newark Conference. He had had three years of administrative experience as State Secretary of the New Jersey Y.M.C.A. At the time of his election he was Superintendent of the Newark District. "He was a man of marked personality," says his biographer, the Reverend A. H. Tuttle. "He had a commanding and magnetic personal presence, tall and erect, compactly built. . . . Every movement indicated perfect confidence. . . . He was something more than an educated man. He was a man of marked mentality, quick of discernment, and ready to assimilate. . . . He was fond of details and was really a genius in organization. All who followed him in any of his Churches found the machinery complete in every particular and in running order."

The combination of these factors leads to no snap conclusion of "bright prospects." Rather it arouses a fascinated curiosity as to the outcome of their interaction.

C. C. I. and her President did not stand alone facing the problem of change. Pennington Seminary and Blair Hall were collaborating with her in a careful, practical study of the whole matter. What they found can be summarized thus: The judgment of an increasing number of distinguished educators in Europe and America, based on consideration of the physical and psychological aspects, on observation, and on experience, was that better intellectual results were obtained in single sex schools above the eighth grade. Public sentiment was demanding the change, as was proved by the fact that increasing numbers of parents were deciding against co-educational schools. Blair and C. C. I. were both falling short of their former registrations of boys. Many colleges and schools had changed from co-education with very satisfactory results. Peddie had done so in 1907.

At that time there were in New Jersey several large and prosperous schools for boys, whereas for girls there were but few schools, and these were of the smaller and more expensive kind. About this time the Girls' Latin School of Baltimore had been closed, and this encouraged the decision to make C. C. I. the greatest preparatory school for girls under the auspices of the Methodist Church, conducted on such broad Christian principles and charging such moderate fees as to win the favor and patronage of all denominations. It could serve to prepare students for Goucher College and for the colleges for women in the North Atlantic States, for almost all of which it already had certification privileges. A final reason for making this a school for *girls* rather than for *boys* was the increasing number of avenues

Centenary Collegiate Institute's Last Football Team, 1909

Standing, left to right: Whittle, Kidney, Thompson, Lansing, Seger, Johnston, Buckley, Coach Denman; Seated, left to right: Hockenbury, Penny, Snedecor, Capt. Gregory, Woolley, Wade, Kidd. "Togo."

of professional and other service opening to women and the increasing demand for more thoroughly trained young women capable of taking responsibility in commercial fields.

It was felt that the location, and the type of buildings and furnishings were especially suited for a girls' school, as were also the excellent facilities for teaching the extra subjects largely taken by girls, such as music, art, and elocution, subjects which bring in increased revenue so much needed by a school where endowment was lacking.

It was only logical therefore that on March 31, 1910, the Trustee presented to the Newark Conference the following Resolution:

Resolved, That we, as the Board of Trustees of the Centenary Collegiate Institute, approve the recommendation to make this school one for girls only, and refer it with power to the Executive Committee to carry out this purpose.

At a special session held on April 1, the Conference by a unanimous vote indorsed this and gave legal sanction to change C. C. I. from the co-educational school which it had been to a girls' school—to quote the words of its President "a young Ladies Female Seminary for Feminine Girls." In the same year Pennington Seminary became a school for boys only.

As June, 1910, approached, the days were full of sadness for the boys, and on the part of some, of indignation. It was especially hard on those who were being pushed away from their Alma Mater before they had completed their course. The last baseball game, the last track meet, the last contests in Oratory, the last meetings of Alpha Phi and Whitney Lyceum all marked the end of thirty-six years of men students, nine four-year student generations.

On the evening before Commencement, at the President's reception, John Lee Brooks, a member of the graduating class and President of Whitney Lyceum, made a mournful address in which he presented to the school a large framed portrait of Dr. Whitney, the most cherished possession of the original literary Society, now disbanding forever, which had so proudly carried the name of Centenary's first President.

During the Commencement dinner the boys, dressed in black, formed a procession, marched through the dining-room singing mournful dirges, shook hands with the Faculty, and then marched out again for the last time.

The valedictorian of that historic class of 1910 was, appropriately, a boy, Steward Franklin Custard.[1] "As I spoke the final words of farewell," writes Mr. Custard, "I felt I was speaking for a great and noble army of men, giants of a former day—now become 'martyrs.' My valedictory was for all of them, not my class alone. For the young men the announcement of making Centenary exclusively for girls came as an order similar to 'Abandon Ship!' and caused dismay, especially for the Junior Class. The Seniors had had three great years before that change hit. Well, we have survived that order of change and are well content with the present Centenary." Let us hope he speaks truly for all that

[1] Now the Reverend S. F. Custard, Rector of Grace Episcopal Church, Allentown, Pa.

band of Alumni of whom C. C. I. and its present successor, Centenary Junior College, are so proud. Five hundred and eighty-six men have graduated from Centenary and many others have attended but not graduated. Of these, many have become eminent in the professions and in business.

It is interesting to note that this change had the full approval of the President Emeritus, Dr. Whitney. He was President Meeker's ablest counselor. But not for long, for, says his biographer, "After this last and radical change was successfully effected he felt that his work was finished and hastened to his rest." He died on June 6, 1913.

The Trustees had reckoned that it would require from three to five years to demonstrate the wisdom of their decision but in 1911 they reported: "A single year has confirmed our judgment and assured the future success of the school." Ninety-two *new* girls had registered, and total registration had increased by twenty. This made it imperative to proceed at once to renovate North Hall, the old "boys' hall." Continues the Report:

> Our very prosperity necessitated unexpected expenditures. . . . The condition of the North Dormitory was such that a thorough renovation was necessary. Fifty-eight new doors had to be purchased, and new window sills placed in every room. The hall walls were in such bad condition that they had to be wainscoted. All the rest of the plaster on halls and in rooms was pointed up and kalsomined, and the woodwork was varnished. Practically none of the furnishings and floor coverings in this dormitory was fit for further use.
>
> All this meant the purchase of large quantities of

furnishings and items of every description. A number of new practice pianos had to be added.

And how did the girls feel about all this when they returned in the Fall of 1910? These excerpts from an Editorial in the October *Hackettstonian* are revealing:

> At first, indignation was felt in many places. C. C. I. and co-education were inseparable in the minds of the hundreds who had been students there. Fond memories were twined around its halls. Many romances had their beginning in C. C. I.
>
> When one thought of Salamander Night, the anniversaries and commencements, the boys were a part of them as much if not more than the girls. . . .
>
> So, on September twenty-second, only girls, girls everywhere, were seen. South Dormitory filled to its utmost and North Dormitory received all the younger girls.
>
> Many "old" girls returned, rather skeptical and curious about the new experiment as it was called. . . .
>
> The girls can go down town every afternoon. The farm also, is ours at any time. The tennis courts, basketball ground, swimming pool and athletic field do not have to be shared with any one this year. Some, perhaps, will think we are selfish. No, we were only too willing to share with the boys in everything, but we like to be able to do as we please when we please. . . .
>
> Again, we are at liberty to use the library at any time during the day. Sunday evening, we have in the main parlors an informal song service, in which every girl enters with the right spirit, which is appreciated by all.
>
> Seniors also have some of their privileges now. On Sundays they do not walk in line to church nor have to report before going. More Seniors have heads of tables this year. Last but not least is the privilege of

The Last Graduating Class of the Co-educational Centenary Collegiate Institute, 1910

chaperoning other students on walks every Sunday afternoon....

One could devote many pages to the advantages and attractions of C. C. I. as a school for girls only. Still, we have in our hearts a place for the memories of "days beyond recall."

The girls, exulting thus in their new-found freedom, soon had much more space at their command in which to exercise it, too. For in 1910 the school acquired thirty-eight of the acres lying between the campus and the farm. This purchase forever protected the school from being surrounded by factories or dwelling houses. The campus, containing ten acres, and the farm, 159 acres, thus comprised a continuous strip of land over one and one-eighth miles in length. In 1912 a broad, well-made path over a mile in length was laid out down to the lake and planted on each side with trees and shrubs —the beginning of Centenary's beloved Farm Path. Resting places were provided under the trees. This secluded walk commanded many miles of uninterrupted view of the charming Musconetcong Valley, flanked on the north by beautiful hills skirted by the Morris Canal —a famous place for skating and hiking—and on the south by the Schooley's Mountains. The farm now had well-stocked poultry yards and provided fresh eggs, chickens, and ducks. The girls took up athletics with enthusiasm. At once they formed their Athletic Association and began a vigorous program of hockey, basketball, tennis, swimming, rowing, skating, and hiking.

The change tended to raise the scholarship, too, in a marked degree. Soon, C. C. I. girls who entered the notable women's colleges began to emulate the high scholastic standards that almost invariably had come to be associated with C. C. I. boys in the high-grade men's colleges and universities. In other words, C. C. I.'s glorious tradition of thorough scholarship was maintained. The strong religious tone of the school, too, suffered no lowering. The school spirit seemed never to have been better.

A number of changes had to be made in the Faculty. The word "Preceptress" is now replaced by "Dean." Miss Olive L. Austin held this office from 1910 to 1917. Like Miss Hoag, she was a woman of rare ability, fine dignity, and tact. The Commercial Department was discontinued but Stenography and Typewriting were continued under a special instructor. The Department of Home Economics was introduced in the Fall of 1911 under the direction of Miss Elsie R. Horne.

The aim of C. C. I. was still "to provide a thorough preparation for college for those that choose it, and also a strong course for such as cannot or do not wish to enter college. We desire to make the latter feel that they are not out-classed, or less fitted for the enjoyment and service of life in the spheres of their choosing." And this interesting thought followed:

Our departments of Stenography, Typewriting, Elocution, Music and Art, when earnestly pursued, transform the accomplishment to a profession worthy of the dignity of any woman confronted with the necessity of earning her living.[2]

Students who had been regular in attendance and who had maintained an average of eighty-five per cent

2 Catalogue—1910-1911.

in daily work and unannounced written tests, and whose deportment had been satisfactory, were advanced without examination. This aimed to avoid the evils incident to "cramming."

Diokosophian and Peithosophian continued as before. Centenary now became the home of a third Society, the Callilogian, founded in 1861, now finding refuge here when girl students had departed forever from Pennington. Miss Mary Isabella Breckenridge sponsored this transfer along with her own as teacher of English. She and her Society became very popular here. The Administration purchased the furniture in the former boys' society halls.

Enrolment figures for the years 1911 to 1914 showed satisfactory upward trends and the area of patronage was expanding. In confident anticipation of a steady increase in the number of students, many improvements were made. An ice-house was built, with a capacity of five hundred tons. A concrete vegetable cellar and a brick garage were constructed. A dumb-waiter was installed, connecting kitchen and hospital. The kitchen was freshly equipped.

In the dining room new tables for six replaced the larger ones of co-ed days, and there were bright new runners on the floors as well as in the dormitory halls and the aisles of the chapel. Forty new rugs were placed. The upholstery of the parlor furniture was renewed. The walls of the parlor, dining room, chapel, and rooms of all buildings were redecorated.

Shower-baths completed the swimming-pool and gymnasium and there was new equipment also in the art studio and library. A moving-picture machine and a Victrola were purchased. An inner-phone system was installed.

Fire escapes were provided where necessary. A very expensive iron fence six feet in height was put up to inclose parts of the campus. A threshing-machine and gasoline engine were supplied for the farm.

These and other improvements, however desirable they might be, made heavy demands on the school treasury. Along with them went a number of items of major repairs which had to be made at once. The heating plant required extensive renovations to make it adequate. The boiler was condemned and a new high-pressure boiler was given to the school by Colonel Edward L. Dobbins, who had become President of the Board. In March, 1912, a large section of the ceiling in the chapel fell, leaving the remainder, it was feared, in a dangerous condition. The construction of the dome was examined by several firms and it was found that the wooden beams resting upon the tops of the iron pillars were not sufficiently strong to hold the dome. These had to be replaced by iron channels. The farm barn also had to have a new roof. Of course there were plenty of repairs and replacements that would be classed as minor. No wonder the year 1912 closed with a deficit of $5000. The previous year had seen the funding of the debt of the Institute in the amount of $35,000. In March, 1914, a campaign was proposed for the purpose of raising $45,000 in order to clear up all indebtedness, and President Meeker was requested to proceed with the effort to raise the entire amount. Where could so much money be secured? Dr. Meeker knew of one man who would give $10,000 on condition that the whole amount be raised. C. C. I.'s great benefactor, the Honorable George J. Ferry, had remained in office during the change-over from co-education, but on March 22, 1911, his resignation had to be accepted and he became Honorary President of the Board. Colonel Edward L. Dobbins took his place, serving until 1915, when failing health compelled him to retire. His successor was Mr. Egbert J. Tamblyn.

Mr. Ferry had nothing to offer President Meeker when he approached him, but advice. He wrote in October, 1914:

> I am very anxious for the outcome of the Centenary Collegiate Institute and should be very sorry if it can not be made to pay. It seems you can not afford, nor can the Board of Trustees afford to run further in debt, for if the increase of debt continues there can be but one result in the matter. I can not see myself where you can raise any amount of money under present conditions to reduce the present indebtedness. I should be very happy to come to see you and will when I can, but my physical condition is such that I feel I can not make the trip at present.

Having no vote, he declined to attend the Trustees' meetings, but wrote on November 20, 1914:

> I am very sorry you find your Institution in an uncomfortable financial condition, but I am personally in no condition to help to relieve the situation at present, not being able to make any money myself.

The most disquieting feature of the situation was the fact that under the new regime the school had never been filled to the point where maximum returns could be realized relative to the constant costs. Some girls had transferred to C. C. I. when Peddie, Pennington, and (in 1915) Blair Hall joined the ranks of boys' schools, but the general trend of enrolment was downward. Now, with war in Europe dislocating so much of our business life, the following advice from Mr. Ferry ought to have been blazoned everywhere:

I am glad to know that you have as many students as you have, but wish you had a great many more for I fear that you will have to use great caution in your economies to come out even at the end of the year. You spoke of this matter as one of the things that you can reduce from previous years.

Competition among private schools was becoming "as keen as in the Insurance business." Wrote one of Dr. Meeker's correspondents, "Let us take what comfort we can in the fact that other schools are having difficulty in keeping up their normal enrolments." Centenary's plight was in truth by no means unique, for many schools were feeling the adverse effects of the European War, which was soon to engulf us also, and some notable preparatory schools sooner or later folded up forever under its crippling impact.

One can imagine President Meeker's state of mind as he had to witness the shrinking of his school. Added to this was his anxiety over the prolonged and serious illness of Mrs. Meeker. There was unusual harmony and devotion between these two; and this background of personal grief militated against full efficiency in his school duties.

While this sad state of affairs continued, several events occurred that belong to C. C. I. history. One of them meant a small accession to the treasury. In 1911, the State Fish and Game Commission began negotiations with C. C. I. looking toward the construction of a fish hatchery on the grounds of the Institute. Their request for water rights was granted. Some springs on the farm—some of the largest in the State—were sold, reserving, however, those in the pond. In 1913, a strip of land fifty feet wide was deeded to the State as a right-of-way for a new road from the State Fish Hatchery to the town. On this new road the school would then have frontage for twenty building lots which might be sold later on. Certain advantages resulted also from transfer to the school of a small strip of land. Credit should be given to Mr. Albert E. May, the school accountant, for carrying out these real estate transfers.

A few more strictly school "family" events must also be recorded. The first concerned Miss Charlotte Hoag. With health impaired, as a result, so her friends insisted, of her heroic conduct on the night of the fire, she had discontinued her work in 1908, hoping soon to return to her position. Her death, on September 3, 1909, was keenly felt by the students. At the next Commencement one of the most impressive exercises was the Memorial Service for Miss Hoag. Mr. Carl Price, representing "The Boys Before the Fire," gave an address. Miss Vivian Gordon, '00, spoke of "The Night of the Fire," telling how the alarm was given to each girl personally by Miss Hoag. At the end of the service, Miss Grace Hall, '06, presented a memorial tablet from the Diokosophian Alumnae. This hangs in Diokosophian Hall.

The next year another—and rather overdue—gesture of appreciation was made when, at Dr. Meeker's suggestion and on recommendation of the Board of Trustees, the assembly room in the Administration Building was named Whitney Hall, in honor of the first president and the then President Emeritus. All readers of this history will rejoice that this was done (April 3, 1911) fully two years before Dr. Whitney's death which occurred on June 6, 1913. Four years after this, on the day of Dr. Trevorrow's Inauguration, May 24, 1917, took place the unveiling of the beautiful mosaic Memorial Tablet to George H. Whitney which now occupies a conspicuous place in Whitney Hall.

Words are all too frail to serve as vehicles of appreciation; and in 1916 occurred an event that called for a much more tangible form of recognition—the passing of George J. Ferry. Centenary was in no condition to do more at the time than to spread upon the Trustees' minutes and send to the sorrowing Ferry family the following Memorial:

A Minute Concerning the Very
Valuable Aid Mr. George J. Ferry
Has Rendered Centenary Collegiate Institute

In view of the recent death of George J. Ferry, the Trustees would recall his vital relation to Centenary Collegiate Institute, and express in our records appreciation of his helpfulness.

The Newark Conference projected the School in 1868; its corner stone was laid in 1869; the Trustees proceeded with the brick building through five years as money was gotten to pay for it.

PROVING "WORTHY OF THE TIMES" 145

In 1869 Mr. Ferry was made a Trustee and was an active Trustee for more than forty years. Cornelius Walsh and David Campbell were successively Presidents of the Trustees for short terms, and then Mr. Ferry was made President. When the edifice was dedicated in 1874, he, as President, handed the keys to Dr. Whitney. He was President thereafter throughout the administrations of Dr. Whitney, Dr. McCormick, Dr. Ferguson and Dr. Noble, heads of the School, and throughout the first years of Dr. Meeker's administration.

He gave more than forty thousand dollars toward paying for the original structure; gave from time to time for its needs or improvement until it was burned; and gave for the building and furnishing of the edifice now occupied. He was in the beginning and all along the chief donor for the School's welfare and work. His gifts aggregated more than one hundred thousand dollars. He gave money because he gave hearty interest to the Institute.

Friend, counsellor, sympathizer, stimulating helper of the heads of the School in their perplexities, troubles, difficulties and endeavors, he was a big factor with them in making Centenary Collegiate Institute all it has been and is; and its influence for good may be credited largely to his generosity, interest and zeal. And all that the School will be in the future rests considerably on his fundamental activity.

How can we adequately honor the man who for forty-two years—from 1869 down to 1911—had carried Centenary's welfare next to his heart? From April 22, 1874, down to his retirement on March 22, 1911, he bore the responsibility of the presidency of the Board. No one knows the sum of his gifts. When C. C. I.

needed something, Mr. Ferry's right hand gave it and even his left hand knew not of it. For instance, research has thrown up in its digging that he gave all the silver for the first school dining-room. Other examples could be cited through the years, of gifts many, varied, practical, essential, given quietly and modestly, unadvertised, unmarked. Verily, the school is a monument to his devotion and zealous service and unfailing generosity.

In 1915 it was thought best to consult the Board of Education of the Methodist Church and to secure guidance from the Newark Conference called in special Executive Session. The result was the appointment of an Efficiency Committee, consisting of Messrs. Whitehead, Tamblyn, Jones, Muller, and Urmy, who visited the school, held consultations and made investigations along many lines. As a result, teaching and working forces were reduced in number and all salaries cut. A Budget Committee, meeting monthly at Hackettstown, was made responsible for all details of the various departments of the school, and for producing a balanced budget for the next year. No expenditure could be made without their approval. Special committees worked on restoring the usual harmony between town and school. The Board sent out a letter expressing gratification at the kindly attitude of the citizens toward the school.

In all this, Dr. Meeker's spirit of generous co-operation was spoken of in highest terms. The President was in a poor physical and nervous condition and in the spring of 1915 he had been obliged to go away for a rest of several weeks. By the spring of 1916, the various expedients adopted had proved their worth, for expenses

PROVING "WORTHY OF THE TIMES" 147

were then well within income. "The satisfactory results achieved have been due," reported the Trustees, "in a large measure to the diligent and untiring efforts of Dr. Meeker in carrying into effect the new plans adopted."

The Trustees pursued a policy of not spending any money for commercial advertising. Instead, during 1915 and 1916, 2,670 circulars and personal letters were sent to pastors, each enclosing a stamped, addressed, return postal card. The President sent two hundred and fifty personal letters to members of the Conference with illustrated brochures and return, addressed postal cards. Plainly they were appealing to the wrong constituency, however, for the group circularized sent only eighty-eight replies, none resulting in a registration, and the group receiving personal letters returned thirty-two answers, one of which ended in a registration.

At the request of the Trustees, the President "represented the school in thirty church and Conference visitations." Dr. Meeker was indeed active, going from one community to another seeking contributions to his plan of "modified endowment" and conferring with parents of prospective new students.

During the summer vacations, while the President was away thus busied, Professor Frank V. Stutsman was living in the school in order to look after all its interests. In 1914, the Board of Trustees had given Professor Stutsman the title of "Principal," with the idea that he could act as assistant to Dr. Meeker. This status he retained until well into Dr. Trevorrow's regime.

It was felt that alumni and former students should

come to the rescue of their Alma Mater and that they could best do this if C. C. I. Clubs were formed in central towns. Some work of this sort was done, but the plan was not very practicable because most C. C. I. alumni lived in distant and widely-separated places. Dr. Meeker was a successful leader of the alumni. He brought together on May 16, 1914, a notable group of more than three hundred alumni and former students. This was one of the most successful and enthusiastic reunions in C. C. I. history and it created a precedent for holding future reunions on the campus.

The year 1916 brought a very serious epidemic of infantile paralysis throughout the East. The weight of this last straw carried registration down to the lowest in the school's history. C. C. I.'s halls echoed to the tread of only forty-six "old" students and twenty-eight new students—only seventy-four students on September 29, 1916! As the financial problem became more and more complicated, gossip about the condition of the school went the rounds, magnifying things, as gossip always does. Articles in the country newspapers set forth dark prospects. The uncertainty reacted very adversely on the relationship between the town and the school. The Methodist Church and the school were not on the best of terms. Some of the teachers were seeking other positions. The good-will of the school was definitely at a low ebb.

Late in November, 1916, President Meeker made the following proposal to the Efficiency Committee: that he resign as President, and taking up his residence in New York City or its vicinity, devote himself, as the business agent of the school, to the securing of students.

The New Building—Dining Room of Centenary Collegiate Institute for Girls

He proposed visiting the various churches, and by means of interviews with pastors and parents, and by whatever other ways might be feasible, to increase the registration. He might also attend to the purchase of supplies. It was finally decided that it would be wise to give the proposed plan a three months' trial, but Dr. Meeker was to retain his office and title as President, while Professor Stutsman was given full power of attorney to attend to the administration of all affairs at the Institute.

Dr. Meeker's residence in New York was justified by the results attained, but his intensive exertions probably contributed to the break of his health that made it impossible to throw off an attack of pneumonia. He died after a very brief illness, on January 1, 1917.

Professor Hammond, who was an observer of all these events, sums up his impressions of President Meeker in these words: "He possessed many excellent qualities which attracted hosts of friends. He was a genial companion, entertaining in conversation, and he understood the art of winning friends." Then he adds, as if the words were wrung from him:

> The writer is not unmindful of the old adage, "De mortuis nil nisi bonum," but it seems necessary to say that Dr. Meeker did not excel as a financier; for the records show on his part many unnecessary expenditures and a long list of deficits mounting higher and higher year by year until the Institution was again burdened with a heavy debt and another mortgage was placed upon its property.

Alas for the illusory "bright prospects" seen by Professor Hammond in 1908! Could we but "look into the seeds of time and say which grain will grow and which will not!" In fairness to President Meeker this must not be the final word, however. Actually it would be difficult to invent a more discouraging combination of adverse circumstances for a president to face. To transform the Institute into a school for girls, and without an endowment to equip it for its new career was a herculean task, especially in those years of industrial unrest and world war. It is scarcely surprising that he was lured into a false sense of success by the upswing in the first registrations and that he waded into increasing expenditures that seemed justified in the hope of attracting students in a highly competitive market.

Besides these over-all conditions, there was in C. C. I. itself a very unfortunate combination of personalities all pulling in different directions. Something of this sort was repeated in the town, too, where the minister of the church which should have been his strong refuge was unsympathetic and even hostile to the school and its head. This is not the place to recount tales of old animosities, but they should be included in the picture of these difficult years.

As if this were not enough, the President was suffering direst grief in his own family circle. His son Clifford, a brilliant young research chemist who was at work on an important experiment attempting to develop synthetic rubber, was killed in his laboratory by an explosion. This shock came to a family saddened by the hopeless illness of the mother—a condition that had existed during almost all of her years at Centenary, rendering her increasingly helpless in body and, for the last two years of her life, in mind also. Her death came in June, 1916.

These additional untoward circumstances are features of the total situation which should be taken into consideration by anyone who would undertake to pass judgment on the work of Dr. Meeker.

To find a man qualified to resolve this difficult crisis was by no means easily or quickly done. While the Board was busy at this task, Professor Stutsman became Acting President, serving as the responsible head of the school, an efficient executive and a confidence-inspiring leader. The vacant place in the religious and spiritual guidance of the school was equally well filled by a substitute, the Reverend J. O. Sparnon, an alumnus and a Trustee of the school who had recently become pastor of the Hackettstown Church. He freely gave his time, labor, and friendly counsel.

Before this sad year ended, a new president had been inaugurated.

CHAPTER VIII

"Alma Mater, Live Thy Glory, Alma Mater, C. J. C.!"

FURTHER CHANGES ON THE SAME THEME—

JUNIOR COLLEGE—1917-1943

1. *Beginning of a New Era of Happiness and Progress*

CENTENARY had weathered one crisis in 1900. Now she was facing another, more serious because it was less spectacular and less generally realized. More steps along the same path must inevitably have meant the end. But there were two alternative courses.

One was offered by the Board of Education of the Methodist Church which had been studying the five preparatory schools of the metropolitan area with the idea of possible consolidation of Centenary and Drew Seminary for Young Ladies. At that time C. C. I. could easily have accommodated all the students of Drew in addition to her own. The Trustees from Drew were very unfriendly to the proposition and both groups agreed that there ought to be more rather than fewer schools in this region.

The only remaining solution was to find a strong

efficient leader while yet the Spring of 1917 was young. At this point, Bishop Thomas Nicholson, confident that with strong leadership and proper support this school could be in the front ranks of service, made a recommendation that was speedily acted upon; with the result that on May 24, 1917, the Reverend Robert Johns Trevorrow was formally installed as the new president of Centenary.

Like most of his predecessors, Dr. Trevorrow was a graduate of Drew Theological Seminary. English by birth, he had first seen the light in the historic town of St. Ives, Cornwall. Moving with his family to California, he had prepared for college at Napa Academy and graduated from the University of the Pacific, receiving there his A. B. in 1898, his A. M. in 1901 and his D. D. in 1913. He had studied also in Union Theological Seminary. From the California Conference he had transferred to the New York Conference and had served pastorates there until in 1913 he had become President of Drew Seminary for Young Ladies. He possessed a rare combination of abilities—those of the preacher, the religious thinker and leader, the teacher, the educational philosopher, and—rarest of all in this company—the administrator.

Centenary presented a challenge to all his energies, but as he stated in his Inaugural Address on "A Christian Ideal of Education," he found his chief incentive to sacrifice and effort in the fact that C. C. I. was a school for women. To him the education of a woman is not merely the training of an individual but the education of a whole family. He saw woman in America on the threshold of a glorious future. For her there must be the most thorough preparation, the highest scholarship, the cleanest ideals of morality and unselfish service. "The ideal of all education," he said, "is character building, approaching Christlikeness."

This creed, so similar to that of her first president, was destined to shape Centenary's program for a quarter of a century. The two presidents served Centenary each for twenty-six years, each with single-purposed, unswerving devotion, in sickness and in health. But how different the two administrations—the first, a calm, unhurried unfolding of the original design; the second, an anxious, tense labor of rescue and retrieving, of adaptation to a world torn by wars, in throes of transition.

President Trevorrow faced a complex, many-sided problem. "Every effort must be put forth," urged the President, "to operate a thoroughly fine school at reasonable rates . . . No one wants C. C. I. to deteriorate into a school for merely rich girls. It needs the vigor of the earnest, economical student." Here protruded the principal prong of a dilemma-like problem. Resources must be found for helping worthy students of limited means. To render the finest possible service at a minimum cost, and to provide ample scholarship opportunities, a school must have a proper endowment—the sum of $200,000 at least. But large gifts for endowment do not readily find their way to a school sinking under a burden of debt. Only by prompt payment of the interest and speedy liquidation of the entire obligation

1 Dr. Whitney held the title of president for twenty-six years, five of which were devoted to bringing the school into existence, twenty-one to actual administration.

could Centenary prove herself worthy of being entrusted with endowment funds.

The new President immediately inaugurated a new method of managing school finances along with regular monthly meetings of the Executive Committee of the Trustees to examine the financial statements and transact business. This method soon included a yearly audit of the school's accounts and careful study of the analytical reports of the auditors.

Dr. Trevorrow always made careful comparative statistical studies of his problems. He did nothing on impulse or mere "hunch." His graphs are a very interesting part of the college archives. Comparison of charges for tuition and residence revealed, for example, that the 1913 rate of $500 had been actually too low to cover the year's expenses. In 1919 there was no alternative but to raise the yearly charge to $725, and to $850 in 1921. Changes and adjustments were made from time to time as these studies and the general business conditions indicated.

Another object of constant scrutiny was the school farm. From the first, Dr. Trevorrow was suspicious of it as an income-producing factor but he gave it a chance to prove its value. He sought information from the State Department of Agriculture and secured an expert farmer. It soon became plainly the better part of wisdom to sell the acres that had constituted the original school farm, reserving to the school, however, perpetual right to the use of the entire "Farm Path." The whole amount realized was immediately applied on the indebtedness.

Above all, Centenary needed friends. "Anything

"ALMA MATER, LIVE THY GLORY..." 157

that will cement old friendships and make new ones is important to our school," wrote the President in 1917. An early suggestion had come from Mr. Carl Price of the class of '98, who wrote:

> I wish you all possible success in the school that was my first love. I believe you will be wise enough to cultivate the Alumni . . . Probably they can help in many of the difficulties that you must face there.

The President speedily sought their friendship. All Alumni and friends of C. C. I. found among their New Year Greetings in 1918 a copy of Volume I, number 1 of *The Bulletin of Centenary Collegiate Institute,* which brought them "wishes for a happy New Year, good will, prosperity, and the quiet mind" from the new President of their Alma Mater. Thus began a now familiar and inseparable part of the Centenary pattern.

Meanwhile registration had gradually increased. In 1920, students were once again using Upper North Hall which had been closed off ever since the boys had left.

Sooner than expected the policy of retrenchment and economy and careful management justified itself. By the Spring of 1921 it was possible to pay in full the $37,500 of accrued deficits on the operation of C. C. I. as a girls' school. Any rejoicing over this was sobered, however, by the fact that there still remained a mortgage of $35,000, the aggregate of accrued deficits, repairs and alterations necessitated by the change from co-education.

About this time Centenary lost an outstanding personality, Miss Mary Isabella Breckenridge, who had come from Pennington as a teacher of English in 1910 and from 1914 on had also been Head of North Hall and senior adviser. Her death on July 31, 1923, was a great grief to the school. The Trustees' Resolutions of appreciation of her inspiration, fine scholarship, friendliness and loyalty closed with these words: "Her life among us added to the fine traditions of our school." Her former students and friends placed on the walls of the chapel a plaque in her memory. Her brother, Mr. Karl Breckenridge of Chicago, provided a yearly memorial of her in the form of the Breckenridge lectures on English or American literature which were continued as long as he lived.

During these busy years the President had taken scarcely any vacation, for the World War, too, had made its demands on his time. In September, 1918, the National War Council of the Y. M. C. A. requested that Dr. Trevorrow be released for Army Camp Service. The Trustees replied by authorizing him to give to that work his vacation and such additional time as could be granted without detriment to the interests of the school. And of course the activities of the school were in every possible way so directed as to aid the war effort.

Mrs. Trevorrow, too, from the beginning had devoted herself to Centenary. Always the gracious hostess of the school and its very efficient Dean, she it was who created and maintained the homelike atmosphere, the friendliness and the high tone of refinement that pervaded the place. She always had her hand on the unseen mechanism that was responsible for the general well-being.

In the summer of 1922, the Trustees were wise

"ALMA MATER, LIVE THY GLORY..." 159

enough to grant to Dr. and Mrs. Trevorrow an extra month of vacation. The two enjoyed together a much-needed change of scene by taking a trip to Europe.

With renewed zeal the President returned to his task, determined that C. C. I. should celebrate her approaching fiftieth anniversary with her record clear of all indebtedness. The day of emancipation came on February 15, 1924, when the mortgage was cancelled. In seven years Dr. Trevorrow had paid $81,011.95 on capital indebtedness and interest—a truly remarkable accomplishment.

The deep joy of the President rings through his report to the Trustees:

> Now we have that freedom which comes from a liberated spirit, . . . the inspiration which comes from the consciousness of success . . . Not for more than thirteen years have we been able to draw the free air that we breathe today . . . Today we begin a new era of happiness and progress.

The time had come, he felt, to gather an adequate endowment, since "it is now perfectly safe to invest money for the future in the care of C. C. I." Centenary herself gave tangible thanks for her "liberated spirit" by reaching out to help worthy students. In past years from ten to twenty girls each year had been receiving scholarship aid, largely from funds granted by the Methodist Board of Education. Now the school was able to authorize some additional scholarships.

Centenary's fiftieth birthday was celebrated on June 7, 1924, the nearest possible date to the actual opening in 1874. So many of her sons and daughters came to do her honor that it was difficult even to estimate the number. One of them, Mr. Carl Price, President of the Hymn Society of America, had written for this day his stately "Anniversary Hymn" which has become a feature of every commencement and every anniversary at Centenary. From one of its lovely lines comes the title of this History.

The happiest feature of the program was the burning of all the cancelled mortgages. The most impressive event was the unveiling of the Memorial Tablet honoring the names of thirteen women and fifty-nine men, the record of C. C. I.'s direct part in the World War. These names represent seventeen branches of American service and three of foreign service: the British, Canadian, and French. Mr. G. Roland Monroe had received the Croix de Guerre. Two men, Frank B. Duvall and Charles D. Fuller, had given their lives. C. C. I.'s grand old man, Professor Hammond, made the presentation speech—after a prolonged ovation in recognition of his own long years of devotion to the school.[2] The Tablet was unveiled by Alfred R. Fowler, '07.

This day was the appropriate occasion for the placing of the bronze tablets of C. C. I.'s first two graduating classes, '76 and '77, along also with those of '87,

---

[2] Professor Hammond kept up his interest in C. C. I., to which he had given practically all of his effective life, until the very end. He died on July 20, 1931. In his will he left one thousand dollars and a considerable part of his library to the school he loved. His memory is fittingly perpetuated by the Hammond Memorial Gates erected by his grateful students and appreciative friends in 1940. These bear the inscription:

> In honor of Professor and Mrs. A. O. Hammond
> who taught here faithfully for a total of 58 years.

'06, '08, and '09. The Roll of Graduates which now lines the halls of the Administration Building had been started by the Class of 1911, the first class of girls. It was mutely begging for completion and this task Dr. Trevorrow undertook, with the aid of the class presidents and secretaries. The last of the empty spaces was filled in on May 18, 1929, and now the roster of "C. C. I. Immortals" stands complete and as far as humanly possible, accurate.

A birthday supper on the lawn, a concert recital by Mme. Marie Sundelius of the Metropolitan Opera Company, and an informal reception in the parlors brought to a close this memorable day and C. C. I. confidently moved ahead into her second half-century, restating her ideals in the words:

The broad enrichment and worthy service of a woman's life depend upon her mental and moral culture; therefore scholarship is our watchword, character is our goal.

2. *"Nothing in Education is Final"*

The Nineteen Twenties were filled with anniversaries, it seemed: 1925 marked the fiftieth commencement; 1926, the fiftieth class to graduate and the sixtieth Founders' Day; 1927 rounded out ten years of Dr. Trevorrow's leadership. Before the decade passed into history, it was also to bring to Centenary another opening day—that of the Junior College. Probably in 1924 the President himself had no idea of such a development but we can see now that two important seeds of change were present then. One was Dr. Trevorrow's own belief that "nothing in education is final" and his willingness to take the expedient course. The other was the presence on the campus of a small group of graduate students whose numbers and influence had of late been growing. Of this group more in a moment.

Forces in the educational world were tending to hasten the maturing of these seeds of change. Demand for the four-year preparatory school for girls was steadily decreasing. There was even less call for the work of the upper elementary years which C. C. I. had also been offering. The work of the elementary schools and high schools now located in every town was adequate for ordinary purposes.

On the other hand, the standard women's colleges were insisting upon more thorough preparation, which could not so easily be achieved in public institutions whose teaching staffs and whose accommodations were overtaxed because of the heterogeneous crowds impelled thither by the raising of the legal age of school attendance. As a result, there were girls who needed to strengthen their weak preparation by spending a year or two in a more scholarly school. Others abandoned their college ambitions but were nevertheless eager for some advanced study beyond high school.

Centenary's teaching had long been of the quality that inspires to advanced study. As early as 1887, the records reveal, there were a few "Post Graduate" girls, graduates of the academic course who wished to study a year or two—but not four years—longer. By 1913 it was deemed wise:

> to meet the growing demand of high school and our own graduates for advanced work, . . . to establish a

"ALMA MATER, LIVE THY GLORY . . ." 163

two years' advanced course, offering an attractive list of elective subjects. This will enable the student who for any reason cannot obtain a regular college education to pursue some of the cultural studies offered in the first two years of college work. For the completion of this course a special diploma will be given.[3]

This was called the "Collegiate Department" in the Catalogues until in 1916 it became the "Graduate Department."

The popularity of this department grew, and the 1918 Catalogue announced that the course opened "to women in New Jersey the opportunity of doing college work without the dangers of the unsupervised freedom of the Freshman and Sophomore years. . . Credit may be arranged for the continuation of study in the college chosen."[4] The next year two graduate courses of only one year were offered, in Home Economics and Secretarial Study.

In these days—1913 to 1918—a student could spend seven or eight years in C. C. I.—and some did, especially missionaries' children and others from foreign lands—covering the two upper elementary years, or sub-academic years, as Centenary called them, the high school years and one or two beyond. Ninety per cent of the student body was then in the high school division. The *Bulletin* of December, 1919, stated: "C. C. I. has always been a college preparatory school and we hope it always will be." The President's ideal then was a school of one hundred fifty students, a group which could be housed

---

3 Report of Board of Trustees to Newark Conference, 1913.
4 This credit was arranged with the individual college in question and does not mean general accreditation.

comfortably and still leave room for faculty and staff.

The very next year, however, we find the graduate students organized as "The Collegiates," with class officers and special privileges. Observed the President: "They have a regular place in the school life and athletics and bid fair to have an important influence in the future of C. C. I." As the "Collegiates" increased in numbers and importance, the "sub-academic" group decreased and at last disappeared, making the program four years of high school and two years of collegiate work.

Within this more homogeneous unit a rich and varied and vivid student life flourished. So attractive was Centenary to outside observers that in 1927 she received two invitations to move to a southern location, or short of that, to establish a southern branch in Georgia or Florida. Certain cities wished to see the Centenary design copied in their region.

What qualities elicited this sincerest form of admiration? Perhaps they were summed up by a friend who described C. C. I. as "not merely a school, but a life with an educational emphasis." C. C. I. had never compromised with academic thoroughness, but neither had she ever stopped there. Her ideal has been not that of filling the mind but of enriching life. As her President wrote in 1927: "It is the use of this portentous leisure that marks a school's greatest contribution to student life and also stamps the school as a success or failure." Extra-curricular activities covered all areas of interest.

There was a lively athletic program which featured both extra-mural and inter-class contests in the usual group games and also encouraged the mastery of skills in activities which would be useful after graduation for continued fellowship and health, such as tennis, swimming, golf, riding. Fencing was a popular study. Dancing became a creative art under the enthusiastic teaching of Mrs. Olive Haring, and the original dance forms worked out contributed much to the beauty of the annual May Fetes.

The year's "Social Events" included every type of wholesome fun and cultural interest. Each class had its own traditional party for the whole school: the Senior party honored George Washington; the Junior, Hallowe'en; the Sophomore, Valentine's Day; the Freshmen, St. Patrick. The French Club Cabaret was an annual event, as was also its Soirée Dramatique. Interspersed were illustrated lectures, recitals by faculty members—Mrs. Julia Larsen, violin; Miss Elise Gardner, voice; Mr. Frederick Mets, organ and piano—and by outside professional artists. Generous provision has always been made that the students hear the best in music, expression, oratory, and contemporary thought.

Week-ends meant picnics in Sully's Grove, bonfires and marshmallow toasts at the farm or the quarry, hikes, and snow sports. Groups went often to the Opera and the theater, or visited museums or other places in New York's endless wonderland.

Much of the social life still centered about the three Societies. Each had its big "rushing" tea in the fall. Pledge Day was eagerly awaited. Each in an Open Meeting in its own hall entertained officers and representatives from the other Societies, the Faculty and Staff with an elaborate literary or dramatic program. Each had its Anniversary, or "Ann," as always the most ambitious undertaking of the year, each vying with the other two. The custom at this time was to produce a play with which to entertain the whole school and its friends. Some plays of these years were: "Peg o' My Heart," "Little Women," "The Importance of Being Earnest," "Little Lord Fauntleroy," "Seventeen," "The Governor's Lady." Following the play came the formal reception with long receiving line, in the parlors, and then refreshments in the beautifully decorated dining-room, where the social time continued—with no dancing—until midnight.

To the student of these years her Society was still the central and most vital of influences—just as had been true in the earlier days of C. C. I.[5] A girl felt she must be a credit to her Society and she worked to keep her scholastic record and her conduct up to approved standards. For serious misbehavior she could be suspended or dropped. For the most meritorious service to the Society she could receive a considerable money prize.

The Trophy Contest among the three groups called forth the best masterpieces of literature—prose or poetry —that could be produced. These were read by many judges, both members and faculty. The essays finally selected had to be memorized. Final judgment was made on the basis of both literary merit and presentation. The prize sought so eagerly was the possession for the ensuing year of "The Lady," who first appeared on the

[5] This statement is a conclusion drawn from a number of interviews with former students and faculty members, from letters and from the *Hackettstonians*, the *Hacks*, and newspaper clippings.

campus on May 20, 1910. This is a piece of gold bronze statuary "by a French artist and imported by Tiffany," according to the *Hackettstonian* of July, 1910. It was given by the Trustees, to be held by the winner until the next contest.

Other annual school events were President and Mrs. Trevorrow's entertainment of each of the classes, the Birthday Parties, the Junior-Senior Banquet, the May Fête. Many will wish to add also Mrs. Mary Carpenter's waffle parties.

One important extra-curricular activity went on all the time, week-ends included: the Young Women's Christian Association with its Girl Reserves of C. C. I. Its roster of committees ran thus: program, social, art, service, religious, publicity. The "Y," states the *Hack* of 1924, "means to all the girls an opportunity for enrichment of spiritual life and personality, as well as a happy get-together every Thursday evening." These devotional meetings, largely attended, were led by students, assisted each week by a teacher. Miss Fanny W. Stauffer was for some years their adviser; Miss Margaret Cummings succeeded her. Frequently recurring names of assisting teachers are those of Miss Alexandria Spence, Miss Jessie Wagoner, Miss Caroline Whitney, Mrs. Carpenter. From summer to summer, representatives were sent to the "Y" Conference at Camp Altamont.

The girls were always busy knitting or sewing, or making scrap-books for their Christmas gifts to Bellevue Hospital, to the Association for the Improvement of the Condition of the Poor, or to local recipients. Lent was a period of self-sacrificial giving when South and North Halls were rivals in generosity. Money for the mite-boxes was earned by all kinds of work such as mending, manicuring, darning stockings, making beds, closing windows at 6 A.M. each morning—with no extra charge for waking occupants of room—bringing sundaes from downtown stores, shampooing, tutoring, running errands. The girl who used to polish five pairs of shoes before breakfast had the true spirit.

Appeals for help never fell on deaf ears in C. C. I. When a missionary from Korea described the needs of his hospital, the response was an endowed child's bed over which a C. C. I. banner brightened the room—and "C. C. I. in Korea" continued for some years. Donations were divided between a number of varying objectives such as: Near East Relief, Student Friendship Fund, Scholarships in China, Y.W.C.A. Secretary support in Romania, Pine Mountain Settlement School, Poor White Work in North Carolina, Maine Seacoast Missionary Society.

Peak years for money raising and for concentrated work were those of the first World War. The war work of the school was organized by Miss Geraldine Shields, who through members of her own family was in close contact with a school for refugee girls in France. Each girl "adopted" a child, worked for her and wrote her letters. The girls also made clothing for refugee children in Alsace-Lorraine.

The Junior Red Cross was organized under Mrs. Trevorrow, chairman. For this much knitting was done. Fifty faculty members and students earned Surgical Dressings Certificates. Thousands of dressings were prepared for shipment through the local Red Cross.

In this place should be mentioned the beginning of

the French Club in 1919 and its work through the years under the leadership of its founder, Miss Geraldine Shields, who joined the Centenary faculty only a few months after the coming of the Trevorrows. Le Cercle Français began with small groups who met to talk French, but who speedily undertook a yearly French play and then, at the suggestion of Gertrude Joy, added an annual French Cabaret. The wealth thus acquired was at first used to purchase embellishments for the French classroom: a bust of Molière, a French flag, subscriptions to French papers and magazines. Then, true to the Centenary spirit, the members voted to help some French girl who had suffered in the war. Enthusiasm for the project ran high when Miss Shields returned from a summer in France in 1921 to tell of her visit to Le Foyer Retrouvé, a home for war orphans founded by the women's branch of the American Methodist Church in France at La Tronche, near Grenoble. Here she had talked with a girl of fourteen named Marie Louise Armand. At once the French Club adopted Marie Louise, paying one hundred dollars each year for her keep in this American-directed school until she was grown up. This assignment ended too soon for the girls and next they sought a very small child to help.

Again the Foyer was called upon and the Club adopted three-year-old Jeannette Ignace, who had been nicknamed Noelle because she had been brought to the school by the Mayor of the town just in time to play a baby part in their Christmas play. With regularity the Club provided a complete scholarship for Noelle until depression days forced the Foyer to close. Then Noelle went to live with her brother, but the French Club sent her 1500 francs a year until she had graduated from Normal School and begun to teach. In 1941 the Club began helping a Belgian boy refugee in England through the Save-the-Children Federation.

Fresh interest and incentive were injected into the work of the Glee Club when in 1926 a Radio Chorus, trained by Miss Elise Gardner, began broadcasting over WEAF and WOR in full-length programs that received very favorable notices from the critics.

Dr. Trevorrow in 1927-28 had received the honor of election to the presidency of the Educational Association of the Methodist Episcopal Church. As he watched the school activities of the Twenties, he was busy with his statistical studies, engrossed in developing the pattern of C. C. I. in accord with plainly traceable trends which he kept reporting to the Trustees. Demand for the major product offered by C. C. I.—a good college-preparatory training, a complete education of the whole girl on the high school level—was decreasing to an alarming degree. This change was a general one and it was closing the doors of many a fine private school. In the near-by city of Easton, to cite examples close at hand, the Park School and the Lerch School had already passed into history. The excellent "Bethlehem Prep" and its neighbor, the "Allentown Prep," presently fell victims to the competition of the public high schools. The average family no longer needed to invest money in secondary education. Families of wealth and of exclusive tastes will, of course, always choose a well-equipped private school for their children. The hand writing was on the wall and C. C. I.'s President, interpreting it, devoted much thought to the contrasting

DR. ROBERT JOHNS TREVORROW
President of the Centenary Collegiate Institute, 1917-1940; President of Centenary Junior College, 1929-1943

tendency in the demand for Centenary's minor product —the "Collegiate" courses. In March, 1928, the Trustees laid the issue before the school's sponsors, the Newark Conference.

In reply, the Conference requested the Trustees to be prepared to report to the next Annual Conference as to the need of a standard college for women in New Jersey, organized under Protestant auspices, and "whether or not the same could be operated in connection with the Institute at Hackettstown."

Only a complete statistical survey of New Jersey and the whole region, along with a careful poll of individuals and groups to ascertain attitudes and opinions, could answer this question. The firm of Tamblyn and Brown of New York, to whom this work was entrusted, presented findings of which the salient facts were, in brief, these: New Jersey was below the national average in the percentage of students attending higher institutions either within or without the State. The State was not offering an educational program sufficiently varied to meet the needs of its large population and its diversified social life. It was not supporting higher education in proportion to its wealth. It was sending to schools outside the State about ten million dollars each year. The second richest state in per capita wealth, New Jersey had the lowest proportion of college students educated within its boundaries.

As to the Newark Conference—if the average ratio of college students to general population, which is one to one hundred fifty, be applied to the three million population within its bounds, there should be 20,000 college students within the Conference, of whom nine to ten thousand would be women. There was then within its bounds no college for women operated by any Protestant denomination. The Methodist Church had no college for women within two hundred miles of C. C. I., and the area within that radius is the most thickly populated section of the United States. There was in New Jersey an actual dearth of educational opportunities for women.

Studies had demonstrated that no new college should be located in a region where population is not increasing. In northern New Jersey extensive developments were tending to increase the population. Moreover, the Methodist population in the State alone could easily provide the nucleus for a total college enrolment of two hundred and fifty.

Dr. Trevorrow himself sent letters to practically all of the high school principals of the State, soliciting their opinions on the subject of a proposed Junior College. Of the replies from the first section of the groups so addressed, seven were negative, one held out for co-education, twenty-three were neutral, uncertain, lacking in information, or dubious of the location, ninety-seven expressed approval, willingness to co-operate, confidence that reaction throughout the State would be favorable, or belief in the need for "emphasis on Christian colleges that will stand four-square to the winds that blow."

In the light of this sequence of facts, the Conference members were unanimous in directing the Trustees to begin to operate the Junior College in September, 1929. Centenary's liberal Charter allowed ample scope for this development.

"ALMA MATER, LIVE THY GLORY . . ." 173

The days between April 4, when Conference had given the Trustees the green light, and mid-September were all too few to prepare and furnish the new rooms, to adjust and equip classrooms, to make all buildings gleaming and resplendent. There had to be many new books for the Library. New members of the Faculty had to be carefully selected. The curriculum, which afforded many electives, was organized in six major groups: Liberal Arts, Fine Arts, Advanced Music, Home Economics, Secretarial Science, and Social and Political Science, with special emphasis on History, Public Speaking, and Journalism—a course designed to provide training for civic leadership.

As he went about his preparations, President Trevorrow "often wondered," he told the Trustees, "what the future will think of us and our plans. When there is a great college here with new buildings and rich scholarships, with a host of earnest students, with a great influence for Christian womanhood. I wonder if the future will look back upon us and say, 'Well done, good and faithful servants.' Let us pray that we may be guided into those paths of usefulness and reverence which may make C. C. I. increasingly an instrument for human betterment."

And so to Dr. Trevorrow September 24, 1929, was a deeply-significant day, a cardinal date in Centenary history, the opening of the Junior College, with its forty-seven students. It also began the fifty-sixth consecutive year of the Centenary Collegiate Institute.

At once he urged the Trustees "to think big things and to plan big things on the basis of a college rather than a school . . . in order that big things may be accomplished."

"What is our objective?" he asked. And he answered,

A Junior College of 250 girls—big enough to command attention, small enough for personalized care and instruction,—a college that shall represent the best in scholarship and character, where true culture and womanliness shall be in the very air and where happiness shall abound, a place so beautiful that merely to be there shall be an education, and where reverence for things spiritual shall provoke a consecration to those Christian ideals which shall, through our students, enrich the world. This is the ideal college we have in mind and for which some of us are giving our lives.[6]

The Trevorrows were certainly devoting all their time to the College in these years of its infancy. In addition to his full load of administrative duties, the President was teaching three classes a week in Bible and religion, "which two things," wrote he, "are about all that any human being ought to undertake." But it was necessary to interpret the Junior College to the public, and so during the early Thirties the President was each week addressing some meeting of teachers, parents or Rotarians. Effort went into making Alumni contacts local and general. In 1932, Dr. Trevorrow had been authorized to seek from them a sustaining fund.

From the President's office poured circulars to high school advisers and senior girls, and personal letters soliciting co-operation from every minister in the New-

[6] Annual Report of President, November 1, 1927, Pages 10 and 11.

ark Conference. Everything was done or carefully supervised by Miss Florence K. Black, secretary to the President. The *Bulletin* too was her responsibility. Lights usually burned later in her office, where one found her working alone. Words are inadequate to express the credit due to Miss Black for her devoted work for Centenary.

Mrs. Trevorrow took over the responsibility of introducing the new educational idea to the high school girls of the State. She secured appointments to speak to student assemblies, to senior classes, to groups of interested senior girls, or to confer with individual girls. During the first two winters, she drove to more than eighty different high schools to do this work.

The school vacations of these early years of the Thirties were devoted by the Trevorrows to interviewing the parents of prospective students in their homes. Occasionally a field worker was employed on a very temporary basis but there was no permanent Director of Admissions until in 1935 Mrs. Mabel W. Kelley took office and began to develop that department.

One person who surveyed all this scene with critical objectivity was Mr. Thomas J. Foster, who in 1934 had frankly told the Board of Trustees of which he was President:

> When Dr. Trevorrow started his work here, there was no money for certain administrative work, and it was easier to do the work himself than to look for aid from the Trustees or the Alumni. He has been willing to get under the burden, no matter how heavy, but some load is going to be too great. In that event, you are not properly organized with functioning committees

of the Board, nor have you an Alumni that is accustomed to taking C. C. I. burdens. There is no qualified person or organization to fall back on in case of an emergency.

All of these facts are well known to you, but the knowledge has not caused action. Possibly no damage has been done, but the policy should be changed before Dr. Trevorrow or the institution is damaged. I am satisfied that Dr. Trevorrow is carrying too heavy a burden, and you know that he would be the last one to complain. . . . .

No one, doing the drudgery required to run a plant, can look for Trustees, secure Committee action, find endowments and build up a reputation for an institution. If we had a President of the Board of Trustees, capable, and having the necessary time of assuming the financial burdens, the balance of the work would be simplified. The problem of setting the goal is for the Trustees. It is not the right procedure, nor is it fair, to leave its solution to the President of the college. We are appointed by the stockholders to determine the policies and to provide ways of carrying them out. We can not shift our responsibilities. We are treating no one, Dr. Trevorrow, the stockholders, or the college, fairly, if we do not accept them.[7]

The goals had been set by the President, however, almost immediately after the College had gotten off to a good start. The Wall Street crash of 1929 had ushered in the long depression, but undismayed by it, the President took a long look into the future and drew up a Ten-Year Plan for development, specifying "not so much what we would like to have as what we ought to

---

[7] Report of the President of the Board of Trustees, March 21, 1934, Pages 2 and 3. Of course the term "stockholders" here means sponsors. There are no stockholders as in a corporation.

have and what we may reasonably hope to have." It was a complete blue-print for educational policy, physical expansion, and financial competence.

First, he hoped to be able very soon to eliminate the first two years of high school work. The last two years he wished to continue along with the two college years, a combination of not too greatly differing ages, he thought, to permit uniform student government and an opportunity for two years either before or after high school graduation, or both, to broaden horizons, enlarge friendships and stabilize religion. This would permit consolidation of faculty to include only strong college teachers.

For the courses in Home Economics and Music he sought recognition by the New Jersey Board of Education as a basis for granting public school teachers' certificates. This program would be facilitated, he urged, by simplifying the name of the school to Centenary College or Centenary Junior College.

As the only college for women in all the State of New Jersey under the auspices of a Protestant church, Centenary ought to be in a position to appeal for state-wide—or even wider—support. The charter should be amended, the President urged, so that of the twenty Trustees, a minority of eight might be free of denominational requirements. This change was effected in 1932.[8]

The Ten-Year Program for physical expansion was

[8] Dr. Trevorrow began his administration by making the important innovation of inviting a woman to join the Board of Trustees. In 1919 Miss Letitia Simons accepted this responsibility and she served until 1934, being for many years also a member of the Executive Committee. Miss Esther Hay has also been an effective member of the Board.

planned for a minimum of 250, practically all boarding students. Some ground work for this had been done that very year. The newly completed boiler house with brick stack and three new boilers had much unused capacity. The brick residence adjoining the campus, purchased in June, 1930, could be used either for additional dormitory space or for faculty apartments. Another basic improvement was the rebuilding of the pipe organ, which was rededicated on December 1, 1930.

The Library would need substantial additions. For the gymnasium and swimming pool both immediate and long-range improvements were outlined. At that time the basement was occupied by the college workshop. This could now be moved to the space released by the moving of the heating plant to an outside building. This basement, equipped with showers, dressing-rooms and lockers, and connected by a stairway with the main floor, became thus a suitable adjunct to the gymnasium. The pool was to be retiled and supplied with a filter. Later plans called for certain enlargements including a pillared entrance on the long bare western side to give the building dignity and beauty.

There was crying need of space for more classrooms and laboratories. Home Economics and Speech and Dramatics were important divisions of the new college work, yet all were trying to get along in the Little Theater which was suitable for only one. The Art Department and Clothing Laboratory were very inadequately housed. Science laboratories in the basement of the Main Building were in most undesirable places. The work of the Music Department went on in annoying proximity to the academic classes.

The Ten-Year Plan envisioned a building for Science and Home Economics and another for Music, Art, and Clothing. These two, with the additional dormitory, would insure adequate facilities.

Of course the Plan dealt next with finances—meaning mostly, endowment and scholarship aid. Consistently, education has been sold in America at less than cost, a policy made possible by the income from endowment in generous ratio to what the student pays. Centenary has never had any private pockets to fill. This means, of course, that fees have never been high enough to cover the "rent" of land and buildings. In other words, no return has ever been sought on the $600,000 or more of investment—capital which had come from free gifts. There are no stock-holders reaching for profits. Annual charges have therefore been much lower than would be possible under private ownership. Given good luck, no calamity of any sort, things can break even from year to year. *But* what happens when bad luck comes—as it must, on a general average, sometimes—or when, as now, new and broader fields of education are being entered?

Obviously it was time to capitalize Centenary's substantial reputation in terms of financial support. So, in October, 1930, the President boldly set the goal at $1,040,000: $500,000 for general endowment; $120,000 for special endowment; $420,000 for expansion and improvements. The time was at least favorable for planning!

The Trustees voted unanimous approval of the Plan and proceeded with the easier parts. As for the rest, the President, looking into the distant future, realized that "we are building here one of the permanent forces of the nation; we ought not to be impatient if we do not solve all the problems of American education every year." And he liked to quote the words of Dr. Terry of Garrett, "And what are five hundred years in the founding of a great university?"

Indeed, he had need of all the serenity and patience he could muster for the bad years ahead. The 1930 accounts were in the red, the first time for Dr. Trevorrow, the deficit being due to the scholarship aid that had to be taken from school funds after the Methodist Board of Education sharply cut its usual appropriation. This became a more than twice-told tale. The depression, it was estimated, set the school back about four years in growth, with a loss of $22,500. Teachers' salaries were cut sixteen per cent. Eventually, so were all others.

But nothing of this ever shadowed student life. Nineteen-thirty brought a double graduation—the twentieth of the Girls' School, C. C. I., and the first of Centenary Junior College. The gala occasion was also the first of a series of international contacts and interests that have characterized the college life.[9] The commencement speaker was the Romanian Minister to the United States, His Excellency, The Honorable Carol A. Davila.

Mr. Davila was an appreciative visitor on this campus and an interested observer of American education. He and Dr. Trevorrow became friends. In 1931

---

[9] This is a point of similarity to the Whitney period, when there were many foreign students in the school. Dr. Whitney, too, had broad international interest.

the Romanian government honored the Trevorrows with two of the highest decorations ever given to American citizens. In recognition of his furthering of international friendship, Dr. Trevorrow received the Order of the Crown of Romania in the degree of Commander. Mrs. Trevorrow's work in education was honored with the decoration of "Resplata Muncii."

The next year Dr. Trevorrow received an invitation from the governments of Czechoslovakia and Romania to deliver in their countries a series of addresses on American education. For this the Trevorrows were given a brief leave of absence in the Spring of 1932. This began Dr. Trevorrow's deep interest in Czechoslovakia. He was a member of the Masaryk Institute from its beginning. Proof of Czechoslovakia's appreciation of this friendship later took tangible form when at the Commencement of June, 1937, President Trevorrow received from President Masaryk, through his messenger, Dr. Starch, the Order of the White Lion, the only order given by that country.

Another international contact was the annual visit of Dr. Stephen F. Duggan, Director of the Institute of International Education. As a result, beginning in 1930, a foreign "Exchange Student" came each year to the Junior College on a full-time residence scholarship.

The Junior College quickly achieved scholastic recognition. Approved at founding by the State Board of Education, it was speedily admitted into the American Association of Junior Colleges. In 1932 it was approved by the Middle States Association of Colleges and Secondary Schools—being one of the first two Junior

Colleges to be approved by them—and in 1934 by the University Senate of the Methodist Episcopal Church. Similar action had been taken by the Board of Regents of the State of New York and by the United States Department of Education. In four years and a half C. J. C. had won every approval possible to an institution of its type. Her graduates were being transferred with full advanced standing to four-year colleges and were receiving degrees on schedule time. These were the laurels worn by the old school on her sixtieth birthday in 1934.

The substantial scholastic ingredients of college life needed, of course, the seasoning and flavoring of a careful blend of extra-curricular activities. Of these there had always been a plentiful variety. The College girls identified themselves with the traditional interests which they found on the campus. In 1927 the Y.W.C.A. had been discontinued and its place taken by a local religious and philanthropic organization called The Guild, which had been a worthy successor to the "Y." The Athletic Association, the Glee Club, and the Societies all had a fresh lease on life.

So too did Le Cercle Francais. There were also at different times Der Deutsche Verein and El Circulo Castellano, later renamed the Spanish Club.

Girls interested in reviewing and discussing current literature formed The Book Club under the leadership of Dr. H. Graham DuBois of the English Department. They enjoyed the hospitality of the DuBois home and the delicious refreshments always served in such profusion and so graciously by Mrs. DuBois.

Another new venture was the International Relations Club founded in 1930 at the suggestion of Dr.

Roucek of the Social Science Department. This at once became a unit in the world-wide chain of clubs sponsored by the Carnegie Endowment for International Peace. With an enthusiastic yearly membership averaging around thirty-five, the Club had lively discussions and debates on the changing international situation and also brought to the campus interesting guest speakers and lecturers. Appealing mostly to the more serious and thoughtful students, it became one of the most active on the campus. It could always be depended upon to lead dignified commemorative services in Chapel and even in Vespers. The Club assumed sole responsibility for the campus observance of the sesquicentennial of the Constitution and the Bill of Rights. It put on several widely-commended radio broadcasts on various subjects, frequently featuring the foreign students and their countries. Whenever possible, the Club sent delegates to the Regional Conferences of the International Relations Clubs of the Middle Atlantic States and Canada.

For several years a Business Club flourished. It made yearly visits to the Stock Exchange and similar places of interest. A Camera Club, too, had its appeal. There have been also Hiking Clubs and Outing Clubs and Aquatic Clubs. There was even a Kin Club, open only to those who had at least one relative who had attended Centenary in the past.

Girls of literary turn of mind had the fun of founding a Junior College newspaper, called "Campus Chatter," which survived during 1930 and '31. The next year they made a fresh beginning, calling it "Spilled Ink." Published in some years as a magazine, in others as a newspaper, "Spilled Ink" has done what was hoped for "Campus Chatter"—lived and grown into the traditions of the school.

And the devotees of dramatics? Yes, there was a field for them and a big one. In 1932, the C. C. I. Players, composed of the members of the two play production classes, began a long career in the Little Theater. Guided and directed by Miss Ellen Claire Couch, teacher of Dramatic Arts, they undertook various ventures even beyond Centenary's campus, participating in the North Jersey Intercollegiate Dramatic League, presenting one-act plays in Nutley, Newton, Blairstown and other places, and also playing three-act drama for a series of nights here at College for audiences from Hackettstown, Washington, Mendham, Denville, and from nearby schools and colleges. There grew up a program of exchanges with other dramatic groups such as Peddie, Blair, and Nutley. The Players were turned into traveling troupers for a time, after *Barriers,* written by our own Dr. DuBois, had been presented in our Little Theater before the meeting of the New Jersey State Federation of Women's Clubs. This brought many invitations to repeat *Barriers* in nearby places. There was a final triumphant performance at Haddon Hall, Atlantic City.[10]

Choral speaking was another field entered and good work was done by a verse-speaking choir.

For many years an ambition had been cherished in Centenary—doubtless with the complete approval of President Trevorrow, who was an ardent lover of the classics—to present a classical Greek play done in the

---

10 The Glee Club, too, was invited here for a number of years to present programs.

ancient manner. This dream was realized in December, 1930, when Sophocles' "Electra" was presented by the Callilogian Society on its seventieth anniversary. It was an inspired performance and valuable experience, interpreting as it did a type of literature not generally familiar to the modern audience. It was carried through most successfully under direction of Miss Couch. The May Fête of the following Spring was also in the Greek tradition, presenting "The Festival of Dionysos," with rituals, dances and processions done under careful direction of Mrs. Olive Haring.

In 1939 and 1940, the Centenary Players carried on the interest in Greek plays by presenting distinguished performances of "The Medea" and "The Trojan Women" of Euripides, using the translations by Gilbert Murray. In out-door settings these were very beautiful.

The three Societies were accepted as traditional but were gradually transformed into almost purely social groups. By 1935, the Open Meetings were a thing of the past. At about the same time the "Ann" week-ends were featured by dances which began immediately after the brief reception that followed the "Ann" play. The first one was the Christmas dance, December 15, 1934, that followed the "School for Scandal" given for the fifty-fifth anniversary of the Peithosophian Society. Later on a Tea Dance and "open house" on the halls for the boy-friends filled the Saturday afternoons of those week-ends.

One entirely new organization of course there was, the Student Council, the governing body of the Junior College. Its membership comprised: hall presidents, two representatives from each class, class presidents.

From 1935 on, the Academy was represented by the Senior class president and the Academy hall president. President and secretary of Council were elected by the entire College. Meetings were held once or twice a month to resolve difficulties. The Dean was always present.

The Faculty, too, had its "Club," a forum organized in 1930 for discussion of educational problems. At its monthly meetings special papers were presented by faculty members and often there were visiting speakers. Dr. DuBois was the president. Miss Shields should be mentioned for her constructive work.

But not alone the Faculty were adventuring toward the new horizon opened by the Junior College. No longer obliged to take orders from college or university, as in the running of a preparatory school they had had to do, all were freed—Faculty, President, Trustees—to consider how best to serve individuals, to prepare "the whole student for the service and joy of a complete life." Said President Trevorrow, "The question ever before us is: What new and yet safe things can we do to make our institution a more perfect servant of our times?" And he warned that next to smug content, the greatest danger is to do something foolish just for the sake of doing something.

The President of the Board during the first half of the Thirties, Mr. Thomas J. Foster, was an unusually searching, probing thinker, pragmatic, even iconoclastic. Criticizing traditional education as impractical and detached, he urged continuous curriculum revision.

We need an education that will teach us to eliminate

the frictions in our relationships, build and care for physical and mental health, show us the secret sources of our power, give us an idea of the economical use of our abilities, reveal the cost to us of our unscientific planning, and provide us with methods for giving better service to our fellows.

I cannot give you the name of the course that most of our young women should take, but my description of the course would be, "The science of creating the next generation." This covers the health, the dress, the abode; the family relationships, personal and financial; and the external relationships to community, church, business and society. A Junior College, with resident students, could give practical demonstrations of much of the course.[11]

He suggested an Educational Conference at Hackettstown to consider the needs of the women of today. Instead of this, questionnaires were formulated by a special committee of Trustees and sent to groups of graduates, to parents, to students and to faculty members. Careful studies were made of the returns under the guidance of the new teacher of Psychology, Dr. Louise Omwake. One tangible outcome was an experimental course in Home Economics intended as preparation for home management, later named Modern Home-Making. Various departments collaborated with Home Economics in presenting this course. Another new departure was "Cultural Reading," designed to stimulate interest extending beyond the classroom and graduation. Later additions to the curriculum were Family Relationships, Child Psychology with laboratory kindergarten, and Consumer Education, also a co-operative course.

11 Letter to Board of Trustees, March 21, 1934, Page 6.

The circumference of Centenary's helpfulness was enlarged to include service also to persons who had finished school days but were interested in keeping intellectually alert. In 1931-32, faculty members went on the air over WOR in bi-weekly broadcasts. In 1934, two adult extension courses of lectures were given: one in Hackettstown and the other in Newton. In addition, frequent addresses were given each year by members of the Administration and Faculty before Parent-Teacher Associations, Women's Clubs and similar groups.

Each year Dr. Trevorrow raised the question: "What new project shall we undertake this year? What thing can we do, *out of routine,* to enrich faculty and student life?" For a few years the answer was the Centenary Forums. The plan was to free every Tuesday afternoon of all classes in order that the time might be devoted to interesting lectures by different faculty members on topics not covered in any course. For example, in 1937-38 the series consisted of choices from the "Hundred Best Books" then constituting the core of study in St. John's College. These afforded a wide range of general culture and uncommon information. Forums were required, for which reason they were not popular—much to Dr. Trevorrow's disappointment.

Actually there were very few requirements, for the purpose was to create individualized courses. Centenary's plan has been to secure all information possible concerning the student—from friends, teachers, reports, tests, the ambitions of the student and the hopes of her parents; on this basis to plan an individual program of present and future value to the student. The counselor

"ALMA MATER, LIVE THY GLORY . . ." 189

must bear in mind not so much the student who is as the woman who is to be. The vocational motive was never allowed to eclipse broad general education. Wrote Dr. Trevorrow in June, 1938:

We must think of our students as mature women in the community with appropriate culture and usefulness, rather than as temporary wage earners. Our instruction must fit them for that larger service. Their general culture, then, their knowledge of household problems, their physical fitness and their abilities to contribute to their churches, their clubs and their communities must not be eclipsed by a narrow hysteria over temporary wage earning. The purpose and plans of our Junior College are centered in the preparation of young women for enriched service, in whatever environments life may give them.[12]

But to Dr. Trevorrow even more important was the need for moral guidance. At no time in history, he thought, had it been more necessary that religion should go hand in hand with education. Certain current social trends and relaxations of conduct, especially as they bear on the ideals and mental processes of young women were making very difficult the achievement of womanly poise and moral self-government. It therefore seemed to him that:

In the midst of this unrest many young women need a quiet place for the sake of self-discovery and for the recognition of the permanence of spiritual principles. This is the distinct opportunity of the Christian college today. Just as Christ spent forty days apart from human contact to determine the principles and objectives of his life activities, so our young people need a time and a place to "think things through," and thus to acquire

12 Report of President, June 11, 1938, Page 2.

not only knowledge but convictions and definite plans for successful lives in a complex age.[13]

And the Trustees, too, stated it to be their belief

> that education in these days should be actively religious, not merely in the matter of courses of instruction. Daily chapel services and Sunday vespers contribute to this end and it is our belief that the religious emphasis at Centenary is not only sane but helpful and inspiring.[14]

In 1934, Centenary again had to trim her sails to an educational wind then blowing. There was a belief on the part of some that it was unwise to educate preparatory school students and college students in the same schools. College girls did not relish having high school students on their campuses. It was difficult to maintain two different standards of student self-government. In Centenary the high school division had proved to be in no sense of the word a feeder for the college—quite the reverse, in fact. Enrolment was dwindling. It was voted in 1934 to discontinue the first two years of academy work. In 1936, the preparatory school classification in the accrediting agencies was dropped. The academy was no longer profitable and therefore in 1940 the preparatory school ceased to exist.

The decade was rounding to the full but much of the Ten-Year Plan remained unrealized. Lack of funds hampered progress. This was the principal criticism of those on the outside evaluating what was there. Hear one observer:

13 Report of President, November 8, 1934, Page 3.
14 Report to Annual Conference, Newark Conference Journal and Year Book, 1942, Page 209.

Other than the purchase of some books for the Library, I believe I have no further suggestion beyond the possibility of your Board becoming active, man by man, in aiding you in securing an adequate endowment fund so as to deliver your budget from the consequences of fluctuating enrollment and also to enable you to finance a thoroughgoing student campaign annually, though it be quiet and wholly unspectacular.[15]

But the situation continued. Mr. Foster had warned that all should accept their responsibilities. For some reason, the Trustees and the President did not work as a unit fired with an irresistible zeal for a great cause beyond themselves. There seems to have been an underestimation of the abilities and good-will of Centenary's "giving" public. Something blocked the resolution to take the bold initiative in going after funds.

Some gifts had been coming in during the years. The Carnegie Corporation of New York had studied the library along with a number of other junior college libraries and in 1937 had given it a $1500 grant-in-aid. In 1941 a further sum of $2000 had been allocated by the Corporation to be spent for books in the field of art and for art equipment. By organizing the "Friends of the Library," numbering over two hundred members, the President had mobilized individual gifts with the slogan: "A book a year for C. J. C." Collections of autographs, of ancient Babylonian manuscripts and of foreign flags were presented as nuclei for a museum. Sums for endowment of prizes came in, such as the J. D. Flock prizes in expression and music, the Cath-

---

[15] Report of President, November 8, 1934, Pages 11 and 12, quoting from letter from Dr. William J. Davidson, Secretary for Institutions of the Methodist Board of Education, October 23, 1934.

erine Matilda Cutler Science prize, the Heath Chemistry prize, the Tamblyn essay contest prizes, the Newman bronze plaque for "First Honors." This is a sampling, not an exhaustive list.

By careful management the President had gradually accumulated a modest surplus. Now it seemed that a further step in the Ten-Year Plan might be taken. Came then prolonged discussions of the possibility of a new science building. Hopes rose,—then sank when postponement was voted, and flared again when in early 1940 an architect was often much in evidence. At long last appeared plans and drawings; the site chosen was near the southeast corner of the campus.

Instead of the customary cornerstone laying there was the placing of the final stone, the feature of the Annual May Fête and Alumni Day, May 24, 1941. What joy and satisfaction shone from Dr. Trevorrow's face on this day! Not even the remembrance that there had to be a sizable mortgage on the new building could cast a shadow over his enthusiasm nor over that of the Faculty, students and friends of C. J. C. Now at last there was adequate housing for the Departments of Science and Home Economics, while the Art Department glorified in its sky-lighted spaciousness and its gallery for special exhibits. With appropriate celerity the Faculty petitioned the Trustees that the new building might be named Trevorrow Hall. This petition the Board granted unanimously and announcement of the action was received with much applause at Commencement on June 7, 1941.

Even if he had not realized it before, certainly on December 7, 1941, Dr. Trevorrow must have known that he would never be able to complete another major unit in his plan for C. J. C. Indeed, the burden of paying off the mortgage on the last unit was pressing all too heavily upon him.

War conditions necessitated again a policy of utmost caution in financial matters. Besides this, much thought had to be given to possible curriculum changes. New classes were added in First Aid, Home Nursing, Foods and Nutrition, and "Women and Responsible Citizenship." Radical revisions did not seem to be indicated, nor did summer sessions, acceleration, nor lengthening of the college year.

In the program of complete co-operation with the town the gymnasium became an emergency First Aid center and hospital. The Annual May Fête was omitted for the duration in order that the energy usually expended on it might contribute to projects useful to the war effort.

It was a time of stress for all. Increasingly, the strain of the long years of unremitting, many-sided work began to tell on Dr. Trevorrow. Anxiety over the incomplete realization of his Ten-Year Plan, worry over the mortgage on Trevorrow Hall, disappointment over the slow growth of the College during depression and war years—all these were taking their physical toll.

At their annual Commencement-day meeting in 1939 the Trustees for the first time missed the greeting of President Trevorrow, whose physician had ordered him to remain quiet until the hour of commencement—which service, however, he conducted as if nothing had ever been amiss. Because of what the doctor called his "tired heart," he now had to limit and presently to forego playing his beloved golf, and to turn to his indoor hobbies; his stamp collection and his Greek classics.

Still he carried on his work, missing few of his daily chapel services and almost always there on Sundays with his inspiring Vesper talks which the girls loved so sincerely. As the semester drew to a close in January, 1943, the President was plainly not well, yet for the concluding Vesper service he was in his place, leading the Centenary family in worship in the Chapel, delivering an inspiring message—"Carry on! Make the most of yourselves, for your own sakes, for your country's sake." It was his last.

Exactly one week after, at that very Vesper hour, —on January 31—the heart that must have had "Centenary" engraved on it, ceased to beat and Robert Johns Trevorrow was at rest. His reach had far exceeded his grasp, but he had restored the school to a firm financial condition; he had recognized the necessity and quickly effected the change to a Junior College; he had charted the initial course of the new institution and taken the first step in essential physical expansion; he had struck the keynote of her future service —the idea of the individualized, or personalized program for developing the total personality. In doing this he had literally given the best of his life to Centenary.

3. *Conclusion*

The Executive Committee ten days later unanimously appointed Mrs. Editha Trevorrow to be the supervising head of the school, with all administrative powers. With great energy and skill Mrs. Trevorrow

Mrs. Editha Trevorrow
Dean, 1917-1943; Administrator and supervising head of Centenary Junior College, February 1 to August 15, 1943

"ALMA MATER, LIVE THY GLORY..." 195

maintained an unbroken continuity in every division of the school's life and inspired increasing confidence in all. There could have been no greater tribute to the quality of the Trevorrows' work for Centenary than the smooth efficiency with which the institution carried on. Feeling no need for haste, therefore, the Trustees resolved that ample time should be taken to find a truly worthy successor; and it was not until well after the close of the college year that they found the man whose education and experience seemed uniquely to qualify him for the needs of the modern Centenary.

Mr. Hurst Robins Anderson differed from all his predecessors in being a specialist in the field of education. He had graduated from Ohio Wesleyan with a Bachelor of Arts degree in 1926 and from Northwestern University with a Master of Science in 1934. Beyond that he had studied in the University of Michigan School of Law and in the University of Chicago Graduate School of Education. His experience had included every kind of work done on a college campus except the actual keeping of the accounts. Beginning in Ohio Wesleyan, he had performed the double duties of the Alumni office and the office of Admissions; continuing in Allegheny College, from 1929 to 1943 he had progressed from an instructorship through the ranks of teaching and into the work of Registrar and Dean of the Summer Session. In 1942, he had held the General Education Board Fellowship granted by the Rockefeller Foundation for study in General Education. This afforded him the opportunity to travel for six months, studying all phases of education. At the conclusion of this survey, his enthusiasm was all for the Junior College as the most significant educational development of this century.

On August 15, 1943, Mr. Anderson assumed the office of President. Within a few weeks, President Anderson had prepared his first report and his proposed budget for the year, both of which were felt to constitute a master-statement of a modern Christian educator who knew where he wanted to go and exactly how he expected to get there. The Trustees felt that a new and inspiring note had been sounded. Another cycle of Centenary history had begun.

HURST ROBINS ANDERSON
President of Centenary Junior College, 1943

CHAPTER IX

"The Golden Haze of Student Days"

> "Those days of yore
> Will come no more
> But through our many years
> The thought of you,
> So good, so true,
> Will fill our eyes with tears."

"THE golden haze of student days" truly "is round about us yet." Only a touch, a word, a phrase, a name,—and click! instantly appear pictures of persons, whole scenes, complete to the last detail of accompanying sounds and smells. So marvelous a gift is Memory. And, fortunately, it brings smiles, chuckles, laughs, and serene delights, more often than tears.

The sons and daughters of Centenary have supplied most of the material for this chapter, in response to requests for recollections, reminiscences, appreciations, tales of pranks, incidents, anecdotes.

Beginning, then, at the beginning, here is the picture of the very first day of C. C. I. painted from memory by Flora Green (Mrs. Richards), the very first girl to register. This is her letter; and would that the fine, firm, beautifully legible handwriting could be reproduced, too.

I wonder if I am the only living *antique* who was present the very first day of the opening of C. C. I.

The day was perfect—one of God's rare gems. A great throng was present—speeches of course—and a great bountiful dinner followed.

The building then was a great bare-looking structure—more like a jail in appearance, but the surrounding scenery then—as now—was captivating. As a "co-educational" institution, the strict rules were not enforced, and it was a very attractive sight to see the girls and boys wandering here and there around the beautiful grounds—but that was only for a day.

Enough cannot be said of Dr. Whitney's presidency —his oft-expressed "Indomitable Will" proved what he expected of his students in behavior, in studies, in strict observance of rules, and all that was uplifting. He was a grand man.

We were all proud of Dr. Whitney, and his influence as a deep thinker and spiritual leader has remained with us through the years.

God bless and prosper C. C. I. We are proud of what she *was* and *now* is as "Junior College."

And she adds this postscript:

If this poor attempt is not worth printing, please do not hesitate to destroy it. I will not care.

Destroy this? My dear lady, this letter belongs to Centenary's archives forevermore. Beside it place the memories of the same day from a letter written in 1925 by William J. Davis, the first boy to register on that opening day:

It seems like a dream to me as I sit in my law office and my mind running back over fifty years when I entered the C. C. I. I was the first boy that registered

The Old Building—The Chapel

in the institute. Well can I recall the scenes in the dining-room, with the shavings lying around on the floor, as the building was not quite completed in all of its details. I took my first meal in the institute with Dr. Whitney, Mrs. Whitney, their son Irvin, and the younger members of the family, and I dined with the Doctor for several days before I was assigned to a regular table with the rest of the students when the school opened.

One can even sniff the fresh woody scent of the unfinished room. He continues:

To travel back over fifty years was quite a shock to me, although a pleasant reminder in every detail. I wish to say I owe much of my success in life to the fact that I was under the instruction and influence of Dr. Whitney, and the rest of the faculty of the Centenary Collegiate Institute. I have recommended the Institute to a number of friends.[1]

Next comes a voice from the class of 1884:

The outstanding memory of my three years at C. C. I. is Doctor Whitney. What a man! He was a college and fraternity mate of my father's at Wesleyan University. I had been led to expect much, but realization far outran anticipation. Every student was uplifted by his splendid leadership and his patient willing service. He inspired the highest and best in us. We all "rise up and call him blessed."[2]

From Eugene A. Noble of the class of 1885 come memories of the great schoolmaster:

[1] From the letter to Robert J. Trevorrow, December 22, 1925.
[2] From the reply of William L. Clarke, C. C. I. '84.

Dr. Whitney stood for one great principle. Some of us who saw him day after day, and who heard his inimitable expressions, look back now to those school privileges with deep gratification, and are pleased to declare that the best lesson learned at "C. C. I." came from the repeated injunction, "Govern yourself." That was the burden of his word and work—to make every student feel a deep sense of responsibility in the conduct of life, to awaken a personal pride that would permit no deformity of character, to inspire a self-confidence that would lead to achievement. The phrase of his message was frequently varied—sometimes it was solemnly impressive, for Dr. Whitney knew how to inspire awe in an appeal; at other times it was intentionally ludicrous; but back of the phrase was the great thought of self-control. If the educational process has been wise there has been, from the lower school onward, a gradual abdication of authority on the part of both teacher and parent, an increasing insistence upon self-activity and self-direction. This was Dr. Whitney's first principle; it was his best principle. Day after day we heard it announced; and, more emphatic than any announcement, day by day we saw it exhibited.

Besides this one supreme principle and quality which in my judgment was in evidence at Hackettstown I should like to mention the unfailing urbanity, the deep and sincere piety, and the matchless patience of the great schoolmaster.

Many recall the "hobby expressions" of Dr. Whitney: "Backbone!" "Be a man;" "Stand on your own feet;" "I place you on your honor;" "Govern yourself;" "Don't be a jelly-fish!"

Ordinarily suave and gentle of speech, he had, relates Mr. Clarke

"a choice vocabulary"— of invective for use from the

Chapel platform as he raked fore-and-aft students who violated the rules or behaved in an unworthy way. "Putty backbone"—"snake in the grass"—"craven"—"pusillanimous"—or "cowardly poltroon" occasionally struck fire.

One morning he was laying down the law as to good housekeeping. An unscheduled inspection had shown some rooms in bad order, one in particular. This was occupied by a little Latin American who lived like a pig. After words of general counsel Dr. Whitney described one certain room as a pest-hole, so unclean and disorderly as to be unfit for animals. Then he wound up a flight of invective with the question, "Who now is the dirtiest boy in the whole school?" Without hesitation the boy himself arose and said, "I am." The crash of laughter and applause marked a sudden change in the trend of that boy's domestic habits!

From Mexico Mr. Julian Aznar of the class of 1890 writes:

All I can say is that I lived a happy life at the old school—made many friends, remember kindly Doctor Whitney and my teachers—Hammond, Slaughter, Smith, Mrs. Jones, Miss Schermerhorn, Prof. Ingham. As to my classmates, I have a good recollection of a fine fellow, Issa Tanimura who did not control the King's English, but who notwithstanding constantly spoke at prayer meetings with such fervour and enthusiasm that we listened and understood him.[3]

The clear consenting voices of all who speak or write express appreciation of Dr. Whitney. Invariably,

---

[3] Issa Tanimura, a Japanese student, attended C. C. I. the full four years and graduated with highest honors, taking nearly all the prizes. He took the four-year course at Yale in three years with Phi Beta Kappa honors. Returning to Japan, he entered government service and became secretary of commerce. Until his untimely death he corresponded regularly with Dr. Whitney.

too, alumni speak with admiration, even veneration, of Professor Hammond, the scholar and gentleman, dignified, kindly, serious, yet with a sense of humor. One of his students back in 1898-1900 took the trouble to send him from France as late as 1925 his long-overdue thanks. Here is part of his letter:

> Perhaps you never knew how much I am indebted to you for the many fruitful and very pleasant things that have come to me during my life time.
> While I was at C. C. I., I never did very much with my Greek; I gave too much time to other things and especially foot-ball, but later I realized, as you told us one day in class, its inestimable value to one's education and from that time on I made Greek and Greek culture as much a part of myself as possible. So that during the war, serving for two years and four months as a Y.M.C.A. secretary, I was able to entertain and instruct the boys with many a pleasant Greek story; this was especially true during the time I was serving at the front. So you see that you too were serving unwittingly. I wanted you to know this and to thank you for all you have done for me, even though my gratitude is expressed rather late.
> In closing permit me again to thank you for all you have done for me and let me say with all my heart that you shall always remain a most pleasant memory to me.[4]

Doubtless this alumnus speaks the mind of many others, especially of those who came to C. C. I. expressly to study Greek with Professor Hammond preparatory to entering Drew Theological Seminary. His students who went to Yale used to be told that either they had special

---

[4] Letter from Benjamin F. Seldon, September 15, 1925.

PROFESSOR ALBERT O. HAMMOND
Professor of Classical Languages and Literature, 1878-1918; Professor Emeritus, 1918-1931

aptitude for classical languages or else they had had a remarkable teacher. Few felt they dared enter his classes unprepared.

Let no one think that students lived saintly lives in those days, however. There is too much evidence to the contrary. It came out readily in interviews, but only in dark hints at first in written replies, such as this one from William Lawrence Clarke, class of 1884:

> As I read your letter of July 18, 1944, and cogitated upon it I realized that the upheaval of 1910 which banished *boys* from the old school, had completely changed my attitude. What could C. C. I. mean to *me* when I couldn't locate "Home Plate" out there on the campus, where I had led our nine for three years as catcher?
>
> I could regale *boys* (now men) with livid stories of ball games, boxing-matches, pillow-fights, shirt-tail parades, nocturnal ascents of icy fire-escapes; of clandestine correspondence with dear young things on the "other side" through patronage of the "grape-vine" post office system operated by Manuel and Mary Wilson, etc., etc., but most of this would be punk stuff to the feminine contingent of the present day.

A reminder that this History is intended for *all* Centenarians, both boys and girls, brought out two or three anecdotes. "Then," wrote Mr. Clarke, "I simply couldn't stop."

> Brain cells forgotten for many years began to wiggle, and before I knew it I had written about thirty separate items. I have tried them on the dog (several in fact) and the response has been favorable.
>
> The result has been that your fortunate historian has a wealth of material from which to select. Much

that will be woven into this chapter has been taken from this source, not all of which will be credited directly.

Mr. Clarke's collection of C. C. I. Stories, bound in an attractive leather cover, has been presented to the Centenary library where it is available to students and alumni at any time.

And so we must record that despite his academic excellences, poor Professor Hammond's nights in Room 1 at the head of the stairs were frequently made miserable by the "crockery fights" on the halls. Lights would be obediently out according to rule, and deep quiet reigning. Suddenly, out of the darkness would come booming down the hall a piece of crockery from one of the fully-appointed wash-stands with which each room was supplied. Its careening career ended in a smash against the door of Professor Hammond's room. When the Professor emerged, no one was ever in sight and the halls were still. After awhile, crash!—came another wash bowl. Again peace. Presently a water-pitcher was hurled into the darkness. Morning found the hall littered with broken bed room china. The pay-off came when costs were assessed against the rooms where such items were missing, but even this did not mean the end of nights made hideous by the rolling crockery.

Years later, the girls substituted for crockery several balls from the bowling alleys. Midnight was the appointed hour. The heavy missiles as they bounced from side to side of the curving corridors made a thunderous noise. And what chance had the bewildered teacher of locating offenders in crescent-shaped halls?—or even of dodging the on-rushing balls!

Occasionally there was an unilateral midnight

"THE GOLDEN HAZE OF STUDENT DAYS" 205

prank. This is how William L. Clarke's "inspiration" worked out:

From boyhood I loved fire-arms, loved to shoot them. I covet a "luger" right now! At an early age I acquired quite an arsenal. I missed these weapons so much at C. C. I. that I took them with me at the start of my second year and kept them carefully locked at the bottom of my trunk. One of my treasures was a big smooth-bore muzzle-loading horse-pistol bearing date of the Civil War. The instant I unpacked my trunk it occurred to me what a grand thing it would be to fire that young mountain-howitzer in the 4th Hall at about 1:00 A.M., so I did it! It was a complete success. It awakened the whole school and brought the entire "Boys' side" double quick to the 4th floor to "view the remains." Of course there were no "remains" except the acrid smell of burned powder, and no damage had been done. Of course I was "sleeping the sleep of the just," and that was probably unfortunate, for I may have been *missed!* Nothing happened that day, but at Chapel the next morning Dr. Whitney, just at the close, announced "I would like to see Clarke in my office immediately after Chapel." Now why he picked on me I can't imagine, but with a fluttering heart I tapped on the door at the left of the chapel platform. A key was turned, the door was opened by Dr. Whitney, who greeted me coldly and pointed to a small table on which —to my horror—was displayed my treasured arsenal— two revolvers, a single-barrel cap pistol, a tiny 1-shot, 22 calibre Remington vest-pocket pistol, a 4-barrel derringer, the young cannon (mentioned above) which still smelled of burned powder, and a beautiful pistol which I had borrowed from a former town pupil who lived next door to the Methodist Church on Main Street. They had used a pass-key to my room (old 47), picked the lock on my trunk, removed the tray and had taken my small arms to the chapel office. Now what could I say? Well, that's just what *I said,* and Dr. Whitney said the rest and a *lot!*

But the truly popular pranks were those that attracted the attention of the whole school. Students of the early '90's will recall the tombstone that seemed miraculously to have started from the ground one morning when they looked out on the front campus. Dr. Whitney did not share the general amusement. If he had any suspicions he did not divulge them but he placed the perpetrators—whoever they might be—on their honor to do the right thing. So in the dead of night the band stole forth with none to say them nay and by dint of hard labor with a wheelbarrow restored the stone to its place in the cemetery.

This was all very quiet and simple, however, as compared with the more pressing problem of restoring to its rightful place a greased pig that was grunting about one morning on fifth floor when the boys got up. It was announced that the pig was to be the property of the man who could catch it and hold it. Everyone joined in the chase. The panicky creature ran from floor to floor letting out unearthly squeals, while the boys—who also were vocal enough—succeeded in nothing but acquiring a thicker coating of grease on hands, arms, and clothing. Waste-paper boxes were upset in the scramble. No one could stop the frantic animal until on the first floor a boy was able to gain a hold on the creature—now considerably divested of its thick coating of grease—long enough to claim it as his. Even then there was considerable commotion before the pig was finally out of the building.

"THE GOLDEN HAZE OF STUDENT DAYS" 207

Equally out of place was the snake that one day appeared in chapel during the prayer. Let a student of the old days relate the story.

A bull in a china shop seems no less appropriate than a snake in chapel. Both are matters of record.

I was assigned at chapel an end seat next the side-aisle at about the center of the room. Otis Houghton ('78-'83) had the seat directly in front of me. The long pews were supported by uprights at both ends, and, in addition, by a vertical board from end to end, the lower edge of which, when pew was heavily loaded, might rest on the floor, but when the load was light might leave a small opening.

One morning at regular chapel exercise, during prayer my forehead rested on the back of the pew ahead of me. My eyes, usually closed, opened for a moment, and right there on the floor between my feet, to my horror a live snake was cavorting up and down as though about to attack me. It was Houghton's latest escapade. He had caught the snake the day before; had kept it in his room over night, then with the snake in his pocket had sallied forth for breakfast, chapel and classes. Otis held the snake by the tail, leaned clear over and poked its head under the vertical board which brought its whole body between my feet. I had never handled snakes, but three or four boys who sat on my bench came very near disturbing chapel exercise when they saw that snake. Had they been girls, there would have been a panic. The poor snake was finally withdrawn (pulled back by its tail) and restored to Otis' pocket. He played with it for a day or two, flashing it on unsuspecting boys, and finally dropped it down the back of one of them.

June-bugs were excellent creatures to be used for

teasing the timid and the less hardy. Here is a June-bug episode:

At a certain time during the spring term June-bugs abound at C. C. I. Big fat black bugs an inch long which make a noise in flight like a motor-cycle. They were something of a nuisance and some timid girls were afraid of them. The light from our open window was a magnet, and we often found a half-dozen in our room. They were easily caught and thrown out. By chance chum and I heard a big sissy tell how they frightened him, and a plot was quickly hatched. He lived conveniently near on the hall below ours. We opened our window wide, with all lights on. The June-bugs sailed in by the dozen. We gathered almost a pint and repaired to the room above the one occupied by our victim. One of us hung far out of the window while chum clung to his feet. Sure enough, the window below was wide open and the room lighted. A well-directed shot sent a whole handfull of June-bugs into the room. Then another and another. You have heard of:

"The yell that rent the mountain air
of fierce defiance and despair."

This we heard as our victim rushed to the window and closed it tightly. We repeated this adventure several times, but the big sissy never suspected that the sudden influx of June-bugs was inspired!

More effectual from every point of view was the use of bats, however. The story is told that one Sunday afternoon a number of boys went on an excursion to a cave from which they gathered enough bats to fill several suit cases. Biding their time till they knew a certain favorite dessert was due to be served, the plotters and their accomplices sallied into the dining-room with their pockets full of bats. Just as the dessert had been served —lo! suddenly the room seemed to be full of swooping wings. The result was all that could have been desired. The girls fled in panic and the boys remained to eat all the desserts at their leisure.

More than once a visiting "grad" has been heard to say, "I wish I could have just one more day at Centenary!" So, let us trace a day, a week, a year,—in a general way. What day of these would you choose to live again?

The rising bell that awoke you students of the earlier years was rung every morning by one of the boys. Promptly at seven-fifteen you were at breakfast hearing Dr. Whitney asking the blessing. You heard him do the same at dinner and at supper. You had besides your meals and classes, two other fixed engagements every day including Saturday: chapel, at eight forty-five every morning and seven in the evening. Remember how you sat—boys on one side of the chapel and girls on the other? The men of the faculty sat on the platform each in turn conducting the service and leading in extemporaneous prayer.

If you were here soon after the girls' school began, you recall the short period after breakfast for making beds and tidying rooms and then the daily walk—under faculty supervision—all the way around the outside of the campus before classes began. When class periods were lengthened the walk was taken right after lunch.

Girls and boys were carefully segregated in all housing arrangements but there were occasions when they met socially. If these were deemed insufficient, ingenuity and inventiveness rose to the occasion. The result? So many marriages of C. C. I. schoolmates that Dr. Whitney used to call the school his Match Factory. Many were the weddings of his former students at which he officiated. Occasionally he recorded in his diary christenings of C. C. I. babies.

Hear the opinion of a young man who in 1889 began his first teaching here about the time he was eligible to cast his first vote, Mr. William Barnard Smith:

I have always thought that the system of co-education then existing at C. C. I. and other Methodist secondary schools was an excellent one. Boys and girls were brought together at meal times and at fraternity and sorority gatherings in a healthy way, I think, and many happy marriages were the result. My father and mother met each other while they were students at Wilbraham, where the school was very similar to the one at Hackettstown, and as a result I am here and writing to you today. I feel rather sorry that these schools and others like them have become non-co-educational.

This same Professor Smith—incidentally—has the distinction of having selected Centenary's school colors. He writes:

When I first came to C. C. I. the school had no official colors. A committee was appointed to make a selection and I suggested to it the colors blue and black. (Our Wesleyan college colors were red and black—selected my freshman year—and I thought that Yale blue with black would be excellent.) These colors were adopted and I understand are still the school colors.

He also contributes a little anecdote that shows how even in the classroom a budding romance could not be unobserved nor go unassisted. He relates:

For a while Miss S——, a very bright student, and Benjamin M—— were "steadies" at the school. One day in Latin class I asked Miss S. to compare "bene" pronounced ("bennie"). The class laughed, or smiled, the young lady hesitated, said she 'thought she couldn't' and sat down. After the class one of the boys stopped and said to me, "Benny is incomparable."

Much more helpful and delicately tactful was the teacher who is the central figure in this recollection sent by a girl student of 1910:

I have thought many times about what I should write. There are many things in my mind. Of greatest importance to me is the fact that I met my husband there as so many did, I suppose. This resulted in twenty-five years of happiness with him in the Methodist ministry. We had our Friday night socials and if both were on the Honor Roll then two other nights we could see each other for half an hour in the small parlor. As we were on the Honor Roll, this continued during the year except for two months when Mr. M. edited the *Hack*. Then Miss Gray one night sent me a note to come to her studio. She would like to see me two nights a week. When I got there she had summoned Brad also to do stencils for her. So those two months we had our dates in the art room, Miss Gray going to a corner far remote and reading out loud.

Naturally Miss Gray was her favorite teacher, sharing honors with "Prof" Hammond who had been her father's teacher, too. She remembers how Tommy Howell used to make a fuss over the children of the "old boys" and how very important he made her feel when introduced to him in this way.

What did the student think of the social regulations? Here is a reaction dating back to the '80's:

Looking back over the vista of sixty years to "the golden haze of student days" at C. C. I., I doubt if any Heidelberg student ever found less to criticize than I. One thing troubled me during my three years, and for years thereafter. There were too few opportunities for social contacts with the girls. We had a scant hour at meals, really contacting only a half-dozen. A signal tossed perhaps across chapel; a 'kerchief waved from a window; little else except a real "Parlor Social" two or three times a year, and those merely a walk-around with your "steady;" seldom a break in the parade in the interest of wider acquaintance. Great pity "cutting in" had not been invented.

Of course, come what may, boys and girls met three times a day in the dining room, but whom you met thus frequently—that lay in the lap of the gods. Or did it? There were "tricks." Let the "authority" just quoted speak:

In the days of co-education the long dining room tables had boys on one side, girls on the other, and a professor at one end. Everything depended upon our surroundings at the table, for it was difficult to change. You were settled for a term, and probably for the school-year. A congenial group of four, six or eight made each meal a "party," and close friendships frequently resulted. The personality of the teacher was an important factor. Some were austere, some friendly.

Obviously the question of your dining room seat was very important. At the beginning of a school year the girls were admitted first. The "old students" took their old seats unless a new one had been requested. Then the boys were admitted, under the same arrangement. Many new students, probably fifty or more, were utter strangers. The girls took the seats which were not claimed. Then came the boys, privileged to take any vacant chair. With the girls it was "now or never." As a boy's hand would touch the opposite chair there would be a smile of invitation or a dead-pan vacant look which showed lack of interest, and the poor boy would pass on. Some tall girls, by sitting low, could reach with a slipper the chair on the other side of the table, and would *hook it,* and if a boy who did not pass muster would take hold of it, she would hold it and look the other way. If a nice-looking boy came along, she would unlock the chair and welcome him with a smile. There in those tender years we learned that "there are tricks in all trades but ours."

In later years it was the custom for the boys to move on to another table every two weeks, while the girls remained in their same places, wondering what their "opps" would be like. Boys would sometimes buy off an "opp" in order to get the place across from the lady of his choice. In this way an "opp" could be lined up for weeks ahead. The word "opp" became a very meaningful localism. After Easter, Seniors could choose their own places.

There were strict rules, strictly enforced, about table manners. For twenty-five years a French table was maintained in the dining room—a feature that students found, by their own admission, very valuable.

The dining room was attractively decorated with a long row of hanging baskets of plants down the center of the room. "The tables are bounteously covered with food of the best quality prepared in a manner equal to any first-class hotel that we ever visited," wrote a visitor in 1881. Dr. Whitney wrote: "This was my decree— all through the years—always ice cream one dinner *every* week and the 'plate of cream' *must be* and was always a very large one." This was home-made. So also were the "magnificent" bread and rolls made by the famous cook, William Finger, who came into the employ of C. C. I. twelve years before Dr. Whitney retired and remained here for more than forty years, passing away after he had completed the feeding of the commencement guests in June, 1926. William was a character whom many will remember—simple, genuine, much beloved, never angry, never behind time, the faithful servant,—"a prize indeed," to quote Dr. Whitney.

Who that ever knew it can forget William's "goo-cake?" What an event when one was placed upon the table and what insistence on accuracy in cutting the slices! "Oh," wrote one student, "ain't it a grand and glorious feeling when you're all nerved up to devour a dessert of prunes and they bring on goo-cake!"

After lunch and after dinner occurred a major event of the day—the giving out of the mail by a teacher in the North and South Hall Parlors. Carrying mail to and from the Post Office was a paying position for some boys.

Afternoons after school were never alike two successive days. When the boys were down town, between three and six, the girls remained on campus, and vice versa. Never were they allowed to go down town on the same day. Only on Class Day were boys and girls allowed to go out together. On the day school closed the boys would take their best girls on a picnic or a sail.

Life-long friendships grew out of those daily associations,—as well as romances and weddings. Here is an illustration, not written for this history, by the way,

"THE GOLDEN HAZE OF STUDENT DAYS" 215

but in a business letter to Dr. Trevorrow dated April 13, 1931:

Have you on your mailing list an alumna who for outstanding service to mankind will rank with the very best? I refer to Mrs. Ella Johnson Kinnear, who spent thirty years as a medical missionary at Foochow, China, now retired. "Ella Johnson" was my "opp" at Professor Hammond's table in '83 and '84. I have kept in touch with her work and have recently received a most interesting letter from her, together with an article from the November number of the *Missionary Herald,* which summarizes her work in China.

And here is a story on the same theme which is guaranteed to bring to dozens of Centenary alumni and doubtless many faculty members too—a nostalgia composed of almost pure rapture. It is about spring time among the silent hills, and—arbutus.

Arbutus is a "weakness" with me. I developed it in C. C. I. days and it has become more virulent with the years. Every spring, do or die, I must find a bunch of arbutus.

At C. C. I. we kept the approximate date on our calendar, and some intimate chum and I would start out before dawn for Mine Hill, which the gods had blest by dropping the seeds of the lovely Mayflower. Others followed and we searched diligently for the fragrant flowers, frequently brushing the snow aside as a leaf gave us a sign of beauty beneath. Each coveted the largest bunch and we hastened back in order to lay the glorious flowers on the breakfast table at the place of our "opp." And the oh's and ah's from the entire section when that marvelous tribute was observed! No unusual thing to see a huge bunch six or eight inches in diameter.

Years after graduation I used to send a bunch of

arbutus to my erstwhile "opp" every spring, and finally thirty years after complete separation, I "plunged" for a big bunch, took them to the superintendent of the Botanical Gardens and asked if they could be packed for a journey of three thousand miles. The box was sent with no identification card, but I got a letter post haste, and my old "opp" wrote, "I knew what was in the box before I opened it, and the arbutus was perfectly fresh."

"The waiters were a very special group," writes William L. Clarke,

> usually older students from modest homes, many studying for the ministry, all working their way through school. It was quite an honor to be asked to substitute when the "regulars" were absent—for example, preaching at small country churches. They ate in the kitchen after the tables were cleared and they had "the best in the house."
>
> I remember that while substituting as "waiter" for one of the "regulars," I filled all of the glasses at my own table with boiling water instead of ice-water. There was some excitement, and I think my transfer to Dr. Whitney's table followed, but soon I was forgiven and was back with the old gang! I think it quite likely that I did not "fit" in that older high-brow group and that they gladly released me.

And now for a voice from the girls' side of the table:

> At table, we were seated girls on one side and boys on the other. Who was to be our "Opposite" was a vital matter. One morning most of the boys came more promptly than usual, but when one of the couples sitting opposite each other arrived and could not pull their chairs out so as to be seated a laugh went up from the males present. Grace was delayed until the young man could reach into his pocket, pull out a knife, open it and cut the cord that held the two chairs together.

"THE GOLDEN HAZE OF STUDENT DAYS" 217

On the wall of the far end of the dining room were these words: "Eat Thy Bread With Joy." One bright girl remarked that she thought the last word was "Jam."

She writes of those far yesterdays:

Those were the days of the original red brick building. When we entered the front door, on the opposite wall facing us was a statue of Atlas bowed down with the weight of the world that rested on his back. On either hand stretched the long halls, that to the right leading to class rooms and the dormitory for boys, the one of the left to the girls' dormitory and the parlors.

In these parlors when the boys were allowed to spend an evening with us girls, there was much chatter and discussion of affairs present and things to come. These "Sociables" as they were called, often marked some particular event, but once when the boys asked for such an evening to celebrate the addition of another unabridged dictionary to the library, Dr. Whitney did not see eye to eye with the young men.

The "gym sociables" featured a variety of activities usually in the form of a program including a promenade or a grand march to music, games, and "a sing." Part of the time was given over to chatting, for here the boys had a chance to sit beside their "opps." Mrs. Whitney was always there along with the "Profs" and the teachers, who enjoyed the occasions only less than the students did. For many years these programs were directed by Miss Martha Barbour, teacher of elocution. Dr. Whitney sometimes honored them with his presence.

There was never any dancing, even of the girls together. Miss Charlotte Howard relates of her student days in C. C. I. how on one of these occasions she joined the edge of a group surrounding Dr. Whitney and out of sheer joy and exuberance began dancing about *alone*. Immediately in a most kindly, yet firm manner Dr. Whitney reproved her, saying that was not done in C. C. I.

Dr. Ferguson was very insistent on increasing the number of Friday night "socials" and "gym socials" and making them regular occasions for bringing the boys and girls together.

These social occasions were not frequent enough to suit some and there was always a temptation to meet down at Tommy Howell's ice cream emporium, or "out of bounds," or right at home in the Library, out of hours, or in society rooms. Faculty were warned to be on the alert! Then too, there were fine town girls who welcomed calls from C. C. I. boys with no questions asked—active students, ex-students, members of church choirs, sisters of students, etc. etc. The method employed is thus described by one who was a past master of the techniques of "French leave":

A permit for an "evening out" was hard to get, but there were no sentries, the gates were open, and the night very dark with few street lights. The trouble was *getting back,* for doors were tightly locked.

At each end of the building was a large porch, the height of the first floor, with square pillars topped with large ornaments and extended cornice. The fire-escape started from the roof and extended to the end hall-window in the fifth floor. How students in case of a fire were expected to get down to the ground from the roof of the porch was not made clear, and there never was a fire-drill. But my problem was not to get *down* but to climb up— say at midnight, returning from a call down town. I learned the trick after practice, and from the roof it was an easy jaunt up the fire-escape to the 5th floor, then around the edge of the mansard roof to a classmate's room near the stairway. He was warned not to be shocked if he saw me entering his window. Donning a bath-robe and slippers then, and waiting for perfect silence in the hall, it took but a moment to go down one flight to the 4th hall and to my own room. No one else to my knowledge ever climbed those ugly square pillars. It was deadly dangerous, especially in icy weather. That very fact led to an improved technique: Piano rooms were on the first floor back. One day as I heard piano practice, the window was wide open. Aha! said I, if I could climb into that window at night I could go upstairs direct to my room and my problem would be solved. But how! Windows and doors carefully locked. It was easy to borrow a key, make a pattern and a duplicate. Then after supper, when the 1st hall was silent, to use the key, unlock the window and raise the sash so that a pry could be inserted. Door locked again and all serene. It was quite a gymnastic feat to cling to the stone cornice below the window while the window was raised and entered. Then window closed and locked.

It would have been foolhardy to go from the 1st floor to my room on the 4th floor in street attire, so most of my clothes were left on the grand piano, to be retrieved in the early morning before ordinary traffic commenced for the day. It worked perfectly until one morning—curses! I overslept and heard the big gong ring for breakfast. My clothes *had* to be retrieved and I rushed downstairs in terror. I turned the key softly and entered, thinking that I was safe. But horror! There stood Doctor Whitney and Jimmy Titus, the superintendent, examining my well-marked linen! Nothing but my well-established good-behavior (?) and my scholarly attainments (?) saved me from expulsion!

Another experienced "leave taker" tells of the difficulty of clambering up the pillars to find "Prof" Stutsman waiting at the top to catch him. The result would be: demerits and campusing.

Seniors had more privileges, one of which was more freedom to go down town. But there were more important places to go than down town. Always the canal was luring, with its miles of good skating or hiking along the tow-path beside the still, mirroring water; there were the Musconetcong River, Sully's Grove, Buck Hill, and mountains to climb. What wonderful places for hikes—and picnics, all day Saturday from ten to five. Each Society had its day to go. The boys would get an old buggy, fill it with eatables guarded by a weaker or perhaps a crippled boy, and pull it through the streets, up Schooley's Mountain, to Budd Lake. Horns and noise makers would attract crowds to line the way. A Professor always accompanied—usually Mr. C. F. Cuykendall or W. B. Smith. The day passed with games and swimming, and all too soon it was time to pull the buggy back again.

In autumn the girls went on hay-rides through Rutherford Woods.

"There was also the senior picnic at Budd Lake," writes Mrs. Miller of class 1883.

This was a very happy occasion, and we know of only one mishap during the years. Then a boat capsized but the only casualty was a camera, that being near the shore was promptly rescued.

Just before commencement Dr. Whitney used to sponsor a day's excursion to the Delaware Water Gap.

The students would march two abreast to the special train of four coaches plus a baggage car to carry the provisions. It was said that as part of the luncheon a barrel of boiled eggs went along. There are extant long and poetic newspaper accounts of these adventures.

One girl who was here at the turn of the century speaks of the popularity of Mrs. Whitney with the girls and describes Mrs. McCormick as much the same sort of person, "very charming and sweet to the girls." To her, Mrs. McCormick and Miss Hoag were the two outstanding personalities of those days. A boy of this period describes Miss Hoag as "a little lady who wore her grey hair swept back and piled up, very aristocratic and very firm, but very human." And the girl already referred to says: "She was always a lady, a perfect lady. She had a way of looking at wrong doers and saying, 'Well, you knew better!' The boys all loved her."

The writer may add that one of the first things she heard about C. C. I. was her brother's description of Miss Hoag, which tallies with the above. He considered it a great honor to carry a message for her.

The weeks, like the days, had certain fixed events, almost unchangeable. One was the Wednesday night Prayer Meeting, which was never long.

Friday afternoon for a quarter of a century meant the rhetoricals already described. On rare occasions Dr. Whitney would spring a Surprise Lawn Party in place of rhetoricals!

Friday evening chapels often featured outstanding speakers. Dr. S. Parkes Cadman enjoyed coming to visit the "dear school among the hills" as he always called it. Friday evening was always given to a lecture or entertainment of some sort.

The Sunday pattern of life has already been described in President Whitney's own words. If you were a boy, the morning found you in the Methodist Church in the gallery at the left, looking down on the girls, conveniently seated at the right. Good singers went in the choir. Students of other denominations could of course attend their own church, but there were at that time few non-Methodists.

In the years 1889, 1890 and 1891 C. C. I. was the center of an expanding circle of religious influence that took in this whole countryside. Members of the school's Y.M.C.A. organized a Praying Band composed mostly of students for the ministry. Presently these young men were called upon to assist ministers of local churches to conduct a series of special services. Dr. Whitney was highly pleased to give this group every encouragement and he selected certain of the older students for this task. Charles L. Mead, later Bishop of the Methodist Church, Benjamin Meredith, George Graff, Grant C. Tullar, Andrew M. Shay, Henry D. Trinkaus, T. S. Molyneaux, and Frederick C. Mooney composed the octette of leaders. Special meetings were held at the Guard Lock Chapel, in Flanders, Drakestown, Port Murray, Tranquility and other places, at the request of the pastors. Two weeks of evangelistic services were also held in the C. C. I. chapel which was crowded every night. Choir and orchestra assisted. As a result, many joined the churches of the towns. The report to the Newark Annual Conference held in Washington in 1891 showed more than a hundred new mem-

The Chapel—New Building

"THE GOLDEN HAZE OF STUDENT DAYS" 223

bers enrolled in the various churches, due to the earnest, humble, and consecrated work of these young men.

Young preachers in training were always available for services in Rockport, Mount Hope, Mount Bethel, and Drakestown, where their compensation would always be a big chicken dinner in homes of the parish where good food abounded. For two months in 1890, when Dr. John Lowry of the Hackettstown Presbyterian Church was ill, the pulpit was filled by Benjamin Meredith, Frederick C. Mooney, Charles Mead or Grant C. Tullar,—with Dr. Whitney always present as a kindly supporter and critic. Dr. George Smith of Trinity Methodist Church was also assisted by members of this group.

It was in connection with these activities that "up in old Whitney Lyceum Hall" Grant Colfax Tullar discovered that he could compose hymns. This is how he tells the story:

One day I was playing for some of the young men hymns which were set before me on the piano. My opinion was asked of a certain hymn which I had just played and I remarked, "I could make a better setting to those words than that one." Someone said, 'Well, why don't you?" to which I responded, "If you will get out and leave me alone for half an hour, I will." When the time was up, they returned with a "Ha-ha, let's hear your tune," but upon hearing it they all admitted that I had done all that I had promised to do, and the one who dared me said, "I didn't know you could write music," to which I replied, "Neither did I, till I tried."

His memories of C. C. I. must be mostly those of hard work, for he writes:

Never having studied English grammar, I found my

initial recitation a serious problem, for it was in Latin. Imagine, if you can, trying to master Latin without knowing a thing about English grammar.

Spending six or seven hours a day on that one study, I would flunk while other students put fifteen minutes on the same and passed. I was forced to work from early morning till late at night to grasp that subject.

Mathematics came more easily. However, spending six terms at the school, I managed to pass all my studies, although I was ill and under the doctor's care more than a third of the school years. During this time I did not have twenty-five cents spending money at any one time. To help out with my daily board and tuition I waited on table and did evangelistic work, until at the end of the second year I was physically unfit for further studies.

His name therefore does not appear among C. C. I.'s graduates but it is in a place which will assure him immortality as the author of the more than three hundred Gospel Hymns which have been selected for permanent preservation in the library of the Washington Cathedral.

It was at C. C. I. that Mr. Tullar met Mr. Isaac Meredith who was later to become his partner in the music publishing business of which Mr. Tullar was president and general manager for a third of a century until in 1927 he retired to devote his strength to religious work. This chance meeting Mr. Tullar describes in a letter of August, 1944.

You mention Isaac Meredith in connection with C. C. I. and his only connection (which I know about) was on the occasion when Ike and I first met. His brother, Ben, was a student there and Ben and my brother Edgar had been roommates during the time my brother attended C. C. I. With my brother his health and his money ran out and he had to leave to recuperate both. Old "W. L." was to have its Anniversary and Ben Meredith invited his brother "Ike" as his guest and my brother Edgar was returning for that occasion and took me along with him—we four slept—I should say tried to sleep—in the one room and under those "trying circumstances" "Ike" and I became acquainted.[1]

Music was a prime interest in the good old days. There survive dozens of programs of musical events. Professor Baumann from 1879-1883 and his successor, Mr. C. F. Thomsen with his assistant, Mr. E. L. Stivers, masters of pipe-organ and piano, were mighty impulses to *good music*. A student of these days recalls:

For those who sang, there was a welcome musical treat at chapel service Sunday evenings. After some formalities, all of which have been forgotten, "those who sing" were invited to meet about the grand piano on the platform. Twenty-five to thirty usually responded. Professor Baumann or Thomsen had just presided at the pipe-organ for the formal service, and frequently both organ and piano led the group as they sang the grand old hymns of the church. And *did we sing!* Many of us in these hallowed hours memorized scores of hymns which have been priceless treasures ever since.

Later, May Vincent Whitney, one of the president's daughters, sometimes used to play the piano for these "sings."[2]

[1] A brief autobiography of Mr. Tullar is to be found in his book *Written Because*, a copy of which is in Centenary Library. It is an intensely interesting story.

[2] May Whitney graduated from C. C. I. She was for three years assistant to the Director of Music in C. C. I. and for two years Director of Music in Drew Seminary. Later she was a concert pianist. Now Mrs. Benjamin H. Thompson, she resides in Ocean Grove where she is still teaching music and taking a leading part in the many musical activities of a busy town.

The favorite hymn, according to a graduate of 1880, was "Sun of My Soul."

This gentleman remembers also the trains on the girls' dresses. So do the girls! One writes:

When we entered the school, the seniors wore dresses with trains and we eagerly looked forward to the time when we too might be thus arrayed. But alas, after four years had passed trains too had passed and were no longer fashionable. They just were not worn at that period by girl graduates.

Clothes had to be conservative, though. No décolleté. High shoes were the rule from Thanksgiving to Easter.

What besides "high shoes" did Thanksgiving mean in those years? For more than half the students it was a day celebrated at school, attending Union Services at the Church, feasting at noon, enjoying an entertainment by professionals in the evening. Friday was free for devouring contents of "boxes" from home, for resting, for reviewing the term's work or for completing preparations for the student entertainment that evening. Parents sometimes came to visit their children. Even in the early 1900's each year a considerable group remained at school, secretly expecting to be home-sick but afterwards all agreeing "that to stay at C. C. I. was just as nice as going home." Very homelike was the atmosphere of the Girls' Parlor where chapel was held, followed by games and impromptu fun where all became well acquainted. Dinner was served banquet style. The afternoon was given over to fun on the canal or to long hikes.

Friday was then a school day but there was fun all

round the edges and a joint Society meeting with Dr. Noble presiding. "The vacation was unanimously declared to be one of the happiest in the experience of each. In many respects it was an ideal way of spending a vacation," states *The Hackettstonian* of December, 1904.

In these years Washington's Birthday was a major holiday observed at school. Morning chapel featured a patriotic address and there were appropriate exercises in the evening. Usually several large sleighing parties went out during the day. In the 1900's there was the Annual Parade in the morning and the Washington's Birthday Banquet in the evening, complete with toastmaster and toasts, serious and humorous, Societies' representatives alternating with faculty members on the program. A few sample toasts: "Civil and Religious Liberty—May they go Hand in Hand"; "The Two Largest Ladies of America: Miss Ouri and Mrs. Sippi"; "Three Greatest American Generals: General Peace, General Prosperity and General Satisfaction"; "Martha, the American Woman, or the True Source of George's Greatness"; and "Columbia: Be She What She Will, With All Her Faults, She Is Our Country Still"—this toast given by Dr. McCormick.

The football games were played on Saturday, with the kick-off at 2:30. Pennington was the chief rival. There was no admission charge but donations to the local team were gladly received. Many townspeople attended. One senior, an over-pious divinity student, would never witness a game but stayed in his room praying all the while that C. C. I. would win. There was a lady, on the contrary, who would never miss a game, whether on the home field or away. There she was, carrying a first-aid kit, an over-anxious mother who lived in constant dread during football season. She took up residence on Church Street in order to be near her son.

For the baseball fans the story of Mr. William L. Clarke must be included:

C. C. I. had a good nine and we stood well with opposing teams. I was catcher and captain. Our "BIG GAME" was with the freshmen of Lafayette College at Easton, Pa. They were big guys, older than our "prep" group and I remember beating them only once.

The big moment of that game is a vivid spot in my memory today. We were one run ahead and two men out in the last half of the 9th inning. The whole school was there, boys and girls, yelling like mad. At this critical moment a huge Lafayette man met one of "Deacon" Morris' ('82-'83) fast balls fairly, and it sailed far above 2nd base and center-fielder's head—over the distant fence! I can see Marvin Shields ('86), whose men's furnishing store is well known in Hackettstown today, as he sped after the ball, vaulted the fence, and dug around in the long grass for it. No ball had ever been batted over that fence before. As Marvin found the ball, the Lafayette runner was rounding 3rd base. With no time to climb the fence, Marvin made a mighty throw for home plate. It seems unbelievable, but that ball, straight as an arrow, landed in my hands a half-second ahead of the runner. As he sailed by in full stride I struck him hard on the shoulder with the ball. The umpire yelled "out" and the game was over. In later years, as I stood on that home-plate many a time, I marveled that any prep school boy could make that miracle throw!

There were during each year four occasions about which the strictest secrecy was maintained and the

"THE GOLDEN HAZE OF STUDENT DAYS" 229

keenest speculation rife—the Anniversary programs of the four Societies. The following lines from a newspaper report dated March 6, 1884, ought to awaken recollections of similar events participated in by all whose experience covers the days when the Societies were central in school life.

At no society anniversary have we known of greater excitement and speculation as to who the president, editor and other officers might be, and, indeed, in regard to the whole literary program. No definite conclusion, however, was reached, and all was successfully kept secret till the president, F. W. Hannan, entered the chapel door upon the arm of Dr. Whitney, followed by the others on the program.

These programs were formal, beginning with an Invocation and a Salutatory Address, followed by an alternation of musical numbers, essays and orations, leading up to the Debate, on some such serious subject as: "Resolved, That the Evangelical Denominations should seek to become united." Finally came the long-awaited society paper presented by the Editor. This contained some serious articles but it featured satire, jokes, "cuts," and other humorous matter—all very mirth-provoking. Whitney Lyceum had its "Lancet," Philomathean—later Alpha Phi—its "Journal," Diokosophian, its "Scroll," Peithosophian its "Meteor," and Callilogian, its "Star."

These occasions brought back many old students and were a kind of "Old-Home" week-end. On Saturday after chapel the "old grads," the Faculty, the members of all the Societies, and the school at large would visit the different society rooms in turn, participate in a half-hour of addresses of welcome and congratulation and general conversation and finally adjourn to the library and reading-room for another program, for conversation and visiting of the museum until the bell summoned the happy company to dinner.

Smoking and card-playing were strictly "taboo," but the record shows that there were those who knew that "stolen fruits are sweet." Room 47, we are told, never started a game without having a "hand" of "Authors" ready for each player in case of a sudden call from a professor.

Students seem to have been very adept at entertaining themselves in a legitimate fashion, however, that must have consumed in preparation most of the time left over from necessary study. An interesting instance is the Mock Trial which sought to establish the innocence of C. V. Dutcher and Thomas Simms of the charge of wilfully depositing fraudulent ballots. This must have involved the whole student body in one capacity or another. All the '"legal documents" survive, with the student signatures, along with a drawing of the trial scene done by Mr. Kuchiki, a clever Japanese student.[3] There were mock weddings frequently, after the girls took over. In 1885, C. C. I. even had its Student Entertainment Company, drawn from the best students of elocution and music, that sometimes took outside engagements. One was a successful amateur mesmerist who was even allowed by Dr. Whitney to give a Friday Afternoon Public Performance. In 1887 the C. C. I. Quartette was received in neighboring towns with great enthusiasm and given urgent invitations for return engagements.

[3] This occurred April 15, 1876.

Numbers of students tried their hand at writing verses and songs—society songs, class songs,[4] football songs, marching songs, humorous songs, odes, carols, songs of the different seasons of the year, parting songs, and—after the first—Salamander songs, which were sung at the Salamander Ceremony on Hallowe'en.

Beginning in 1901 Hallowe'en became the date for this unique, poetic school tradition. The students that year began it spontaneously after the Hallowe'en party in the dining room had ended in a grand march and all had—presumably—gone to bed. The *Hackettstonian* [December 1901] relates:

About midnight on the 30th of October, the second anniversary of the fire of old C. C. I., objects in a variety of costumes appeared one by one from the windows of the first floor of the boys' dormitory. Having assembled on the campus the boys marched around to the back of the building where they kindled a large bonfire. Around this they danced and sang for an hour, after which, with the permission of the faculty, they retired to their rooms.

Of course this idea "took" and was soon elaborated into a formal ceremony. Before Hallowe'en the boys would build a large replica of the original building. The girls elected a boy to be the Fire Orator; the boys chose a girl to be Vestal Virgin. A faculty and student committee planned the program. The "Boys' Gym" was decorated with leaves, pumpkins, cornstalks and lanterns. The masqueraders paraded before the judges and the prize winners were chosen. There were selections

[4] The Class Song of 1883 was in 1923 presented to C. C. I. as a general school song.

by Glee Club and Orchestra, sometimes an address by a visiting alumnus. Of course refreshments were served. Then began a procession to the rear campus: Seniors, Juniors, Underclassmen, Faculty, in order and last of all the Vestal Virgin, the Fire Orator, the President and guests of C. C. I. The Fire Orator—one of the honor events of the year—eulogized C. C. I. as an indestructible spirit that rose more gloriously from its ashes than the fabled phoenix of old. Here was scope for expression of the finest loyalty and school spirit. The Vestal Virgin then reviewed the history of the fire and applied the torch to the model of the old building. The students watched in silence and then when the flames rose high, C. C. I. songs and mighty cheers rent the midnight air. As the fire died they returned to the dormitories.

Class Days have always been memorable minglings of frolic and the sweet sorrow of parting. The Seniors turned a mock-serious face toward the Junior Class so soon to take their places, as they made over to them their "Deed of Trust" and presented admonitory gifts such as a model canoe, a mammoth tin horn, a huge target, a large rusty old plow, or an immense key.

It was for several years the custom to prepare a casket containing Class Day exercises and other class work, with programs, catalogs, songs, class secrets and mysteries; lock it and bury it with appropriate exercises of songs and speeches under a tree on front campus. In 1886, the class of '76 resurrected its box and used it in its reunion. Only one such box remains above ground here at school—that of '77, and it has made its contribution to this history.

The class of '76 planted a purple beach tree and

thus began a custom that was long continued. In the Eighties the impressive farewell exercises of the class were held after supper under the Class Tree, with singing of the class songs. The red maples are class trees of the Trevorrow period. When there were too many trees classes took to planting rambling roses to adorn the back fence of the campus. Ivy planting too was a feature of class day until very recent years.

Memories of school days—the golden haze grows mellower with the years. Hear the tributes of a student of only one semester back in 1882—taken from two letters far apart in time:

Well, among all my days—now past 82 years of them—*absolutely* none happier, richer in spiritual aspirations than those few fall months of 1882.

and

So farewell memories of C. C. I. Although I was there only three months and a long, long time ago—I recall it all happily—among the brightest and most beautiful in the Hall of Memory.

"I still have my Whitney pin and my '84 ring," writes another, who comments on the value of *The Bulletin*:

What a lot of happy memories are awakened as each number reaches me. I hesitate to open it for it means immediate abstraction from all the elements of time and space as I ponder over the names.

Often the experience resembles this one:

Instantly as I saw your name in Miss —'s letter your photograph popped up like a Jack-in-the-box.

Also the *old* name; your oratory; and the fine warm personality. Golly, I wish that I had been living near you all of these fifty years.

The magic of the common school experience in these impressionable years produces friendships that stand in a class by themselves for bright warmth, strong fiber and resilient exuberance. Stephen Leacock expressed it so beautifully and simply in his last book:

It is a commonplace, as often repeated as it is true, that the friendships formed at school are different in kind, different in meaning, than ordinary friendships. And how they last! I am thinking of those who were boys together at school and for uncounted years, for long decades, never saw one another, life passing separately for each of them, yet bring them casually together after twenty years, after forty years if you like, and the passage of the years is just as nothing, the call of the past bridges it in an instant. Such has often been my experience, meetings with boys of the old school whom I had neither seen nor much thought about for half a lifetime.[5]

With enthusiasm Mr. William L. Clarke was able to illustrate this paragraph from his experience at the Alumni Reunion held on the campus in May, 1946:

How I laughed as I read how Leacock met the boys of "Upper Canada" "after half a lifetime." Barriers down; "Hello Jim," "Hello Tom," meeting again as though separation had occurred a few weeks ago! I have had scores of similar experiences but none more acute than "Hello 'Chummy'" (Carmichael Miller '83) at C. J. C. on May 4, 1946. Hadn't seen her in 62 years but we dropped right back into the atmosphere of 1882-4 although we had scarcely known each other.

[5] The Boy I Left Behind Me, page 125.

"THE GOLDEN HAZE OF STUDENT DAYS" 235

Here are a few recollections of Dr. Noble's times: a studious atmosphere, with quite stiff courses; much congregating of the boys in each others' rooms; study hours, with faculty members checking to see that all students were in their own rooms—except the recipients of demerits, who would be studying in the "coop" under the eyes of a teacher, usually "Prof" Denman; the Friday evening musicals—formal affairs—tense hours for the advanced music students, each ready with memorized selection wondering whether this or some other would be the evening for appearing on the program; following the musicals the social times in the drawing rooms. Then there were the tea parties given each month by Mrs. Noble, to which every student went. Prolonged through days were the banner contests, with Senior boys struggling to fly their banner from the top of the boys' gymnasium and to maintain it there in the face of all attempts of the Juniors to tear it down. In those years very few ever went home for a week-end.

And now the girls who since 1910 have "owned" the school are beginning to gain perspective through the golden haze of memories. For in their willingness to help produce this chapter they have supplied a wide enough variety of recollections of events and personalities to bring the light of these days too about us again. Here is the sequence of suggestive replies, the first from a 1918 girl:

My first knowledge of C. C. I. dates back to the time about which I have heard when my Aunt Edith Wallace attended the school in the old building—before the fire.

I went to C. C. I. a heart-broken "little girl"—an

only child who had just lost a young, beautiful and beloved mother. I was spoiled, lonely and in need of the surroundings and friendships conducive to happiness—which I soon found.

I remember Miss Howard buttoning my dresses and generally mothering me. She was a dear. I remember the "haunted house" and our forbidden visits there; the hot home-made cinnamon buns certain breakfasts during the week.

Brecky (Miss Breckenridge) was one of my favorites as she was with all. I recall her informal teas when under the influence of her charm and sense of humor we were taught some of the graces young ladies should have. I remember the Society week-ends, in the stiff pillowed "parlor" soon to have its "face lifted" by the Trevorrows. I recall the visits in the Trevorrows' homey apartment and the special distinction one felt when invited there to dine.

The hour at night between study and lights out was full of fun; unexpected feasts and visits; reducing exercises in the hall in preparation for the next college week end; confidences about the newest beau; exchange of serious problems regarding the war, studies, personalities, etc. More than one world-wide problem was completely settled at these conferences!

School was fun. We learned amid pleasant surroundings, interesting and interested people. The trips to New York were something to anticipate and then dream about; each new event, new friend made, stimulating.

Mine are the fondest of memories. Dr. and Mrs. Trevorrow were charming and kind and so understanding of the busy world at school and the problems and personalities of each of us—and equally aware of the big world outside and the qualifications necessary for young women preparing to enter it. Theirs was the wide vision—and wide has been their influence!

"THE GOLDEN HAZE OF STUDENT DAYS" 237

A 1923 student writes:

Although I was only at C. C. I. a year—having just completed High School—I have many pleasant memories. Among these and really at the top of the list was Dr. Trevorrow. Centenary lost a grand person when he went away. I'm sure he is missed very much. He was a friend to us all.

And she continues:

One of my very pleasant recollections is a sleigh ride we went on—horses, bells and all. It was beautiful. The country was glistening with snow and made a lovely sight.

Then there was the play "Green Stockings" put on by the Diokosophians in which I played the part of the butler. Had a stiff neck for a week after wearing the high collar but it was swell fun. All in all I gained a lot in my year at C. C. I. and have pleasant memories.

Another student of the Twenties remembers especially the Seniors singing Christmas carols as they moved very slowly through all the corridors, each with her lighted candle, very early in the morning of the last day before all went home for Christmas.

Writes another girl of the Twenties:

Our Society was the most important thing in our lives. We almost lived for it. It was a great honor to hold an office. There was competition between Societies in every respect, particularly in scholarship. There was much rushing of girls. The initiations were serious matters.

The initiation of the Freshman class was held in the gym on a Friday night early in the term.

The Y.W.C.A. was another strong feature of the life.

Shakespearean plays and operettas were given in these years.

Class rivalry took the form of painting numerals on the barn, the Seniors stealing a march on their rivals by getting theirs up first.

Miss Breckenridge, the senior class adviser, was the outstanding teacher on the faculty. She was affectionately called "Brecky."

A high point of interest for the Senior Class each year was the trip to New York by train as a class to be the guests of Dr. and Mrs. Trevorrow at the opera, where they occupied a box.

One of the most vivid letters is this from a member of the Academy class of 1930. Unfortunately, no one of that first Junior College class has contributed recollections.

My memories of C. C. I.—there are so many of them, that it is rather difficult to sort them out.

First and foremost, of course, would be Dr. and Mrs. Trevorrow. For in my mind they and C. C. I. are inseparable. It was our class who petitioned Dr. Trevorrow to give our Baccalaureate Address, instead of inviting some "distinguished outsider." We thoroughly enjoyed the Vespers when "Dr. T." was the speaker. I remember many of Mrs. Trevorrow's kind ways. In particular I remember Sunday evening suppers in her apartment and a trip to the "Green Barn" as her dinner guest.

Since I was a music major, I naturally have many happy memories connected with the music faculty: Mr. Mets, Miss Howard, and Miss Gardner. We had many good times when the C. C. I. chorus would broadcast or give a concert at the Women's Club. Miss Howard was Senior Class adviser the year I graduated, and no class could ask for a better one. Mr. Mets had an ensemble class and we surely had fun there.

The banner hunt!—Each Senior Class had a banner. The day it arrived it was hung in the auditorium during chapel service. The entire student body would lustily sing "Fling Out the Banner!" Then the Juniors, of course, would get it from the Seniors—hide it—and then the fun began. The Seniors were given a certain length of time in which to find it. And of course they always did. I wonder how many of the present day students have been under the front porches, in the cellars, etc.

The painting of the Numerals was another big time. The Seniors painted their numerals on the old barn, and of course the Juniors tried to stop them. Usually the numerals were all on before the Juniors realized what was happening. Then there was much fun, ending with a snake dance over the campus.

Dances at Blair Academy were highlights, too. We would go in a large bus—well guarded by many able chaperons!

Saturday afternoon we would go downtown (if we had no demerits). There were shopping lines—and teachers who checked you out, checked on you downtown, and checked you in again! Occasionally, someone did manage to sneak some ice cream home to the girls with demerits.

Here are the significant memories of a 1932 girl. Any repetition of topics has the effect of underscoring their importance. For her:

Two important occasions were Sorority Anniversaries and the French Club Cabaret. Your own Anniversary was a thrill because once a year you overcame stage fright in spite of yourself to stand before the assemblage of students, faculty, and parents. Just being in the audience was fun, too, because it was one of the only occasions for evening clothes at C. C. I. Each of us felt as glamorous as a movie star on Anniversary nights. The Cabaret was gala, too, but in another way. Our old Methodist School gone "Left Bank" with red checked tablecloths and esoteric lighting was an anachronism that thrilled the least adventuresome. The main interest in spite of an excellent show by the French Club was the French pastry imported from New York—and how we wallowed in it!

Painting the numerals on the barn our class missed. That was a keen disappointment.

Hockey games at other schools were loads of fun—also the trips to the Opera in New York. We always had lunch at an Italian restaurant—Giolitto's I think it was, but Miss Gardner will know—seven course lunch we got away with! Excursions to Blair for dances were most exciting of all. How we talked and talked of what our blind dates would be like—always supposed to be the epitome of good looks, sartorial perfection, athletic prowess, and Arthur Murray dancing. Weeks after the dances we discussed our none-too-mild disappointment. We always went back for more—we enjoyed it!

A popular custom was the Saturday trip down town. We spent our time gorging at the new sandwich shop—Batchelor's was passé. We ate some *very* interesting things—double thick chocolate floats, so thick with ice cream they couldn't be drunk, and strawberry sundaes with chocolate cream. I can vouch each customer had at least three orders of something, and we parted with the better part of a dollar bill. The "store" helped satisfy our wolf-like appetites. Each week I treated myself to the delights of chocolate covered grahams—something very new.

I'll always hold out, if anyone asks my opinion, for small classes such as we had—only four in our Virgil class, and we had a whooping good time. Miss Stearns tried to humor us as long as we did our Latin, but Shorty, Smitty, Betty Taber and I got out of hand plenty. Betty used to give some very quaint interpretations of Virgil, which sent us off into gales of laughter.

To me the most glorious day of the year was graduation—not my own particularly, but each one I witnessed. I was impressed by its solemnity, the dignity and prestige of those officiating, the tears and smiles on all faces. Then there were the long-anticipated awards for athletics and scholastics and the *Hack* to be hastily glanced through before hurrying home for the summer. One of the loveliest traditions of the day was the carrying of the long-stemmed roses by graduates. The girls talked of those roses long before they carried them— they were a symbol of the beauty of achievement to us.

Personalities not before mentioned appear in these reminiscences.

Miss Whitman was quite a character. She spoke so rapidly we didn't get a word for a month. She was tremendously interested in nature and told daily of the visits of birds and bees to her window. When a bat got in Smitty's room, it was Miss Whitman who carefully caught it and freed it.

Mrs. Monohan was famous for combining brains with culinary skill. Her waffles were out of this world.

Don't leave out Jack, who taught us horse-back riding. When you fell off, he yelled, "Get up there on that thar horse, and don't you let the poor creature stumble again." Dazed, you obeyed.

One final word about personalities. I think Dr. and Mrs. Trevorrow were the dominating personalities— always so poised and gracious. They were full of sound advice; I still remember many words of wisdom from Dr. Trevorrow's Vespers' Sermons. They filled the school with a spirit of gentility and culture and counseled us to be "complete" people, giving attention not only to the development of our minds, but our bodies as well —and our manners that we might be ladies—and our appearance that we might look our best.

From this 1938 correspondent we are afforded a glimpse behind the scenes. She writes:

> I recall the "midnight snacks" in "Cal" Hall. After the last gleam from the night watchman's lantern had disappeared down the hall, about fifteen giggling girls would slip from the shadows of their rooms and, laden with "coke" and crackers, etc., tiptoe from dark corner to dark corner up three flights of creaking stairs (you can't tell me the night watchman didn't know what was going on) to the sanctity of our Society Hall to munch and talk. Oh, these were sacred times!
>
> The times I loved best were the gatherings in various rooms to talk! *(Of course,* after assignments were accomplished.) Each individual would have some form of occupation—knitting, writing letters, reading, or trying to, one perhaps cleaning and attempting to climb around us, and, of course, one who affords the "laughs" and "clowning." These are the times we became fast friends and to me one of the themes of school life!

Could anyone forget:

The "Butt House," the den of sin (so to speak) where most everyone, sooner or later, took up the horrible habit of smoking—just to belong, perhaps!
The Carlon Shoppe—as it was called then.
The trembling line outside Mrs. Trevorrow's office

"THE GOLDEN HAZE OF STUDENT DAYS" 243

—waiting to know what she wanted or asking for late "per."

The time the Leading "Man" of one of the plays got laryngitis a week before the play was to be given.

And of course the sadness of graduation!

Dr. Trevorrow's talks, always inspiring, always leaving deep impressions.

We wonder sometimes if Dr. DuBois still rises on his toes as he lectures. He was so loved by all!

From the most recent classes little material has been forthcoming. The last contribution in this sequence, from a 1940 graduate, consists of a series of vignettes, of which the following may awaken sleeping memories:

Mr. Knapp's shy manner; "Dr. T's" navy blue golfing beret; motherly, studious Miss Stearns serving tea to her girls on upper South during "exam" weeks; moody, friendly Mr. Dilts and his hourly rounds to the fire box stations; gentle, smiling Theresa in the front office at dinner time; the beautiful annual Christmas pageant; chapel every day and better still the vesper services.

Limitations of space and time have prevented the inclusion in this chapter of many more anecdotes and other material of interest which has been submitted by alumni and former students. From the wealth of contributions it has obviously been necessary to make a selection which serves to illustrate the variety of the students' activities and to typify the rich experience of their life at Centenary. In acknowledging these contributions, the author expresses the hope that the reader has enjoyed these reminiscences as much as she has enjoyed selecting and arranging them.

CHAPTER X

"Ever Shall Her Children Love Her"

WE have but paused midway in our song to glance backward—to trace the sequence of progress through three-quarters of a century, to catch the rhythm of the stride into the future. Thanks to this experience, richer and deeper meanings will cluster about the name "Centenary" forevermore. Associated with them is nothing that is cheap, flashy, opportunistic. No claim has been made for originating brilliant educational theories or inventing remarkable devices. There have been more important aspirations than these.

The desire of the founding fathers was to erect "an institution that shall be an honor to the church and a blessing to future generations." The actual record is one of sincere, whole-hearted, consistent effort, the doing of the thousand tasks that have reached fruition in lives enriched and prepared for service in this waiting world.

Only one half, then, of Centenary's history has been written. The other—the record of service—is now woven into the world-wide story of humanity. Some strands of it could be traced in the lives of many sons of C. C. I. who became bishops, missionaries, ministers of the gospel, diplomats, doctors, teachers, and members of other professions and of business organizations. There would be a roster of notable daughters, too. A chapter on these personalities would round this story to the full. With it should go interesting facts and figures on the less spectacular but no whit less essential careers of the wives and mothers, responsible American citizens. But limitations of time and space forbid this difficult but interesting investigation.

One thought in conclusion. Centenary and change are by now old friends. Had her leaders stubbornly refused, on any one of the several different occasions, to fit the school to the needs of the times, her graduates would long since have been orphans, with an Alma Mater that existed only as a memory. Her adaptability is a measure of her strength. It should attach to her with bonds of enduring loyalty all those who have ever worthily lived under the spell of her spirit. This means that the boys who swore allegiance to the Blue and Black have exactly as much reason as the girls of their day and of all succeeding days to be proud of their identification with the Centenary spirit.

And, by a happy accident, the boys never did say their formal and final farewell to their Alma Mater. The unimpeachable authority for this statement is none other than the valedictorian on that historic last commencement day for the boys, Mr. Steward Franklin Custard. Feeling that he represented the boys, not only those of his own class but those of all the years, he had prepared his speeches of appreciation and farewell, to the Trustees, to the Faculty, and especially to the President, the real symbol of the continuity of the school. There had to be goodbyes to schoolmates, friends, and last of all to classmates, too. The long commencement essay on "Political Corruption, Past and Present" had been presented and most of the farewell speeches made. Then, as Mr. Custard relates, something for an instant distracted his attention and, blithely unaware, he completed the farewell to his classmates and did not realize until after the exercises were all over that he had forgotten the all-important address to the President.

In great embarrassment he sought Dr. Meeker, to apologize. But the President, in reassuring manner, put him completely at his ease. The omission, he felt, had feen providential, even symbolic. He, and doubtless many others, had been dreading to hear those words that would express—and perhaps for some listeners embitter—the sadness of final separation. As it turned out, the boys had simply walked away as do those who expect to come home soon—most any time. "And that," said the President, "is exactly what we hope they will do."

Today's commencement programs have no valedictories. Why should they? One may bid farewell to places, to buildings, and to persons, and perhaps never return to see them again; but one who has truly caught the spirit of Centenary will carry its blessing through life, and in gratitude will wish to make it possible for others also to live Through Golden Years.

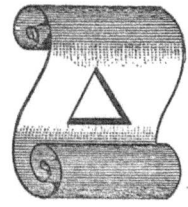

APPENDIX I

Board of Trustees, 1946-1947

*Mr. William J. Birdsall, ex '00
Former Vice-president, New York Trust Company, New York, New York.
Residence: Maplewood, New Jersey
  Treasurer of the Board

Rev. Howard R. Breisch
Minister, Bloomfield, New Jersey.

Mrs. Samuel H. Clark
Maplewood, New Jersey.

Dr. Fred P. Corson
Bishop, Philadelphia Area of the Methodist Church, Philadelphia, Pennsylvania.

Rev. George Y. Flint
District Superintendent, Newark Conference of the Methodist Church
Residence: East Orange, New Jersey.

Mr. Donald S. Good, ex '11
President, Lackawanna Leather Company, Hackettstown, New Jersey.

Miss Esther M. Hay, '08
Brooklyn, New York.

Mrs. S. Ainsworth Hird, '08
Ridgewood, New Jersey.

　　　Deceased, March 1, 1947.

Dr. Parker B. Holloway
Minister, Madison, New Jersey.

Mr. Marion L. Lewis
President, Lewis Historical Publishing Company, Inc., New York, New York
Residence: Nutley, New Jersey.

Mr. Charles E. Lotte
President, National Dyeing and Printing Company, Paterson, New Jersey.
President of the Board

Rev. Roland L. Luerich, ex '11
Minister, Elizabeth, New Jersey.

Rev. Charles L. Mead
Minister, South Orange, New Jersey.

Dr. G. Bromley Oxnam
Bishop, New York Area of the Methodist Church, New York, New York.

Dr. Elmer E. Pearce
Minister, Newark, New Jersey.
Vice-President of the Board

Dr. Karl K. Quimby
Cultivation Secretary, Board of Missions of the Methodist Church, New York, New York
Residence: Ridgewood, New Jersey

Mr. William L. Swenson
Sales Manager, General Dyestuffs Corporation, New York, New York
Residence: Hackensack, New Jersey

Mr. Charles S. Van Auken
Vice-President and Trust Officer, Citizens Trust Company, Paterson, New Jersey.

Mr. Charles A. Van Winkle, ex '00
President, Rutherford Trust Company, Rutherford, New Jersey.
Secretary of the Board

Dr. J. Edgar Washabaugh
Manager, Methodist Publishing House, New York, New York
Residence: Morristown, New Jersey

APPENDIX II

Faculty, 1946-1947

HURST ROBINS ANDERSON, President

B.A., Ohio Wesleyan University, 1926; School of Law, University of Michigan, 1927-28; Northwestern University, 1934; Workshop in Higher Education, University of Chicago, summer, 1939; General Education Board Fellowship, Rockefeller Foundation, second semester, 1940-41. Assistant alumni secretary, Ohio Wesleyan University, 1926-27; instructor in English language and debate, Allegheny College, 1928-31; assistant professor, 1931-32; assistant professor of speech, 1932-39; associate professor, 1939-40; professor, 1940-43; registrar, 1940-43; director of the summer session, 1942, 1943; president, Centenary Junior College, 1943-

---

MARGARET ELLEN HIGHT, Dean

B.A., Woman's College of the University of North Carolina, 1925; summer session, Columbia University, 1926; University of North Carolina, 1927; University of Virginia, 1928; M.A., University of North Carolina, 1931; summer session, University of Wisconsin, 1939; Ohio State University, 1941; New York University, 1945. Teacher of social science, Stantonsburg, N.C., high school, 1925-30; instructor, social science, Chowan College, 1931-37; acting dean and registrar, 1932-33; dean and registrar, 1936-37; instructor, social science, St. Mary's Junior College, 1937-42; registrar, 1938-42; registrar and assistant dean, Centenary Junior College, 1942-43; dean 1943-

VICTOR G. MILLS, Dean of Religion

Ph.B., Western Reserve University, 1904; Union Theological Seminary, Diploma, 1910; M.A., Columbia University, 1911; D.D., Wesleyan University, 1920. Clergyman, 1910-1946; Dean of Religion, Centenary Junior College, 1946-

ALEXANDRIA SPENCE, Home Economics, Assistant Dean; Chairman of Applied Arts Division

B.A., University of Toronto, 1919; dietitian interne, Wellesley Hospital, Toronto, 1919; M.A., Teachers College, Columbia University, 1932. Instructor in foods, nutrition, home management, Beaver College, 1920-22; Centenary Junior College, 1922-

HAMILTON GRAHAM DuBOIS, English; Chairman of Humanities Division

B.A., Johns Hopkins University, 1912; graduate school, 1915-17; M.A., Columbia University, 1924; Ph.D., New York University, 1926. Instructor in composition and literature, St. Paul's School, Baltimore, 1914-17; assistant in freshman English, Johns Hopkins University, 1916-17; instructor in composition and literature, Newark College of Engineering, 1919-20; assistant professor, 1920-22; associate professor, 1922-24; professor, 1924-29; visiting professor of English, Colorado State Teachers College, summer sessions, 1926, 1928; Centenary Junior College, 1929-

LEILA R. CUSTARD, Social Science; Chairman of the Division

B.A., Goucher College, 1909; Pd.B., Syracuse University, 1912; M.A., University of Southern California, 1929; Ph.D., 1934. Instructor in history, University of Southern California, 1933-34; instructor in history, sociology, and economics, Maryland College for Women, 1934-37; exchange professor, Santiago College, Chile, 1945; Centenary Junior College, 1937-

ROBERT B. GARBER, Psychology; Chairman of Natural Science Division

B.A., Bridgewater College, 1937; B.D., Union Theological Seminary, 1941; M.A., New York University, 1943; Candidate for the Doctorate, New York University. Internee in vocational counseling, Young Men's Christian Association, New York City, 1944; instructor in psychology, New York University, summer session, 1946; Centenary Junior College, 1944-

W. NORMAN GRAYSON, Director of Music; Chairman of Fine Arts Division

Juilliard School, 1925-26; B.S., Teachers College, Columbia University, 1928; M.A., Teachers College, Columbia University, 1932; pupil of Mme. Berta Thomason and Karl Ulrich Schnabel in piano, Miss Lilian Carpenter and Dr. T. Tertius Noble in organ. Director of Music, Brookside School, Montclair, N.J., 1928; teacher of music, Montclair Academy, Montclair, N.J., 1928-33; director of music, Carteret School, Orange, N.J., 1928-46; instructor in the Music Demonstration School, Teachers College, Columbia University, summer sessions, 1929-31; Centenary Junior College, 1946-

PATTY SMYTH, Health and Physical Education; Chairman of the Division

B.S., New York University, 1942; Ed.M., Boston University, 1945. Director of health and physical education, Westbrook Junior College, Portland, Me., 1942-44; instructor in physical education, Boston University, 1944-45; Centenary Junior College, 1945-

ELISE GARDNER, Music

Hunter College, 1910-11; pupil of Matja Niesson Stone, 1915-21; Luis Espinal, 1921-22; Joseph Regneas, 1925-28; George Fergusson, 1928-. Recital, Aeolian Hall, New York City, 1921.

APPENDIX II 255

Teacher of voice, Peace Institute, Raleigh, N. C., 1922-23; Centenary Junior College, 1923-

AGNES L. SHEEHAN, Secretarial Studies

B.S.S., College of Practical Arts and Letters, Boston University, 1927; Hunter College, summer, 1938; College of Liberal Arts, Boston University, summer, 1944. Instructor in secretarial subjects, Katharine Gibbs School, Boston, 1928-37; instructor in typewriting, Centenary Junior College, 1938-39; instructor in secretarial subjects, The Windle School, New York City, 1939-43; Centenary Junior College, 1943-

ELIZABETH GREGORY, Home Economics, Assistant Dean

B.S., Kansas State Teachers College, 1934; Traphagen School of Design, summer, 1936; M.A., New York University, 1944. Teacher of clothing, Field Kindley senior high school, Coffeyville, Kansas, 1934-37; dress designing, New York City; Centenary Junior College, 1940-

CHARLES HAMMOND BLATCHFORD, JR., Social Science

B.A., Yale University, 1925; Geneva Institute of International Studies, summer, 1927; M.A., Columbia University, 1929; Columbia University, summer sessions, 1930, 1938, 1939. Instructor in social studies, Hopkins Grammar School, New Haven, Conn., 1929-1930; assistant to the executive secretary, College Entrance Examination Board, 1930-1942; assistant to the president, Centenary Junior College, 1942-45; instructor in social science, 1944-; comptroller, 1945-

G. MARGUERITE CARLSON, Dramatic Art

B.A., Alfred University, 1942; M.A., Cornell University, 1944. Graduate assistant in department of speech and drama, Cornell University, 1943-44; assistant to Alexander M. Drummond, director, Cornell University Theatre, 1943-44; director of dramatic art, Queen's University, Canada, summer, 1945; assistant in research to Alexander M. Drummond, director, Cornell University Theatre, summer, 1946; Centenary Junior College, 1944-

MYRTLE GODDIN, Languages

West Virginia University, first semester, 1917-18; B.A., Davis-Elkins College, 1918; Université de Grenoble, 1923-24; M.A., Columbia University, 1924; Universidad de Santiago, 1925-26; Columbia University, 1927-30, 1931-33; New York University, 1928-29; summer sessions, Université de Paris, 1923, 1929, 1935; Columbia University, 1924, 1928, 1936, 1937, 1938; College International, Faculté de Aix, Cannes, 1939; Universidad de Mexico, 1940, 1941, 1942, 1943; Université Laval, Quebec, 1944; Instituto de la Lengua Espanola, Mexico, summer, 1945; research in postwar conditions in France as guest of French government, summer, 1946. Head of French and Spanish department, Columbia College, Columbia, S. C., 1924-25; Fassifern School, Hendersonville, N. C., 1934-37; Stuart Hall, Staunton, Va., 1937-44; Centenary Junior College, 1944-

GILBERTA DANIELS GOODWIN, Art

Diploma, Yale School of Fine Arts, 1912; B.S., Teachers College, Columbia University, 1939; M.A., Teachers College, Columbia University, 1940, in fine arts and fine arts teaching; Art Students League, student in life drawing with George Bridgeman, in composition and painting, with Hayes Miller and Thomas Hart Benton, 1924-27. Teacher of art, The Bentley School, New York City, 1939-40; supervisor and teacher of art in Richardson Park Junior High School, Wilmington, Del.; teacher of design in Wilmington Art Center, 1940-44; Centenary Junior College, 1944-

ALICE H. BOUTON, Secretarial Studies

B.S., Syracuse University, 1941; summer session, Teachers College, Columbia University, 1942; spring session, Hofstra Col-

APPENDIX II 257

lege, 1943; Teachers College, Columbia University, 1943-44, 1944-45. Instructor in secretarial studies, Baldwin High School, Baldwin, N. Y., 1942-45; Centenary Junior College, 1945-

GUSTAV SIVAK, Social Science

A.B., Columbia University, 1927; A.M., Columbia University, 1945. Instructor, Blawenburg School, Blawenburg, N. J., 1928-30; instructor in history, English, and philosophy, Middlesex Junior College, Perth Amboy, N. J., 1933-42; instructor in history, Peekskill Military Academy, Peekskill, N. Y., 1942-44; Centenary Junior College, 1945-

MARGUERITE MORSE SHAW, Physical Education

B.A., Bates College, 1940. Head of speech and dramatics department and assistant instructor in physical education, Westbrook Junior College, Portland, Me., 1940-43; recreation director, American Red Cross, 1943-45; Centenary Junior College, 1945-

ENID BEVER, Natural Science

B.S., Pennsylvania State College, 1939; M.S., University of Pennsylvania, 1940. Research assistant in biological chemistry, University of Pennsylvania, 1940-43; instructor in biology and chemistry, Stevens School, Germantown, Pa., 1943-46; Centenary Junior College, 1946-

MILDRED PANGBURN, Natural Science

B.A., New York State College for Teachers, Albany, N. Y., 1940; M.A., Cornell University, 1945; research in University of Miami Marine Laboratory, 1945; research in Atkins Institute for Tropical Research, 1946. Assistant in New York State Health Laboratory, 1940; instructor in science, Altamont High School, Altamont, N. Y., 1941-42; Deposit Central School, Deposit, N. Y., 1942-44; graduate assistant, Cornell University, 1944-45; instructor in science, Ruston Academy, Havana, Cuba, 1945-46; Centenary Junior College, 1946-

JOSEPHINE ELIZABETH WIBLE, Speech

B.A., Ohio Wesleyan University, 1927; summer session, University of Pittsburgh, 1928; University of Wisconsin, summer session, 1929; Kent State University, summer session, 1932; graduate assistant in speech, Ohio Wesleyan University, 1933; Lakeshore Playhouse, Massachusetts, summer, 1935; M.A., University of Iowa, 1940. Instructor in speech and dramatic art, Dover High School, Dover, Ohio, 1928-38; private studio of speech and dramatic art and director of Little Theatre, Dover, Ohio, 1938-39; instructor in speech and dramatic art, Rochelle High School, Rochelle, Illinois, 1940-42; Delaware High School, Delaware, Ohio, 1942-43; Stephens College, Columbia, Missouri, 1943-44; assistant professor of speech and drama, Salem College, Winston-Salem, N. C., 1945-46; Centenary Junior College, 1946-

RACHEL FLOCK SCOTT, Assistant in Art

Académie Delacluse, Paris, 1900; Chase School of Art with William Chase, Luis Mora and Frank du Mond, 1903-4; School of Modern Art with Ilonka Karasz, 1914; design with Ralph Pearson, 1934. Art experience with Vogue, Butterick Publishing Company, and Ladies' Home Journal, 1905-12; Centenary Junior College, 1945-

Index

Index

A

Academic Course, 31, 106
Adult extension courses, 188
After Chapel Club, 118
Albertson, Samuel, 96 n.
All-Round Athletic Championships, 111
Allen, J. C., 19, 127
"Alma Mater", xxi, 107, 121
   (See also Runyon, Harry H.)
Alpha Delta Tau, Zeta Chapter, 105
Alpha Epsilon, 118
Alpha Phi Annual, 38.
Alpha Phi Fraternity, Zeta Chapter, 38, 114, 134
Alumni Association, 61, 77, 88, 118, 148, 157, 174-176
Alumni Day, 192
American Methodist Church in France, 169
Anderson, Hurst Robins, xvi, 195
Andrews, Bishop, 104
"Animal Cracker Club", 118
   (See also "Eating Clubs")
"Aniversary Hymn" (Carl Price), 160
Anniversary Programs, 115, 166, 185, 229, 239
   (See also Literary Societies)
Aquatic Club, 183
Armand, Marie Louise, 169
Art Department, 34, 94, 178
Ashley, Miss, 118
Athletic Association, 75, 111-113, 137, 182
Athletics, 44, 45, 74, 75, 94, 106-113, 164, 165, 228
Axford, Daniel, 95n.
Aznar, Julian, 201

B

Bacheler, William H., xi, 110
Backus, Miss, 118
Bacon, R. W., 110
Baker, Miss, 118
Bancker, "Bob", 117
Banner hunt, 239
Barbour, Martha, 217
Barriers (Dr. DuBois), 184
Base Ball Club, 44
Bass, Thomas James, 34n., 44
Batchelder, Professor L. H., 25, 29, 63
Baumann, Professor, 225
Benedict, C. S., 37
Bi-Centenary of John Wesley, 103, 104
Black, Florence K., 175
Blain, The Reverend J. C., 14
Blair Academy, 107, 108, 132, 142, 184, 239, 240
Blanchard, Milton E., 86n., 94, 126
Blatchford, C. Hammond, xi
Board and tuition, 30n., 122, 156
Board of Censors, 77
Board of Education of the Methodist Church, 153, 159, 180
Board of Trustees, 5, 11, 13, 17-20, 23, 44, 60, 62, 65, 68, 77-80n., 85, 87-90, 93, 94, 99, 100, 109, 122-126, 129, 130, 135, 141, 144, 147, 156, 158, 159, 163n., 170-173, 175, 176, 179, 186, 187n., 190-196
Bolles, Enoch, 12, 13
Book Club, 182
Bowers, R. Q., 8
Bowman, Bishop, 104
Boynton, Arthur, 111
Breckenridge, Karl, 158

Breckenridge, Mary Isabella, 139, 157, 158, 236
Breckenridge Lectures, 158
Brice, A. L., 8n., 13, 22
Brooks, John Lee, 134
Brown's *Grammar*, 41
Bryan, J. R., 8n.
Bryant, H. L., 110
Budd Lake, 119, 220
Budget Committee, 146
Building Committee, 1900, 86, 92
Bulletin of Centenary Collegiate Institute, 157, 163, 175
Burgess, Annie (Mrs. Yerkes), 96n.
Burgess, George 96n.
Burr, J. K., 6
Business Club, 183
"Butt House", 242
Byrnes, Miss, 118, 120, 121

C

Cabbage-Head Dramatic and Musical Club, 116
Callilogian Society, 137, 185
Camera Club, 116, 183
Camp (mem. of relay team), 110
Campbell, David, 12, 15, 17, 145
"Campus Chatter", 183, 184
Carlon Shoppe, 242
Carnick, Miss, 118
Carpenter, Mrs. Mary, 167
Carter, Colin S., 24
Carter, George, 24
Catalogue, Annual, 30, 31, 73, 74, 105n., 128, 163
"Cauldron and Pestle", 118
 (See also "Eating Clubs")
Centenary Forums, 188
Centenary Junior College, xiv, 135, 161, 162, 172-174, 177, 180, 186, 187
Centenary Players, 185
 (See also Little Theater)
Cercle Francais, 116, 169, 182
Chapel Exercises, 46, 105
 (See also Religion)

Chaplain, Miss, 40
Chronicle, The, 75n.
Circulo Castellano, El, 182
 (See also Spanish Club)
Clark, "Walt", 117
Clarke, William Lawrence, xi, 203-205, 216, 228, 234
Class Day Ceremonies, 232, 233
Class tree dedication, 120
Classical Course, 104
Clawson, Alpheus, 8
Clawson and Haszen, contractors, 8
Clothing Laboratory, 178
 (See also Home Economics)
Cobb, George T., 6, 7, 13, 14
Cokefair, Mrs. C. C., 96n.
Cole, The Reverend J. A., 92
Cole, Robert A., 88
College Preparatory Course, 53, 54, 89, 90, 104
"Collegiate Department"
 (see Graduate Dept.)
"Collegiates" (see Graduate Dept.)
Commencement, 49, 53, 78, 90, 103, 134, 143, 180, 181, 192, 193, 246, 247
Commercial Department, 73, 104
 (See also Evening Commercial School)
Committee of Examiners, 54-56, 62
Concert Band, 116
 (See also Musical Clubs)
Coonrod, Miss, 118
Cornerstone, Laying of, 10, 92
Couch, Miss, 185
Cranberry Lake, 119
Crane (football captain), 108
Crane, Isaac W., 8
Crane, J. T., 8n., 13
Cricket Club, 44
Cummings, Margaret, 167
Current Topics Club, 76, 115, 116
Curtis, J. H., 8
Custard, Dr. Leila, xiv
Custard, The Reverend Steward Franklin, xi, 134, 246, 247

INDEX

Cuykendall, Professor E. F., 63
Cutler, Catherine Matilda, Science Prize, 192

D

Dalrymple, R., 44
Dashiell, The Reverend Dr., 15, 16
Davidson, Dr. Wm. J., 191*n*.
Davila, The Hon. Carol A., 180
Davis, Miss, 118
Davis, William J., 198
Day, John Crane, 109, 111, 117
Day School, 89-91
Dedicatory Services, 1901, 93, 95
"Deiks" (*see* Diokosophians)
Delawater Water Gap, 119, 220
Delta Lambda Pi, 117
  (See also "Dormitory Societies")
DeMott, B. H., 109
DeMott, W., 109
Denman, Professor George Edward, xi, 106, 107, 111-113, 119, 235
Department of Classical Languages, 63
De Ponthier, Miss, 118
Derry, Miss, 118
Deutsche Verein, Der, 182
Dill, Mrs. Nancy, 95*n*.
Dilts, Mr., 243
Diokosophians, 39, 40, 42, 79, 115, 137, 143, 237
Director of Admissions, 175
Dobbins, Colonel E. L., 87, 88, 140, 141
"Dormitory Societies", 116, 117
Dramatics, 185, 238
Drew Seminary for Young Ladies, 153, 154, 225*n*.
Drew Theological Seminary, 71, 88, 131, 154
DuBois, Dr. H. Graham, xi, 182, 184, 186, 243
DuBois, Mrs. H. Graham, 182
Duggan, Dr. Stephen F., 181
Dunlap, Miss, 118
Dunn, The Reverend L. R., 13

Dutcher, C. V., 230
Duvall, Frank B., 160

E

"Eating Clubs", 118
Eckman, Geo. P., 65
Educational Association of the Methodist Episcopal Church, 170
Educational Committee, Board of Trustees, 12
Educational Conference, Hackettstown, 187
"Educational Society", 99
Efficiency Committee, 146, 148
Ege, H. N., 13
Elliott, T. J., 75
Ellis, Miss, 40
Endowment, 147, 155, 159, 179, 191
Epworth Leagues, 84
"Eutaws" (*see* Base Ball Club)
Evening Commercial School, Washington, N. J., 73
"Evergreen" Society, 39
  (See also Peithosophians)
Exchange Students, 181
Executive Committee of Board of Trustees, 134, 194

F

Fact and Fiction Club, 116
Faculty, first, 29, 30
Faculty Club, 186
Faraday, H. W., 108, 110, 111
"Farm Path" (*see* School Farm)
Ferguson, The Reverend Wilbert P., 32, 71-73, 77, 78, 83, 85, 86, 145, 218
Ferry, The Hon. George J., vii, 8*n*., 12, 15, 17, 19, 20, 23, 65, 79, 86-88, 90, 94, 104, 120, 125, 126, 128, 129, 141, 142, 144-146
"Festival of Dionysos", 185
Field Day, Annual, 111

264 INDEX

Fiftieth Anniversary, 159
Fiftieth Commencement, 161
Financial Agents, 13, 14
Finger, William, 83, 214
Fire of 1899, 79-84, 107
Fletcher, Miss, 118
Flock, J. D., prizes in expression and music, 191
Foster, Thomas J., 175, 186, 191
Founders' Day, 161
Fowler, Alfred R., 160
Freeman, Dr. J. M., 78, 87
French Club, 116, 165, 169, 239
   (See also Cercle Francais)
Fretz, "Abe", 117
Friday Rhetorical exercises, 105
"Friends of the Library", 191
   (See also Library)
Fuller, Charles D., 160
Fusser's Club, 116

G

Galloway, W. J., 44
Gardner, Elise, 165, 170, 240
Garrison (football captain, 108
General Conference of the Methodist Church, 3, 99, 122, 137
Geoffroy, Miss, 118
German Club, 116
Getchius, Mrs. Olive, xii.
Gillette, H. M., 19
Glee Club, 76, 170, 182, 184n.
   (See also String Glee Club)
Golf Club, 128
Gordon, Vivian, 143
Gorham (football captain), 109
Goucher College, 90, 132
   See also Woman's College of Baltimore)
Graduate Department, 163, 164, 171
Graduation Exercises (see Commencement)
Graff, George R., 42, 222
Graves, Carrie, 58
Graves, Mrs. Mary F., 58

Gray, Mary, 106, 211
Green, Flora (Mrs. Richards), 24, 197
"Green Barn", 238
Griffen, Miss, 118
Grobé, Professor Charles, 30
Guild, The, 182
Gulick, Fanny, 30, 63
Gymnasium, 44, 59, 111, 178

H

Haanes, Winnifred, xi
Hack, The, 107n., 113, 116, 120, 121, 166n., 167, 211
Hackettstonian, The, annual, 42, 75n., 113
Hackettstonian, The, monthly, 75, 76, 84, 91, 112, 115, 120, 121, 124, 136, 166n., 167, 227, 231
Hackettstown, N. J., x, xi, 1, 7-9, 16, 19, 23, 47, 53, 60, 74, 77, 79n., 83, 84, 86, 88, 91, 97, 115, 123, 125-127, 130, 146, 151, 171, 184, 187, 188
Hagerty, Miss, 118
Hall, Professor Clifford W., 112, 120
Hall, Grace, 143
Halls, Mr., 88
Hammond, Mrs. Albert Overton, 63, 160n.
Hammond, Professor Albert Overton, ix, 36, 63, 64, 67, 72, 74-76, 79n., 80, 88-90, 98, 106, 127, 149, 160, 201, 202, 204, 211, 215
Hammond Memorial Gates, 160n.
Hanlon, Laura J., 30
Hanna, Miss, 118
Hannon, Fred, 41, 229
Haring, Mrs. Olive, 165, 185
Harmon (football captain), 108
Harris, Miss, 118
Hart, Elmer, xi
Hatch, S. B., 8

INDEX 265

Hay, Esther, 177*n*.
Hay, Miss, 118
Heath, Mrs., x
Heath Chemistry prize, 192
Hemmingway, C., 44
Hiking Clubs, 183
Hoag, Charlotte, 76, 81, 106, 116, 143
Hoaglund, Hudson, 87
Holden, Dr., 84
Holidays at C. C. I., 225-227, 231-232
Home Economics, 138, 163, 178, 187, 192
Houghton, Otis, 207
Howard, Charlotte, xi, 106, 217
Howell's Tommy, ice cream emporium, 218
Hurley, Mrs. and son, 77, 96*n*., 128
Hurley, Memorial fund, 128
(*See also* Hurley, Mrs. and son)
Hutchison, Miss E., 118
Hyde, Professor, 116

I

Ignace, Jeannette, 169
Inaugural Addresses, 22, 23, 25-28, 71, 97, 104, 154
Inaugural Exercises, 23, 71, 91, 103, 104
Infantile paralysis epidemic, 148
International Relations Club, 182
Irving, Arthur B., 111

J

Jackson, J. W., 88
James, Bishop, 23
Johnson, George W., 8
Johnson, S. A., 34*n*.
Johnson, William L., 8
Jones, Mr., 146
Jones, Susan George, 63
"Journal" (Philomathian), 229
Joy, Gertrude, 169

Junior Banquet, 119
Junior Red Cross, 168
Junior-Senior Banquet, 167
(*See also* Junior Banquet)

K

Kavanagh, Abram S. (later The Rev. A. S.), 65
Kelley, Mrs. Mabel W., 175
Kilpatrick (mem. of track team), 110
Kin Club, 183
King, Miss, 118
King's Daughters, 114
Kinnear, Mrs. Ella Johnson, 215
Knapp, Mr., 243
"Knife, Fork and Spoon", 118
Kuchiki, Mr., 230

L

"Ladies Classical Course", 73
(*See also* Classical Course)
Ladies College, 31, 32, 53
Ladies Female Seminary for Feminine Girls, 133
(*See also* Centenary Junior College)
"Lady, The", 166, 167
"Lancet" (Whitney Lyceum), 229
Larsen, Mrs. Julia, 165
Latin-Scientific Course, 104
(*See also* Science Dept.)
Le Foyer Retrouvé, 169
Lecture courses, 35, 100
Lewis, Marion L., xiii
Library, 59, 96, 173, 178, 191
Linder, Fred E., 111
Literary Societies, 90, 94, 100, 113-115, 165, 166, 185, 229
(*See also* names of societies)
Little, The Reverend C. E., 14, 18
Little Theater, 178, 184
Lockwood, Mr. and Mrs. W. F., 96*n*.
Lowry, Dr. John, 223
Ludlow, J C., 20

M

McCormick, The Reverend Charles Wesley, 74, 82, 83, 85, 86n., 89-94, 97, 98, 145
McCormick, Josephine, 94, 98
Mack, Laura, x
Maclay, Miss, 112, 118
Malvern, Hill, 1
Mandolin-Banjo Club, 116
  (See also Musical Clubs)
Mandolin Club, 76
Martin, Josephine McCormick, x
Masaryk, President, 181
Masaryk Institute, 181
Massey, Mrs. C. D. (Anna Vincent), 95n.
Mathews, Robert O., 81
May, Albert E., 106, 143
May Fête, 119, 165, 167, 185, 192, 193
May Queen and King, 119
Mead, Bishop Charles L., 90, 222, 223
Meeker, Clifford, 150
Meeker, Mrs. Jonathan Magie, 142, 144, 150, 151
Meeker, The Reverend Jonathan Magie, 126-128, 130, 135, 140, 142, 145-151, 247
Memorial Tablet, World War I, 160
Memorial Tablet to Dr. Winthrop, 144
Meredith, Benjamin, 222, 224
Meredith, Isaac, 224
"Meteor" (Peithosophian), 229
Mets, Frederic A., xi, 106, 165, 238, 239
Miller, Carmichael, 234
Miller, Julia Carmichael, x, xi
Mine Hill, 215
Mirteenes, Anna May, 106
Mission Study Class, 113
Mittag, Miss, 118
Modern Language Course, 104
Molyneaux, T. S., 222

Monohan, Mrs., 241
Monroe, G. Roland, 160
Mooney, The Reverend Frederick C., x, xi, 222, 223
Morris, "Deacon", 228
Morris Canal, 137
Morrow, Miss, 40
Mortgage, 18-20, 98, 122, 149, 157, 159, 160, 192, 193
Morton, Miss, 118
Motto, 29, 92
Muller, Mr., 146
Murphy, The Hon. Franklin, 104
Murphy, The Hon. William H., 86, 87, 104, 122
Musconetcong Valley, 7, 137
Museum, 191
Music at C. C. I., 120, 121, 225, 238, 239
  (See also Musical Clubs)
Music Department, 33, 34, 55, 104, 106
Musical Clubs, 116

N

New York City, 148, 149, 165, 236, 238, 240
Newark, Convention in, 6, 7
  See also Newark Conference
Newark Conference, 4, 7, 9, 11, 12, 19, 20, 31, 87, 88, 94, 104, 123, 124, 130, 131, 133, 144, 146, 171-173, 175, 190n., 222
  resolutions of, 3-5, 86
Newman bronze plaque for "First Honors", 192
Nicholl, Anna, 30, 63
Nicholson, Bishop Thomas, 154
Noble, Mrs. Eugene Allen, 235
Noble, The Reverend Eugene Allen, 99, 103-106, 122, 126, 127, 145, 199, 227, 235
"Normal Class", 34
North Jersey Intercollegiate Dramatic League, 184

INDEX 267

Nunn, Harold, x
Nutley, N. J., 184

O

Ocean Grove, 61, 77, 225n.
Olmstead, Miss, 118
Omwake, Dr. Louise, 187
Opening Day, 21-23, 93, 161, 173, 198
Orchestra, 116
　(See also Musical Clubs)
Osborne, Lillian W., 183
　(See also Noble, Mrs. Eugene Allen
Outing Clubs, 183

P

Palmer, Gerald Andrew, 108, 109, 111
Palmer, "Dud", 117
Parker, The Hon. Joel, 23
Parry-Jones, Phoebe, xii
Pearsall, J. W., 96n.
Pedestrian Club, 118
Peithosophian, 39, 40, 42, 79, 115, 137, 185
Pennington Seminary, 4, 21, 107, 132, 133, 142, 227
Phi Delta Delta, 118
Phi Delta Pi, 118
Philomathean, 38, 40, 41
Pledge Day, 165
Porter, Miss, 40
Porter, The Reverend J. S., 13
Pranks, at C. C. I., 203-209, 218-220
Praying Band, 222, 223
Preparatory School, closing of, 190
President's Reception, 49, 134
Price, Carl F., 121, 143, 157, 160

Q

Quackenbush, S., 121

R

Radio Chorus, 170
Registration, first, 24, 33
Religion at C. C. I., 45-48, 64, 65, 113, 114, 190, 220, 222, 223
　(See also Sunday at C. C. I.)
Reminiscences of alumni, 197-243
Richards, Mrs. W. P., 24
　(See also Green, Flora)
Richardson, Miss, 40
Riegel, E. Raymond, 113
Roe, George, 8
Roll of Graduates, 160, 161
Roucek, Dr., 183
Runyon, Harry H., 113, 121
Rusby, H. H., 37
Rutherford Woods, 220
Ryan, Miss, 118

S

Salamander Ceremony, 119, 136, 231, 232
Sanford, Beulah M., 118, 121
Save-the-Children Federation, 170
Schlieder, Professor Frederick, 120
Scholarship Aid, 179, 180
School Farm, 124, 128, 137, 156, 165
School plays, 166
　(See also Dramatics
School songs, 120, 121, 231
Schooley's Mountain, 1, 84, 137, 220
Science Department, 59, 192
Scientific Course, 104
　(See also Science Dept.)
"Scroll, The" (Diokosophian), x, 34, 35, 38, 43, 229
Sea-side Reunion, 61, 62, 77
Secretarial Study, 138, 163
Selden, Benjamin F., 202n.
"Seminary Farm" (see School Farm)
Seney, George I., 19
Senior "Pleasure Trips", 119, 220
Seventy-fifth Anniversary Development Program, xiv, xv

INDEX

Shay, Andrew M., 222
Sheldon House (see Sea-side Reunion)
Shields, David, 8
Shields, Geraldine, xi, 168, 169, 186
Shields, Marvin, 228
Simms, Thomas, 230
Simons, Letitia, 177n.
Simpson, Bishop Matthew, 10
Sims, The Reverend Charles N., 23
Slaght, J. W., 34n., 44
Smallpox epidemic, 97, 98
Smith, Dr. George, 223
Smith, Joseph S., 30
Smith, Mr. and Mrs. Odell, 96n.
Smith, Peter, 8n.
Smith, William Barnard, xi, 210
Sound Money Club, 76
Spanish Club, 182
Sparnon, The Reverend J. O., 151
Spence, Alexandria, 167
"Spilled Ink", 183
"Spook and Spectre", 117
    (See also Dormitory Societies)
"Star" (Callilogian), 229
Starch, Dr., 181
Stauffer, Fanny, 167
Stearns, Miss, 241, 243
Stevens, Miss, 40
Stevens, O. A., 38
Stitzer, H. Emma, 39
Stitzer, J. H., 37
Stivers, E. L., 63, 225
Storm, Frank A., 96n.
Storm, Mrs. Julia A., 96n.
Stoval, Phyllis, xii
String Glee Club, 116
    (See also Glee Club; Musical Clubs)
Stryker and Brother, contractors, 8
Student Council, 185
Student Entertainment Company, 230
Student Friendship Fund, 168
Stutsman, Frank V., xi, 106, 147, 149, 151
Stutsman, Helen Whitney, x, 2
Sub-Preparatory Department, 93, 164

Sully's Grove, 165
Sunday at C. C. I., 47, 48, 222, 223
Sunshine Circle, 114
Sutton, G. W., 110

T

Tabor, Betty, 241
Tamblyn, Egbert J., 141, 146
Tamblyn essay contest prizes, 192
Tanimura, Issa, 201
Teale, O. S., 87, 94
Ten-Year Plan for development, 176, 177, 179, 190, 192, 193
Terrill, Mr., 81
Terry, Dr., 180
Theresa, 243
Thompson, Mrs. Benjamin H.
    (see Thompson, May Vincent Whitney)
Thompson, Laura G., 76
Thompson, May Vincent Whitney, x, 2, 225
Thomsen, Professor C. F., 63, 225
Thorpe, Milton, x
Titus, Jimmy, 219
Togo (Delta Lambda Pi mascot), 118
Track teams, 109-111, 113
Travel Club, 116
Tressler, Professor, 112
Trevorrow, Edith (see Trevorrow, Mrs. Robert Johns)
Trevorrow, Dr. Robert Johns, 144, 147, 154-157, 159, 161, 163, 167, 169, 170, 173-177, 180, 181, 184, 186, 188-194, 236-238, 241-243
Trevorrow, Mrs. Robert Johns, 158, 159, 167-169, 174, 175, 181, 194, 215, 236, 238, 241, 242
Trevorrow Hall, 192, 193
Trinkaus, Henry D., 222
Trophy Contest, 166
Trumbower, W. M., 37
Tullar, Edgar, 224
Tullar, Grant Colfax, 120, 222-224

INDEX 269

Tuttle, A. H., 86n., 131
Tuttle, The Reverend J. M., 14
Twentieth Century Thank Offering, 122
Twenty-fifth Anniversary, 78

U

University Senate of the Methodist Episcopal Church, 182
Urmy, Mr., 146

V

Valden, D. Harvey, 109, 111
Valentine, Caleb H., 8
Van Syckle, A. C., 37
Vancleve, The Reverend Crook S., 2, 10
Van Lorne, Mrs. Richard, 95n.
Vincent, Dr. John H., 58
Vincent Prize Contest in Oratory, 49, 58n.
Voorhees, Hannah M., 90

W

WOR bi-weekly broadcasts by faculty, 188
Wagoner, Jessie, 167
Waldo, Stella, 30, 63
Wall Street crash of 1929, 176
Wallace, Edith, 235
Walsh, Cornelius, Esq., 5, 7, 8n., 12, 13, 145
Welch, Bishop Herbert, 123
Welch, Peter A., 123
Welsh, J., Jr., 8
Wendler, Miss, 118
Wesleyan University, 9, 24, 29n., 53, 69, 91, 103, 110, 119, 131

Whitehead, Mr., 146
Whiting, The Reverend Henry C., 29
Whitman, Miss, 241
Whitney, Caroline, 167
Whitney, Edward A., 29, 30, 63, 66
Whitney, Dr. George H., 2, 8-10, 13, 16, 19, 21-29, 33-37, 39, 41, 46, 47, 49-51, 56, 58, 59, 61, 63, 65-67, 77-79, 86-88, 92-103, 119, 126, 128, 129, 134, 135, 144, 145, 155n., 180n., 198-201, 205, 206, 209, 210, 214, 216, 218, 219, 222, 229, 230
Whitney, Mrs. George H., 22, 25, 68
Whitney, May Vincent (see Thompson, May Vincent Whitney)
Whitney Hall, 144
Whitney Lyceum, xi, 37, 39-42, 115, 134
Willcocks, W., 44
Willing Workers, 114
Wilson, Manuel and Mary, 223
Woman's College of Maryland, 32, 73, 74, 119, 125
(See also Goucher College)
Wragge, Martha A., 30

Y

Yerkes, Mrs. (see Burgess, Annie)
Young, The Reverend J. W., 14
Young Men's Christian Association, 47, 113, 114, 131, 222
Young Women's Christian Association, 113, 114, 167, 168, 182
Young Women's Missionary Society, 114

Z

Zeta Hall, 38, 115

www.ingramcontent.com/pod-product-compliance
Lightning Source LLC
Chambersburg PA
CBHW051747040426
42446CB00007B/251